PRAISE FOR *Justice, Justice Thou Shalt Pursue*

"Ruth Bader Ginsburg was a feminist icon, a legal titan, and an inspiration to so many, including me. Her final work gives readers a glimpse at the person behind the accomplishments and shines a light on her life and legacy as she saw it, from her earliest efforts to dismantle gender discrimination to her unwavering commitment as Supreme Court Justice to fight for equality and a Constitution that leaves no one behind. *Justice, Justice Thou Shalt Pursue* is a gift to readers and a stirring call to continue the fights she waged."

Hillary Rodham Clinton, former United States Secretary of State

"Every word Ruth Bader Ginsburg left us is precious, and this book is a treasure trove. Don't live your days without it."

Gloria Steinem, feminist activist and author

"Want to know what RBG's favorite opinions were? Or hear about her repeated battles with cancer? Or read her message about how important it is for all Americans to play their part in helping to achieve 'a more perfect Union'? Prior to Justice Ginsburg's death, she and her onetime law clerk Professor Amanda Tyler managed to assemble this book that weaves together multiple aspects of Ginsburg's life, both legal and personal, into a wide-ranging yet accessible volume that will leave the reader inspired."

Nina Totenberg, Legal Affairs Correspondent, National Public Radio

"The inspiring and persuasive power of Justice Ginsburg's voice emanates from every page of this book. Her reflections on her own journey as daughter, wife, mother, lawyer are as resonant as her powerful opinions—often in dissent—in telling the story of the struggle of American women for gender equality, and in articulating with penetrating clarity the uniquely stubborn persistence of racial inequality in American life."

Sherrilyn Ifill, President and Director-Counsel, NAACP Legal Defense and Educational Fund, Inc.

"With Justice Ginsburg, Amanda Tyler has compiled a page-turning book that is the perfect tribute to her former employer and hero, the incomparable Ruth Bader Ginsburg. Anyone interested in how the 'notorious' RBG transformed American law to begin the still-unfinished journey

T0052063

toward the goal of securing equality without regard to sex must read this splendid road map through the great jurist's path-marking work. Bringing a legend to life isn't easy. With Ginsburg, Tyler has done that and more—lovingly and with deep understanding."

Laurence H. Tribe, Carl M. Loeb University Professor and Professor of Constitutional Law Emeritus, Harvard Law School

"In this, her final project, Ruth Bader Ginsburg reflects on her life's work— dismantling patriarchy and fighting for all to have the freedom to thrive regardless of gender. As this volume documents, she began this work in earnest during the eight years she spent as director of the ACLU's Women's Rights Project in the 1970s and continued as a Justice on the Supreme Court until her final days. We at the ACLU will use each day to carry forward the legacy built in these pages."

Ria Tabacco Mar, Director, Women's Rights Project, American Civil Liberties Union

"An invaluable volume by the most significant figure in this field that will serve as a reference for decades to come."

Jenny S. Martinez, Dean, Stanford Law School

JUSTICE,
JUSTICE
THOU SHALT
PURSUE

JUSTICE, JUSTICE THOU SHALT PURSUE

MY LIFE'S WORK FIGHTING FOR A MORE PERFECT UNION

RUTH BADER GINSBURG
AMANDA L. TYLER

Simon & Schuster Paperbacks

New York   London   Toronto   Sydney   New Delhi

Simon & Schuster Paperbacks
An Imprint of Simon & Schuster, Inc.
1230 Avenue of the Americas
New York, NY 10020

First Simon & Schuster trade paperback edition March 2023

SIMON & SCHUSTER PAPERBACKS and colophon are registered
trademarks of Simon & Schuster, Inc.

For information about special discounts for bulk purchases,
please contact Simon & Schuster Special Sales at 1-866-506-1949 or
business@simonandschuster.com.

The Simon & Schuster Speakers Bureau can bring authors to your
live event. For more information or to book an event, contact the
Simon & Schuster Speakers Bureau at 1-866-248-3049 or
visit our website at www.simonspeakers.com.

Manufactured in the United States of America

10 9 8 7 6 5 4 3 2 1

Library of Congress Cataloging-in-Publication Data is available.

ISBN 978-1-6680-1381-6
ISBN 978-1-6680-1382-3 (ebook)

To our families, and to all those who work
to make ours "a more perfect Union"

CONTENTS

Photos appear after page 48

PREFACE

OCTOBER 2020

Amanda L. Tyler

On September 18, 2020, three weeks after Justice Ginsburg and I submitted this book to the University of California Press for publication, the Justice succumbed to complications from cancer and passed away at her home surrounded by her family and loved ones.

What follows is the book she and I assembled together before she passed away, with only a few annotations and minor introductory material added during the production process.

In the afterword, I reflect on the loss of Justice Ginsburg and the extraordinary legacy that she leaves behind. What follows here offers the reader a window into how the Justice thought of her legacy and hoped to be remembered.

ACKNOWLEDGMENTS

We owe appreciation to many people who helped make this project come to life. We must begin with Herma Hill Kay, cherished friend and colleague in whose memory we came together for the conversation that is at the heart of the book. Appreciation is owed as well to Professor Pamela Samuelson and Dr. Robert Glushko, who were instrumental in establishing the Herma Hill Kay Memorial Lecture series.

We are grateful to Naomi Schneider at the University of California Press, who worked with us to construct a vision for this book and then carefully shepherded the project to final form.

For research assistance along the way, we are indebted to current and former Berkeley Law students Djenab Conde, Lana El-Farra, Ashley Johnson, and Carmen Sobczak.

We thank Mary Hartnett and members of the Supreme Court Public Information Office for providing invaluable assistance in selecting the images for this book as well as Jane Ginsburg, Justice Ginsburg's daughter, for her wise counsel on this project.

Finally, heartfelt thanks go to our assistants, Kim McKenzie and Lauren Stanley at the Supreme Court, and Matt Veldman at Berkeley Law, without whose unwavering and generous support this project never would have seen the light of day.

Ruth Bader Ginsburg and Amanda L. Tyler
August 2020

INTRODUCTION

AUGUST 2020

Amanda L. Tyler

In 2017, when my beloved colleague at the University of California, Berkeley School of Law, Herma Hill Kay, passed away, another colleague and her spouse helped endow a lecture series in Herma's memory.[1] There was one very obvious choice to deliver the inaugural lecture—Herma's longtime close friend and co-author of the very first legal casebook on gender-based discrimination, Justice Ruth Bader Ginsburg. To our collective great delight, Justice Ginsburg accepted the invitation to deliver the first annual Herma Hill Kay Memorial Lecture in October 2019. As the Justice and I planned her visit, we decided she would begin with remarks about her decades-long friendship with Herma and then we would sit down for a conversation about how the Justice has pursued gender equality through her life and work.

This book stems from Justice Ginsburg's time in Berkeley that fall. Following her visit, she and I decided to assemble a collection of materials that tracked our conversation about her life and work in order to give readers a glimpse into how as a lawyer and federal judge she has worked tirelessly for gender equality and, more generally, achievement of our Constitution's most fundamental aspiration—to build "a more perfect Union."

1

When Joan Ruth Bader was born on March 15, 1933, the law viewed women very differently than it does today. A little over two decades before her birth, the very Court on which she would one day sit issued an opinion in *Muller* v. *Oregon* positing that even if a woman "stood, so far as statutes are concerned, upon an absolutely equal plane with [a man], it would still be true that she is so constituted that she will rest upon and look to him for protection."[2] This was the same Court that late in the nineteenth century upheld a state's refusal to license a married woman to practice law, with one justice going so far in that case to assert that "[t]he natural and proper timidity and delicacy which belongs to the female sex evidently unfits it for many of the occupations of civil life."[3] Through the 1960s, in fact, the Supreme Court upheld legislation drawing distinctions between men and women, declining to disturb, among other things, a law that prohibited women from bartending unless they did so under the auspices of a husband or father,[4] and also laws that excluded women from local jury pools.[5] Speaking to the latter issue, the Court's 1961 decision in *Hoyt* v. *Florida* observed:

> Despite the enlightened emancipation of women from the restrictions and protections of bygone years, and their entry into many parts of community life formerly considered to be reserved to men, woman is still regarded as the center of home and family life. We cannot say that it is constitutionally impermissible for a State, acting in pursuit of the general welfare, to conclude that a woman should be relieved from the civil duty of jury service unless she herself determines that such service is consistent with her own special responsibilities.[6]

Against this backdrop, perhaps it is unsurprising that a young Justice Ginsburg did not even contemplate a career in the law. As she told me in our conversation, "I didn't think about the legal profession for me because women were not there." But, as she and I also discussed, law became her chosen path based on her experience in college during the McCarthy era watching lawyers stand up for the First Amendment rights of Americans to "think, speak, and write as we believe and not as a big brother government tells us is the right way to think, speak, and write." Another pull in her gravitation toward the law came when she chose as her partner in life

Martin D. Ginsburg, "Marty," who would be her beloved spouse for fifty-six years. As she described in our conversation, after they met at Cornell, the two decided they would enter the same profession. After a process of elimination, law won out and both eventually enrolled at Harvard Law School, Marty one year ahead of the Justice.[7]

Justice Ginsburg was one of only nine women in her Harvard Law School class of over 500 students. She was also a mother at the time, with a fourteen-month-old daughter at home.[8] As she described this period of her life in our conversation, motherhood gave her life "balance," ensuring that she would not be completely consumed by her law studies. As we also discussed in our conversation, there were also trying months when Marty was diagnosed with cancer in the winter of his third year and it was not at all clear he would survive. He did, and as the Justice told me, this—and her own more recent courageous battles with cancer—taught her that "if you have survived cancer, you have a zest for life that you didn't have before, you count each day as a blessing."

After taking her final year of studies at Columbia Law School and graduating tied for first in her class, she found job offers hard to come by. She was, after all, Jewish, a woman, and a mother. With the powerful backing of a favorite professor, Justice Ginsburg started her legal career in a clerkship with District Judge Edmund L. Palmieri of the Southern District of New York, after which she gained academic appointments. She joined the Rutgers Law School faculty in 1963, the nineteenth woman law professor appointed to an accredited law school in the United States.[9] But, as she and I discussed in our conversation, even though her appointment occurred the year the Equal Pay Act became law, she was still paid less than her male colleagues. As her law school dean told her at the time, Rutgers could pay her less than her male counterparts because she had "a husband with a well paid job." It was during her time at Rutgers that Justice Ginsburg's path intersected with Herma Hill Kay's and in 1974 the two, together with Kenneth Davidson, published the pathbreaking *Cases and Materials on Sex-Based Discrimination*, the very first casebook on the subject.[10]

Meanwhile, Justice Ginsburg had already begun a litigation career that would lead in time to comparison of her work for gender equality to the work Justice Thurgood Marshall had undertaken to dismantle segregation.

One by one, Justice Ginsburg toppled the stereotypes and assumptions that had provided the foundation for cases like *Muller* v. *Oregon* and *Hoyt* v. *Florida*. It began, as those who have seen the 2018 movie *On the Basis of Sex* know, with a case she jointly litigated with Marty, *Moritz* v. *Commissioner of Internal Revenue*.[11] As she and I discussed in our conversation, their effort began when Marty, a tax lawyer, handed his wife some pages from a Tax Court advance sheet after seeing a report of Mr. Moritz's case. In short order, they prevailed on behalf of Mr. Moritz, a never married man, who had been disallowed a caregiver tax deduction his female equivalent would have been allowed. In time, as Justice Ginsburg noted in our conversation, *Moritz* offered her a roadmap for the series of cases she litigated in its wake as Director of the American Civil Liberties Union's Women's Rights Project, and later, as one of the ACLU's four General Counsels. Throughout the 1970s, she briefed ten Supreme Court cases on behalf of parties challenging gender discrimination, presented oral argument in six of those, and prevailed in seven (with one becoming moot before the Court decided it).[12] Justice Ginsburg also filed friend of the Court, or *amicus curiae*, briefs in at least a dozen more cases.

In one of those cases, the first she argued before the Supreme Court, *Frontiero* v. *Richardson*, Justice Ginsburg explained in her brief to the Court: "Historically, women have been treated as subordinate and inferior to men. Although some progress toward erasing sex discrimination has been made, the distance to equal opportunity for women in the United States remains considerable."[13]

To close that distance, Justice Ginsburg successfully challenged in litigation before the Supreme Court and lower courts, among others: a statutory scheme that preferred men to women as estate administrators,[14] the automatic discharge of pregnant Air Force officers,[15] federal statutes granting disparate benefits to male and female members of the military,[16] the automatic exemption of women from jury pools (effectively winning the overruling of *Hoyt* v. *Florida*),[17] the denial of equal social security benefits to men and women caregivers,[18] the denial of unemployment benefits to pregnant women,[19] the denial of equal social security benefits to male surviving spouses,[20] and the limitation of assignments available to women in the Navy.[21] Mindful that her work was the continuation of efforts by many who had come before her, Justice Ginsburg included the names of Dorothy Kenyon and Pauli Murray on the first brief she filed in the Supreme Court, for the appellant in *Reed* v. *Reed*.

In 1980, President Jimmy Carter nominated and the Senate confirmed Ruth Bader Ginsburg to serve as a judge on the United States Court of Appeals for the District of Columbia Circuit. Then, in 1993, President Bill Clinton nominated her to serve as an Associate Justice of the Supreme Court. In the hearings before the Senate Judiciary Committee leading up to her confirmation, Ginsburg gave opening testimony in which she introduced her family and then offered this self-description:

> I am . . . a Brooklynite, born and bred—a first-generation American on my father's side, barely second-generation on my mother's. Neither of my parents had the means to attend college, but both taught me to love learning, to care about people, and to work hard for whatever I wanted or believed in. Their parents had the foresight to leave the old country, when Jewish ancestry and faith meant exposure to pogroms and denigration of one's human worth. What has become of me could happen only in America. Like so many others, I owe so much to the entry this nation afforded to people yearning to breathe free.[22]

Justice Ginsburg next credited Marty for supporting her choice to become a lawyer "unreservedly" and for believing "when we met, and . . . today, that a woman's work, whether at home or on the job, is as important as a man's." Among many others she also thanked for the opportunity before her, she credited "the determined efforts of men and women who kept dreams of equal citizenship alive in days when few would listen," specifically mentioning Susan B. Anthony, Elizabeth Cady Stanton, and Harriet Tubman.

Finally, in her statement, Justice Ginsburg discussed the role of the judge and more generally what it means to serve as a guardian of the Constitution. "[T]he Justices," she said, "do not guard constitutional rights alone. Courts share that profound responsibility with Congress, the president, the states, and the people." She continued: "Constant realization of a more perfect Union, the Constitution's aspiration, requires the widest, broadest, deepest participation on matters of government and government policy." As we will see throughout the pages of this book, striving for this aspiration—the "more perfect Union"—has always been at the heart of Justice Ginsburg's life's work. As she testified at her confirmation hearings, moreover, she believes that working toward a "more perfect Union" is also the responsibility of all of us.

Following Senate confirmation by a vote of 96–3, Justice Ginsburg took her seat on the Supreme Court on August 3, 1993. In only her third term on the Court, a blockbuster gender discrimination case came before the justices. The case involved the storied Virginia Military Institute (VMI) and its longstanding exclusion of female cadets from its student body. When the time came to assign the opinion, the senior justice in the majority camp initially turned to Justice Sandra Day O'Connor, the first woman to serve on the Supreme Court of the United States. Justice O'Connor, however, believed that Justice Ginsburg should speak for the Court in *United States* v. *Virginia*. Justice Ginsburg's majority opinion rejected the state's newly created separate military college offering training geared to women, holding instead that VMI, with its prestige and far more robust opportunities, must open its doors to male and female cadets alike. In so ruling, Justice Ginsburg highlighted the considerable progress made in the fight for gender equality by this time: "[G]eneralizations about 'the way women are,' estimates of what is appropriate for *most women*, no longer justify denying opportunity to women whose talent and capacity place them outside the average description."[23] Justice Ginsburg's opinion in *VMI* would seem to be, in many respects, a capstone to her career. But she was only getting started.

Indeed, as I write this, Justice Ginsburg has just completed her 27th term on the Supreme Court, during which time she has authored hundreds of opinions, including many more seeking to dismantle various forms of discrimination and open up opportunities to broader segments of our society. In recent years, some of her most prominent opinions have been dissents. One of the best known—the opinion that garnered her the nickname "the Notorious RBG"—is her dissent, joined by three other justices, to the Court's 2013 decision in *Shelby County* v. *Holder*.[24] In that case, the Court struck down as unconstitutional the preclearance requirements of the Voting Rights Act of 1965. In a line that resonates today as powerfully as the day she wrote it, she objected that "[t]hrowing out preclearance when it has worked and is continuing to work to stop discriminatory changes [in voting laws] is like throwing away your umbrella in a rainstorm because you are not getting wet."[25]

In another case, this one involving gender-based pay discrimination, Justice Ginsburg again found herself in a minority of four justices, unable to convince her colleagues on the other side that every time a woman is paid less than her male counterpart, the original discriminatory conduct on the part of her employer is renewed. Ever hopeful, she concluded her dissent in that case, *Ledbetter* v. *Goodyear Tire & Rubber Co.*,[26] by observing that "the ball is [now] in Congress' court" to correct the majority's erroneous interpretation of Title VII.[27] As she and I discussed in our conversation at the heart of this book, Congress wasted little time in taking up her invitation, enacting the Lilly Ledbetter Fair Pay Act soon thereafter.[28]

Another dissent, in *Burwell* v. *Hobby Lobby Stores, Inc.*,[29] chastised the Court's majority for permitting commercial enterprises that employ workers of diverse faiths to opt out of providing congressionally mandated contraceptive coverage based on the employers' religious beliefs. Relying on the Court's recognition two decades earlier that "[t]he ability of women to participate equally in the economic and social life of the Nation has been facilitated by their ability to control their reproductive lives," Justice Ginsburg's opinion, speaking for four justices, maintained that an employer's asserted religious beliefs could not be wielded to the detriment of the rights of their employees.[30]

These opinions—which she has designated as favorites among those she has written while on the Court—are included here, along with her bench statements in which she summarized her position when the Court handed down its opinions in the cases.

In the opinions and the bench announcements that accompany them, one sees that Justice Ginsburg acutely appreciates how the decisions of the Supreme Court impact the everyday lived experiences of all persons. For example, in her dissent in Lilly Ledbetter's case, Justice Ginsburg observes how difficult it can be for someone in Ledbetter's position to uncover the fact that she is the victim of systematic gender-based wage discrimination. Justice Ginsburg's dissent in *Hobby Lobby*, in turn, highlights how expensive it is for working women to obtain contraception coverage in underscoring the government's interest in making contraceptive coverage more accessible. Then there is her *Shelby County* dissent, in which she walks the reader through the ongoing systemic discrimination and second generation barriers that continue to be erected to prevent minority voters from fully participating in the electoral process, making the case for the continuing need for a robust Voting Rights Act.

As already noted, throughout her tenure on the Supreme Court, Justice Ginsburg has remained a tireless advocate for the idea that our Constitution should leave no person behind. All along, she has celebrated, as she did in *VMI*, that "[a] prime part of the history of our Constitution . . . is the story of the extension of constitutional rights and protections to people once ignored or excluded."[31] Beyond the opinions included in this volume, Justice Ginsburg has written countless others advancing these ideals. In one 2003 opinion, for example, she recognized the continuing need to confront the fact that "conscious and unconscious race bias, even rank discrimination based on race, remain alive in our land, impeding realization of our highest values and ideals."[32] In another, she underscored the importance of the Americans with Disabilities Act and Congress's recognition that "including individuals with disabilities among people who count in composing 'We the People' . . . would sometimes require not blindfolded equality, but responsiveness to difference; not indifference, but accommodation."[33] There is also her vote to declare unconstitutional the Defense of Marriage Act, which limited federal recognition of marriages to those between a man and a woman. During the 2013 oral argument in *United States* v. *Windsor*, Justice Ginsburg labeled the Act as problematic for sanctioning "two kinds of marriage: the full marriage, and then this sort of skim milk marriage."[34] Two years later, in *Obergefell* v. *Hodges*, she joined her colleagues in the majority to hold that the Fourteenth Amendment requires states to license and recognize marriages between persons of the same sex.[35] Meanwhile, Justice Ginsburg has consistently endeavored to increase access to justice. On this score, she has written several noteworthy dissents in procedure cases in which she believed her colleagues were putting up roadblocks undermining that principle.[36] And of course, Justice Ginsburg has remained steadfast in her conviction that the law should not discriminate based on gender.[37] Indeed, as I write this, her most recent opinion—the final opinion she issued in the 2019-2020 Supreme Court Term—was in a gender discrimination case. Finding herself once again in dissent, Justice Ginsburg chastised her colleagues in the majority for further limiting the reach of the Affordable

Care Act's contraceptive mandate and leaving potentially half a million women workers, as she put it, to "fend for themselves."[38]

This book is a window into each of these aspects of Justice Ginsburg's life and work. It begins with Justice Ginsburg's remarks about Herma Hill Kay delivered at Kay's namesake memorial lecture at UC Berkeley in October 2019. Kay was, as Justice Ginsburg tells us, an early and enormously influential woman in the legal academy who joined the Berkeley Law faculty in 1960. Their work together launching the field of gender discrimination law with their pathmarking casebook cemented a lifelong friendship. As the reader also will learn, Professor Kay spent the last decade of her life documenting the stories of the first women law professors in the United States, women who paved the way for her and Justice Ginsburg (and countless others, including myself) to join their ranks. Kay's book, *Paving the Way: The First American Women Law Professors*, which includes a discussion of the life and career of Justice Ginsburg, will be published in 2021 by the University of California Press.

Following Justice Ginsburg's remarks in tribute to Herma Hill Kay, the book provides the full text of the conversation I had with Justice Ginsburg on the occasion of her memorial lecture. Our discussion covered much of the Justice's life, starting with how she came to a career in the law. We also explored at length her life partnership with Marty. She described the challenges they faced as he battled cancer while they were both in law school and how they teamed up to litigate and win that first case, *Moritz*. Our conversation also offered a chance to hear about the most important marital advice the Justice received (from Marty's mother) as well as her own advice on choosing a life partner. As she told my students, "choose [someone] who thinks that your work is as important" as theirs. Our conversation also offered a window into Marty's legendary sense of humor, about which I will have more to say below.

From there, Justice Ginsburg and I discussed the difficulties she faced launching a legal career as a woman and mother in the late 1950s and 1960s and how she, like so many other persistent women of her generation, confronted those challenges with determination and ingenuity. After discussing her time in academia, we then turned to her career as a litigator who worked case by case to dismantle institutionalized gender discrimination. Justice Ginsburg talked about some of her favorite cases, including her first Supreme Court argument in *Frontiero* v. *Richardson*, in which she quoted Sarah Grimké's show-stopping line: "I ask no favor for my sex. All I ask of our brethren is that they take their feet off our necks." She spoke before the Court uninterrupted for the entirety of that almost eleven-minute argument, educating the all-male bench about how laws that purport to protect women actually hold them back.

Justice Ginsburg and I next talked about the important work she believes remains to be done to combat discrimination in our society, including the need to confront unconscious bias. Finally, we discussed her time on the Supreme Court and her favorite opinions, which she was at first reticent to name. But in time, she shared that she is particularly fond of her opinions in *VMI* and *Ledbetter*. As I noted at the end of our conversation, I could have kept going with the Justice for hours. Indeed, I never had the chance to talk with her about other topics she and I had planned to cover, including (among other things) her love of opera, her steadfast hope that someday the Equal Rights Amendment will be included in the United States Constitution, whether, as the movie *On the Basis of Sex* depicts, she stumbled in her *Moritz* argument (of course, she did not), and which cases decided by the Court during her tenure she hopes one day to see reconsidered. As to this final point, I suspect one can infer that the dissents she has chosen to include in this book make the list; other cases that might have made that list likely include *Citizens United* v. *Federal Election Commission*,[39] given her criticism of the decision in a speech included in the fourth section of the book and in other settings.[40]

After the conversation, the book collects a range of materials chosen by us together to give the reader a fuller understanding of Justice Ginsburg's life and work. We begin with her time as an advocate. Included here is her very first brief submitted in a gender discrimination case, co-written with Marty, in the *Moritz* case, which has never before been published. In it, one sees the foundation laid for what would become one of the most successful advocacy campaigns ever waged through litigation. In their brief, the Ginsburgs argued that Mr. Moritz should prevail under existing standards while also pushing the appellate court to move beyond those standards and apply heightened scrutiny to gender-based distinctions in the law. Thus, they contended that (1) the exclusion of unmarried males from the caregiver deduction lacked "the constitutionally required fair and reasonable relation to the congressional objective" at issue, while applying the existing standard of review; and (2) distinctions predicated upon gender are inherently suspect and should receive "the most rigid scrutiny" from a court, no less than distinctions predicated upon race. The Ginsburgs likewise argued, as all of her work that followed stressed, that "[f]air and equal treatment for women means fair and equal treatment for members of both sexes." In the follow-on cases she litigated before the Supreme Court, Justice Ginsburg continued to press for heightened scrutiny of gender-based distinctions, ultimately prevailing even if the Court did not go quite as far as she would have liked. Specifically, the Supreme Court in the 1970s came to view gender-based distinctions as warranting so-called "intermediate scrutiny," or, as Justice Ginsburg prefers to emphasize, as demanding "an exceedingly persuasive justification."[41]

We have also included transcripts of the Justice's first and third oral arguments before the Supreme Court in *Frontiero* and *Wiesenfeld*, two of her favorite cases from her time as an advocate. Both established important precedents in the struggle for recognition that the equal protection components of the Fifth and Fourteenth Amendments to the United States Constitution guarantee equality to both genders and that gender-based distinctions should receive heightened judicial scrutiny. In reading the argument transcripts, one witnesses a masterful advocate with encyclopedic knowledge of the field opening the eyes of the justices so they could finally comprehend how gender discrimination holds back both women and men from realizing their full human potential.

From there, the book takes a deep dive into the Justice's time on the Supreme Court. We begin by hearing Herma Hill Kay's testimony at Justice Ginsburg's Senate confirmation hearings, which offers a laudable summary of the Justice's work as a scholar and advocate. Dean of University of California, Berkeley School of Law at that time, Kay stated that "[i]n Ruth Bader Ginsburg, the President has offered the country a Justice worthy of the title." Next, we move on to the cases. Justice Ginsburg has chosen her favorite four opinions for inclusion here, along with the statements she read from the bench on the days the Court handed down its resolution of the cases. The first opinion should be no surprise—*VMI*. The other three are all dissents: *Ledbetter*, *Shelby County*, and *Hobby Lobby*, each discussed above.[42] *VMI* provides a particularly strong window into the Justice's life and work, for there, as a justice writing for the Court, she relies on the Court's earlier decisions hard won by her as an advocate. Her *VMI* opinion likewise speaks of how the concept "We the People," in whose name the Constitution was ratified, has expanded over time. Here, too, she emphasizes how the work to build a "more perfect Union" remains ongoing.[43]

The book concludes with several speeches the Justice has given in recent years, addresses that have not been published before and complement all that precedes them. In one, Justice Ginsburg reflects upon her litigation strategy in the gender discrimination cases and the influence of Justice Brandeis on her career both as an advocate and judge. In another, she speaks of the powerful influence of several Jewish women who have inspired her to be "steadfast in the service" of the "demand for justice, for peace, and for enlightenment [that] runs through the entirety of Jewish history and Jewish tradition." Finally, the book concludes with a speech that affords a window into the Justice's life and love of her country. In her remarks given at a naturalization service held at the National Archives, the Justice spoke once again of the American dream that drew her own family to this country:

> As testament to our nation's promise, the daughter and granddaughter of immigrants sits on the highest Court in the land. In America, land of opportunity, that prospect is within the realm of the achievable. What is the difference between a bookkeeper in New York City's garment district and a Supreme Court Justice? One generation, my life bears witness, the difference between opportunities available to my mother and those afforded me.

As in her testimony before the Senate and in her *VMI* opinion, once again Justice Ginsburg speaks of the work that remains to be done, inviting the newest citizens of the United States to join her and all Americans to play their part in striving to achieve "a more perfect Union."

I had the great fortune and privilege of serving as a law clerk to Justice Ginsburg for one year during the October 1999 Term. Looking back, I count my time as her law clerk to be one of the greatest honors of my life.

Countless aspects of the job made it truly awesome, not the least of which was working with the Justice on pending cases. To her law clerks, "the Justice" (as we call her) is many things—a brilliant, thoughtful, and exceedingly fair jurist; a gifted teacher; someone who through her exacting standards and legendary work ethic brings out the very best in her clerks; a generous mentor who always makes time to offer helpful advice; a friend in good times and a source of comfort and wisdom in trying times; and an exceptional and inspiring role model at each and every turn.

A special perk of clerking for the Justice when Marty was still alive, moreover, was being able to observe firsthand their extraordinary partnership and devotion to one another. One of my favorite stories on this score took place during the summer of 1998, when, having just been hired to clerk for the Justice the following year, I was invited to my first Ginsburg law clerk reunion. It was an event I would not soon forget.

After entering the Court building and making my way to one of the two large, elegantly designed and proportioned conference rooms where these events typically take place, I spied the Justice, her back to me, talking with several of her clerks. Then, out of the corner of my eye, I saw Marty crossing the room toward her with an enormous grin on his face. He proceeded to put his arm around his wife in what I am sure she took to be a loving embrace. It was that, but it was also part of one of Marty's legendary practical jokes, for in putting his arm around the Justice, Marty taped a sign to her back—a sign she wore unwittingly for the balance of the reunion, laughing when she later discovered it.

It read: "Her Highness."

Now here is why I love this story so much: It provides a glimpse into the grand love affair and partnership that was at the center of the Justice's life and shows that even the Notorious RBG can take a joke in stride. It was her marriage, moreover, that played a central role in Justice Ginsburg's ability to argue to the Supreme Court in the 1970s—and later hold for that Court in the 1990s—that outmoded gender stereotypes should retain no place in this country's legal framework. Indeed, no one was more supportive of the Justice's career or prouder of her accomplishments than Marty Ginsburg. It was Marty, after all, who followed his wife to Washington from New York in 1980 because, as he put it, "she got a good job" there.

And, as already noted, it was Marty we have to thank for handing the Justice the Tax Court advance sheets in the fall of 1970 and encouraging her to take on the case of Charles Moritz, thereby commencing the dismantling of gender discrimination in this country.

I should also note that Marty was the family's "Chef Supreme": He made the Justice's dinners, baked cakes for the birthdays of her chambers staff, and prepared a feast at the end of the Court's first sitting to welcome on board each new term's law clerk team and their partners. He was also the preferred caterer for the lunches held quarterly for Supreme Court spouses and provided cakes for when the Justice invited clerks from other chambers each term to tea in her chambers. Indeed, Marty's culinary feats were so exceptional that following his death in 2010, his fellow Supreme Court spouses published a collection of tributes to him along with many of his recipes in the book *Chef Supreme: Martin Ginsburg*.[44]

A second story from my time clerking for her says a great deal about Justice Ginsburg. I joined the Justice's chambers as her law clerk in the summer of 1999. But the initial excitement of working for her soon turned to concern, for in the weeks leading up to the formal commencement of the Court's term that year, the Justice had her first bout with cancer. I recall vividly how the press simply assumed that her surgery and extensive treatment regimen, begun just days before the formal start of the term, would keep her home and that she would listen to recordings of the arguments instead of attending them. As things turned out, I was fortunate enough to be the first to arrive in chambers on the morning of October 4, 1999—the first day of oral arguments for that term—and this meant I was the one who answered the phone when the Justice called chambers from her car that morning. "Amanda," she told me, "call the Chief's chambers and make sure he knows I'm coming."

It was an assignment that I relished.

This story speaks volumes about the Justice's courage, tenacity, and commitment to her life's work. That same steadfast commitment has carried her through her subsequent bouts with cancer, during which she has hardly missed a day's work at the Court. She even participated from her hospital bed in one of the Court's teleconferenced oral argument days during the Covid-19 pandemic this past May.

Justice Ruth Bader Ginsburg is defined by her resilience and unwavering dedication to making our country a "more perfect Union." It is my hope that those who read the materials she and I assembled here will be inspired to join her in that enormously important work.

NOTES

1. My colleague Berkeley Law Professor Pamela Samuelson, and her husband, Dr. Robert Glushko, were instrumental in launching the Herma Hill Kay Memorial Lecture series.

2. *Muller* v. *Oregon*, 208 U. S. 412, 422 (1908) (upholding a state law limiting the hours of women laborers). Justice Ginsburg discusses *Muller* in the first speech included in the fourth section of this book.

3. *Bradwell* v. *Illinois*, 16 Wall. 130, 141 (1873) (Bradley, J., concurring).

4. See *Goesaert* v. *Cleary*, 335 U. S. 464, 466 (1948) ("The Constitution does not require legislatures to reflect sociological insight, or shifting social standards, any more than it requires them to keep abreast of the latest scientific standards.").

5. See *Hoyt* v. *Florida*, 368 U. S. 57 (1961).

6. *Hoyt* v. *Florida*, 368 U.S., 61–62.

7. As the Justice explained in our conversation, the two considered attending business school, but Harvard's Business School did not decide to admit women until 1962.

8. Justice Ginsburg entered Harvard Law School in 1956, just six years after the school began to admit women students. The lives of Justice Ginsburg's female classmates at Harvard are detailed in Dahlia Lithwick and Molly Olmstead, "The Class of RBG," *Slate*, July 21, 2020, https://slate.com/news-and-politics/2020/07/the-women-of-harvard-law-rbg-1959.html. Justice Ginsburg's memories of her female classmates are captured in Dahlia Lithwick, "It's Amazing to Me How Distinctly I Remember Each of These Women," *Slate*, July 21, 2020, https://slate.com/news-and-politics/2020/07/ruth-bader-ginsburg-interview-transcript.html.

9. As Justice Ginsburg's remarks that follow highlight, Herma Hill Kay's final project was a book chronicling the stories of the first fourteen women law professors in the United States. See Herma Hill Kay, *Paving the Way: The First American Women Law Professors*, Patricia A. Cain, ed. (forthcoming, University of California Press).

10. For more details on how the book came together and its reception, see Herma Hill Kay, "Claiming a Space in the Law School Curriculum: A Casebook on Sex-Based Discrimination," *Columbia Journal of Gender and the Law* 25 (2013): 54. See also Kenneth M. Davidson, Ruth Bader Ginsburg, and Herma Hill Kay, *Cases and Materials on Sex-Based Discrimination* (West Publishing Co., 1974).

11. *Moritz* v. *Commissioner of Internal Revenue*, 469 F.2d 466 (C.A.10 1972), cert. denied, 412 U.S. 906 (1973).

12. The ten cases were *Reed* v. *Reed*, 404 U.S. 71 (1971) (won); *Struck* v. *Secretary of Defense*, cert. granted, 409 U.S. 947, judgment vacated, 409 U.S. 1071 (1972) (moot); *Frontiero* v. *Richardson*, 411 U.S. 677 (1973) (won); *Kahn* v. *Shevin*, 416 U.S. 351 (1974) (loss); *Edwards* v. *Healy*, vacated for determination of mootness, 421 U.S. 772 (1975) (vacated as likely moot but consolidated in the Supreme Court and argued in tandem with *Taylor* v. *Louisiana*, 419 U.S. 522 (1975), a win); *Weinberger* v. *Wiesenfeld*, 420 U.S. 636 (1975) (won); *Turner* v. *Department of Employment Security*, 423 U.S. 44 (1975) (*per curiam*) (vacated and remanded on winning terms); *Califano* v. *Goldfarb*, 430 U.S. 199 (1977) (won); *Vorchheimer* v. *School District of Philadelphia*, 532 F.2d 880 (C.A.3 1975), affirmed by an equally divided Court, 430 U.S. 703 (1977) (upholding the lower court's decision as a result of a tie vote, a loss); *Duren* v. *Missouri*, 439 U.S. 357 (1979) (won). Justice Ginsburg presented argument in *Frontiero* v. *Richardson*, *Kahn* v. *Shevin*, *Weinberger* v. *Wiesenfeld*, *Edwards* v. *Healy*, *Califano* v. *Goldfarb*, and *Duren* v. *Missouri*.

13. Brief for Amicus Curiae American Civil Liberties Union in *Frontiero* v. *Richardson*, 411 U.S. 677 (1973), No. 71-1694, 6.

14. See *Reed* v. *Reed*, 404 U.S. 71 (1971).

15. See *Struck* v. *Secretary of Defense*, cert. granted, 409 U.S. 947, judgment vacated, 409 U.S. 1071 (1972). After the Supreme Court granted certiorari to review *Struck*, the Air Force changed its rule.

16. See *Frontiero* v. *Richardson*, 411 U.S. 677 (1973).

17. See *Healy* v. *Edwards*, 363 F. Supp. 1110 (E.D. La. 1973), vacated for determination of mootness, 421 U.S. 772 (1975), and consolidated in the Supreme Court and argued in tandem with *Taylor* v. *Louisiana*, 419 U.S. 522 (1975); see also *Duren* v. *Missouri*, 439 U.S. 357 (1979).

18. See *Weinberger* v. *Wiesenfeld*, 420 U.S. 636 (1975).

19. See *Turner* v. *Department of Employment Security*, 423 U.S. 44 (1975) (*per curiam*).

20. See *Califano* v. *Goldfarb*, 430 U.S. 199 (1977).

21. See *Owens* v. *Brown*, 455 F. Supp. 291 (D.D.C. 1978).

22. Justice Ginsburg's testimony is recorded in *S. HRG. 103-482, Hearings Before the Committee on the Judiciary of the United States Senate, 103rd Cong., 1st Sess., The Nomination of Ruth Bader Ginsburg, to be Associate Justice of the Supreme Court of the United States*, July 20-23, 1993 (U.S. Government Printing Office, 1994), 46. Her testimony is also reprinted in Ruth Bader Ginsburg, with Mary Hartnett and Wendy W. Williams, *My Own Words* (Simon and Schuster, 2016), 181, as is her Rose Garden acceptance speech (see Ginsburg, *My Own Words*, 174).

23. *United States* v. *Virginia*, 518 U.S. 515, 550 (1996).

24. *Shelby County* v. *Holder*, 570 U.S. 529 (2013).

25. *Shelby County*, 570 U.S. at 590 (Ginsburg, J., dissenting).

26. *Ledbetter* v. *Goodyear Tire & Rubber Co.*, 550 U.S. 618 (2007).

27. *Ledbetter*, 550 U.S. at 661 (Ginsburg, J., dissenting).

28. Lilly Ledbetter Fair Pay Act of 2009, codified at 42 U.S.C. § 2000e–5(e)(3)(A).

29. *Burwell* v. *Hobby Lobby Stores, Inc.*, 573 U.S. 682 (2014).

30. *Hobby Lobby*, 573 U.S. at 741 (Ginsburg, J., dissenting) (quoting *Planned Parenthood of Southeastern Pa.* v. *Casey*, 505 U.S. 833, 856 (1992) (internal quotation marks omitted)).

31. *United States* v. *Virginia*, 518 U.S. 515, 557 (1996).

32. *Grutter* v. *Bollinger*, 539 U.S. 306, 344, 345 (2003) (Ginsburg, J., concurring).

33. *Tennessee* v. *Lane*, 541 U.S. 509, 535, 536 (2004) (Ginsburg, J., concurring); see also *Olmstead* v. *L.C.*, 527 U.S. 581, 587 (1999) (writing for the Court, holding that the Americans with Disabilities Act "may require placement of persons with mental disabilities in community settings rather than in institutions").

34. See Oral Argument Transcript, *United States* v. *Windsor*, No. 12-307, 570 U.S. 744 (2013) (argued Mar. 27, 2013).

35. *Obergefell* v. *Hodges*, 576 U.S. 644 (2015). Justice Kennedy wrote the majority opinion in *Obergefell*.

36. See, *e.g.*, *Lamps Plus, Inc.* v. *Varela*, 139 S.Ct. 1407, 1420 (2019) (Ginsburg, J., dissenting) (disagreeing with the majority's holding precluding class arbitration and forcing wronged employees and consumers to pursue arbitration individually rather than permitting them to band together); *J. McIntyre Machinery, Ltd.* v. *Nicastro*, 564 U.S. 873, 893 (2011) (Ginsburg, J., dissenting) (criticizing the majority for denying an injured employee the ability to sue in his home state the manufacturer of a product that caused his injury when the injury took place in that state); *Wal-Mart Stores, Inc.* v. *Dukes*, 564 U.S. 338, 367, 373 n.6 (2011) (Ginsburg, J., concurring in part and dissenting in part) (faulting colleagues for making it harder for Title VII employees to join together to bring class actions and overlooking "how subjective decision making can be a vehicle for discrimination").

37. See, *e.g.*, *Sessions* v. *Morales-Santana*, 137 S.Ct. 1678 (2017) (writing for the Court and declaring a statute unconstitutional that provided for different residency requirements for United States citizen-fathers versus citizen-mothers to transmit citizenship to their children); *Safford Unified School District #1* v. *Redding*, 557 U.S. 364, 381 (2009) (Ginsburg, J., concurring in part and dissenting in part) (disagreeing with the Court's holding that school officials enjoyed immunity from suit for violating a thirteen-year-old girl's Fourth Amendment rights when they subjected her to a strip search); *Gonzales* v. *Carhart*, 550 U.S. 124, 169, 183 (2007) (Ginsburg, J., dissenting) (criticizing the all-male Court majority for disregarding medical testimony in upholding a ban on a particular abortion procedure along with its untested assertion that "[w]omen who have abortions come to regret their choices").

38. *Little Sisters of the Poor Saints Peter and Paul Home* v. *Pennsylvania*, 140 S.Ct. 2367, 2400, 2400 (2020) (Ginsburg, J., dissenting). *Afterword:* This dissent marked Justice Ginsburg's final opinion before her death.

39. *Citizens United* v. *Federal Election Commission*, 558 U.S. 310 (2010).

40. Justice Ginsburg once said: "If there was one decision I would overrule, it would be *Citizens United.*" Jeffrey Rosen, *Conversations with RBG: Ruth Bader Ginsburg on Life, Love, Liberty, and Law* (Henry Holt, 2019), 154.

41. *United States* v. *Virginia*, 518 U.S. 515, 531 (1996) (quoting *Mississippi University for Women* v. *Hogan*, 458 U.S. 718, 724 (1982)) (internal quotation marks omitted).

42. Justice Ginsburg previously published these bench statements in Ginsburg, *My Own Words*, 150, 287, 292, 307.

43. The entirety of the Preamble to the U.S. Constitution reads:

We the People of the United States, in Order to form a more perfect Union, establish Justice, insure domestic Tranquility, provide for the common defense, promote the general Welfare, and secure the Blessings of Liberty to ourselves and our Posterity, do ordain and establish this Constitution for the United States of America.

44. *Chef Supreme: Martin Ginsburg—Created by the Justices' Spouses In Memoriam* (Supreme Court Historical Society, 2011).

HERMA HILL KAY MEMORIAL LECTURE

What follows is the first annual Herma Hill Kay Memorial Lecture delivered by Justice Ginsburg on October 21, 2019, at the University of California, Berkeley. Justice Ginsburg first pays tribute to Herma Hill Kay, her friend of almost fifty years. As Justice Ginsburg says, Kay was her "best and dearest working colleague" during the 1970s. Along with Kenneth Davidson, Justice Ginsburg and Herma Hill Kay wrote the first casebook on gender discrimination, publishing *Cases and Materials on Sex-Based Discrimination* in 1974. Justice Ginsburg chronicles their friendship as well as Kay's important role as a trailblazer in the legal academy and as a scholar who documented the lives of the women law professors who paved the way for both of them and all who followed.

Following Justice Ginsburg's tribute, the authors sat down for a conversation spanning Justice Ginsburg's life, starting with her childhood through her time on the Supreme Court. Here, Justice Ginsburg tells her story in her own words, discussing how she came to the law, her marriage and family life, her work as an advocate, her time on the bench, and what she has learned from her many battles with cancer. Justice Ginsburg also talks about the work that remains to be done to confront inequality today.

TRIBUTE TO HERMA HILL KAY

UNIVERSITY OF CALIFORNIA, BERKELEY
(OCTOBER 21, 2019)

Ruth Bader Ginsburg, Associate Justice,
Supreme Court of the United States

Herma Hill Kay was the fifteenth woman to hold a tenure-track position at a law school accredited by the Association of American Law Schools (AALS). For more than twenty-five years, she devoted her time and talent to bringing vividly to life the work and days of the fourteen women who preceded her in appointments to AALS-accredited law faculties. And in a final chapter, she wrote of the women who came next, achieving tenure-track appointments in the years since 1960. Retrieving this history was a huge undertaking. The University of California Press will publish the book in 2021. It is of great value to all concerned with the well-being of legal education and women's part in making law schools more user friendly.

To tell the stories of the first fourteen, Herma read their publications, personally interviewed the nine still alive when she embarked on the project, and for all of them, elicited the remembrances of colleagues when available, and scores of students. Without Herma's prodigious effort, we would scarcely comprehend how women altered legal education and law itself.

Most of the pioneers, the seven appointed from 1919 to 1949, and the equal number appointed in the next decade, did not think of themselves as exceptional or courageous. Eleven were married, nine had children.

23

Several were family law scholars and reformers, but most taught in diverse areas, including commercial law, corporate law, and oil and gas law. As one of them commented: "We didn't talk about what we were doing. We just did it." Different as they were, they shared a quality essential to their success: perseverance. And all of them overcame the odds against them for the same reason: They found law study and teaching fulfilling.

Reading Herma's manuscript more than four years ago, I found one thing missing. Herma told us almost nothing about herself. It was fitting, I decided, to address that omission by devoting most of my introduction to Herma Hill Kay, law teacher, scholar, reformer nonpareil, and my treasured friend. These remarks convey what I wrote about Herma.

When Herma was a sixth grader in a rural South Carolina public school, her teacher witnessed her skill in debate and suggested what she should do with her life: She should become a lawyer. Undaunted by the profession's entrenched resistance to women at the bar, that is just what Herma set out to do after earning her undergraduate degree from Southern Methodist University in 1956.

Initially told by famed Professor Karl Llewellyn that she didn't belong in law school, Herma rejected that bad advice and became a stellar student at the University of Chicago Law School. There, she worked as research assistant to pathmarking Conflict of Laws scholar Brainerd Currie and co-authored two leading articles with him.[1] On Professor Currie's recommendation, Herma gained a 1959 clerkship with California Supreme Court Justice, and later, Chief Justice, Roger J. Traynor, a jurist known for his brilliance and his humanity. Despite Traynor's strong endorsement of Herma, Chief Justice of the United States Earl Warren wasn't up to engaging a woman as his law clerk in 1960. (Nor were his fellow Justices.)

Traynor's recommendation carried heavier weight with the Berkeley law faculty, where Herma commenced her career in the academy, and in just three years, became a full professor with tenure in 1963. Inspired and encouraged by Berkeley's distinguished Professor Barbara Armstrong, first woman to achieve tenure at any U.S. law faculty, Herma made Family Law her field of concentration, along with Conflict of Laws.

At a young age uncommon for such assignments, in 1968, Herma was appointed Co-Reporter of the Uniform Marriage and Divorce Act. That endeavor of the National Conference on Uniform State Laws launched no-fault divorce as an innovation that would sweep the country in a decade's span. In the ensuing years, in California and elsewhere, Herma strived to make marriage and divorce safer for women.

Herma and I first met in 1971, at a Yale Law School–sponsored Women and the Law Conference. For the rest of that decade, she was my best and dearest working colleague. Together with Kenneth Davidson, then at SUNY Buffalo, we produced, in 1974, the first published set of course materials on Sex Discrimination and the Law.[2]

Before we met, I knew Herma through her writings. She co-authored, with Roger Cramton and David Currie, the casebook I used in teaching Conflict of Laws.[3] Her extraordinary talent as a teacher, I knew as well, had garnered many awards, lectureship invitations, and visiting offers. I was also aware of Herma's reputation as a woman of style, who had a private pilot's license, flew a Piper Cub weekly, and navigated San Francisco hills in a sleek yellow Jaguar.

Herma had a remarkable quality not readily captured in words. A certain chemistry was in play when one met her, something magical that made you want to be on her side.

Herma's skill in the art of gentle persuasion accounted, in significant part, for the prominent posts she held in legal and academic circles. In 1973 and 1974, she chaired Berkeley's Academic Senate. From 1992 until 2000, she served as Berkeley Law School's valiant Dean, meeting budgetary constraints by honing her skills as a fundraiser, planning for the Law School's new home, promoting depth and diversity in faculty appointments, and making the place more user conscious and user friendly. An unflinching partisan of equal opportunity and affirmative action, Herma managed to reset Berkeley Law School's course to advance the admission of African-American and Hispanic students after the initial shock of Proposition 209, California's strident anti-affirmative action measure. Before and after her deanship, she served the University and the University's Senate in various capacities, sitting on or chairing, by her own reckoning, "fifty zillion" committees.

Outside the University, she played lead roles in major legal institutions. She served on the Executive Committee of the AALS for four years, and became AALS President in 1989. She chaired the Association's Nominating

Committee in 1992, and was a member of the *Journal of Legal Education* editorial board from 2001 until 2004.

Herma was Secretary of the American Bar Association's Section of Legal Education and Admissions to the Bar, 1999 to 2001, Executive Committee member of the American Bar Foundation, 2000 to 2003, and both Council and Executive Committee member of the American Law Institute, 2000 to 2007. In the private philanthropic domain, she chaired the Russell Sage Foundation Board 1980 to 1984, and the Rosenberg Foundation Board 1987 to 1989. For many years, she served on the Editorial Board of the Foundation Press, and she counseled Senator Dianne Feinstein on judicial appointments. In that capacity, she strongly supported my nomination to the U.S. Supreme Court in 1993.

Herma was a proponent of interdisciplinary education, team teaching Law and Anthropology with Laura Nader in the early 1960s, and later, Law and Psychiatry with Irving Phillips. As Dean of Berkeley Law School, she launched the Center for Clinical Education, and made clinical experience a mainstay of the curriculum. At the Hague Academy of Private International Law, in the summer of 1989, she delivered a series of influential lectures defending Professor Brainerd Currie's interest-analysis approach to resolving conflict of laws.[4] Showing how stunningly she could perform outside an academic milieu, in 1978, she argued flawlessly before the U.S. Supreme Court the *Hisquierdo* gender discrimination case.[5]

A new chapter opened in Herma's life in 1975 when she married psychiatrist Carroll Brodsky, widowed father of three boys, the youngest, age 12, the older boys in their teens. Carroll was as loving and supportive as a partner in life can be. Each week during Herma's deanship, Carroll sent a gorgeous floral display to brighten the Dean's workspace. And although Herma stopped piloting when she took on the joys and burdens of family life, she became an avid swimmer and an accomplished gardener, growing roses and orchids on the balcony of her Telegraph Hill apartment.

Herma's persistent endeavor for well over a half century was to shape the legal academy and the legal profession to serve all of the people law exists (or should exist) to serve, and to make law a protector of women's capacity to chart their own life's course.

No person was better equipped than Herma Hill Kay to write about the women in law teaching who paved the way for later faculty and student generations, populations that reflect the capacity, diversity, and talent of all our nation's people. Her comprehensive and engaging presentation of the history of women in legal education is cause for celebration.

NOTES

1. Brainerd Currie and Herma Hill Schreter, "Unconstitutional Discrimination in the Conflict of Laws: Equal Protection," *University of Chicago Law Review* 28 (1960): 1; Brainerd Currie and Herma Hill Schreter, "Unconstitutional Discrimination in the Conflict of Laws: Privileges and Immunities," *Yale Law Journal* 69 (1960): 1323.

2. Kenneth M. Davidson, Ruth Bader Ginsburg, and Herma Hill Kay, *Cases and Materials on Sex-Based Discrimination* (West Publishing Co., 1974).

3. Roger C. Cramton, David P. Currie, and Herma Hill Kay, *Conflict of Laws: Cases—Comments—Questions* (West Publishing Co., 2d ed. 1975); Herma Hill Kay, Larry Kramer, and Kermit Roosevelt, *Conflict of Laws: Cases—Comments—Questions* (West Publishing Co., 9th ed. 2013).

4. Herma Hill Kay, "A Defense of Currie's Governmental Interest Analysis," *Recueil des Cours* 215 (1989): 9.

5. *Hisquierdo* v. *Hisquierdo*, 439 U.S. 572 (1979). Herma argued on behalf of the NOW Legal Defense and Education Fund as amicus curiae. Despite the excellence of her argument, the Court held that the Railroad Retirement Act of 1974 prohibits states, in dividing property upon divorce, from treating as community property a spouse's expectancy interest in pension benefits under that Act.

IN CONVERSATION

UNIVERSITY OF CALIFORNIA, BERKELEY
(OCTOBER 21, 2019)

Professor Amanda L. Tyler and the Honorable
Ruth Bader Ginsburg

AMANDA L. TYLER

I have the distinct privilege of speaking on behalf of everyone here at UC Berkeley and saying welcome, Justice. We are thrilled to have you here and to have you here for such a very special occasion, honoring former Berkeley Law Dean Herma Hill Kay.[1]

Now, as everyone knows, you have recently had your fourth bout with cancer, so I have to ask at the outset: How are you?

RUTH BADER GINSBURG

Compared to how I was six months ago, very well.

ALT

Wonderful. Wonderful. Now you've given me my opening to ask you my next question, which I've been dying to ask you. As everyone here probably also knows, I believe you're the only Supreme Court Justice whose personal trainer has published a workout book around your regimen. And I know that you are also a regular at the Justices' gym at the Supreme Court. So I have to ask—are you back at the gym?

RBG

Yes, I never left it. Even in my lowest periods, I couldn't do very much, but I did what I could. Since 1999, I've been working with Bryant Johnson, author of *The RBG Workout* book.[2] We started at the end of my first cancer bout, colorectal cancer. My husband said, "You look like an Auschwitz survivor. You must do something to build yourself up." So I asked around. Bryant, when he's not training, is on the clerk's office staff at the U.S. District Court for the District of Columbia.

ALT

That is fantastic. You'll have to let me know when you're ready to run a marathon with me.

RBG

I've never been up to that, but I do push-ups, planks, front and side, lots of weight-bearing exercises. Bryant, for a time, also helped Justice Breyer and Justice Kagan, and also D.C. Circuit and D.C. District Court judges.

ALT

We'll have to ask him, if we can get him here, who his favorite client is. . . .

Now, I want to say a few words at the outset about Herma Hill Kay, in whose memory we are gathered here today. As your remarks highlighted, you two were friends going back decades, and you two actually graduated from law school the same year, 1959. But as you said, you met years later. It is really exciting and interesting to me—and I think it will be to our audience of law students—that you wrote the first book on gender discrimination in response to requests from your students to do so. And a little-known fact is that the women of Berkeley Law had a huge celebration here when that book came out.[3] Further, as you mentioned in your opening remarks, the first woman appointed as a law professor at an American Bar Association– and American Association of Law Schools– approved law school was Barbara Nachtrieb Armstrong. She was appointed to the Berkeley Law faculty in 1919, which is exactly 100 years ago, and so that's something of which we're very proud here at Berkeley. Now, Herma, as I think you mentioned, was the fifteenth woman law professor appointed at such a school, and you were the nineteenth.[4] You talked in your opening remarks about Herma's book chronicling the lives of the first woman law professors and how important it is that we preserve their stories. I am really excited to see it and to see your introduction and her preservation of the stories of these first women law professors in print. So hopefully, we will see that within the next year, and maybe we'll be able to entice you back for a celebration.[5]

Now, I want to talk a little about your life. I have read that you have said on occasion that you were not thinking that you would be a lawyer when you were a kid. I've also recently been reading a book that you put together, which is a compilation of things that you've written. In it, there is a passage from something that you wrote for your student newspaper when you were thirteen years old. You talked in that piece about the importance of, among other things, the Magna Carta, the English Bill of Rights, and the Declaration of Independence.[6] Now, I'm not sure, but that sounds like somebody who's thinking she might become a lawyer.

RBG

It was the end of World War II, a hopeful time. I listed as the last of the great documents the then-new UN charter. There was a dream of one world at peace, that's what prompted the article. But I didn't think about the legal profession for me because women were not there.

ALT

I'm going to fast-forward a little bit to when you attended college at Cornell. You have told me in the past that that's where you started to think about maybe becoming a lawyer. How did that happen?

RBG

Yes. I was at Cornell from 1950 to 1954, not very good years for our country. There was a huge Red Scare. Senator Joe McCarthy from Wisconsin saw a communist in every closet. People were hauled before the House Un-American Activities Committee, the Senate Internal Security Committee, and badgered about organizations they had belonged to, socialist organizations, at the height of the Depression in the 1930s. I was then a research assistant for a great teacher, Robert E. Cushman. He taught Constitutional Law to undergraduates, and he wanted me to be aware that our country was straying from its most fundamental values. He pointed out that there were lawyers standing up for people called before the investigating committees, lawyers reminding our Congress that we have a First Amendment guaranteeing the right to think, speak, and write as we believe and not as a big brother government tells us is the right way to think, speak, and write, and also that we have a privilege against self-incrimination. So reading about what those lawyers were doing, I got the idea that being a lawyer was a pretty nifty thing. I hoped that I could get a paying job but also spend my time trying to make things a little better in the communities in which I lived.

ALT

Now, something else happened when you were at Cornell. You met a certain handsome member of the golf team named Marty Ginsburg. What was different about him as opposed to some of the other guys on campus?

RBG

Marty was the first boy I ever dated who cared that I had a brain. We started out as best friends. Marty had a girlfriend at Smith College, and I had a boyfriend at Columbia Law School. But there were long, cold winter weeks in Ithaca, and Marty had a gray Chevrolet. We would go to the movies together. We'd go to the College Spa, where drinks were sold, and speak about anything and everything. And it dawned on me after not too long that Marty was ever so much smarter than my boyfriend at Columbia Law School.

ALT

As I don't want to say anything that gets me in trouble with my former colleague who is now the dean of Columbia Law School, I'm going to just move right on.

Now, as I understand things, together, you decided you would pick a profession, and the same profession.

RBG

Yes.

ALT

How did you wind up going into law when Marty entered the picture and you were debating this?

RBG

Early on, medical school was eliminated, thank goodness for me, because the chemistry labs in the afternoon interfered with Marty's golf practice. So then the choices were: business school or law school. For some reason, Marty wanted to go to Harvard. The Harvard Business School didn't admit women in the 1950s. It wasn't until the middle '60s that they did. That left law school.

ALT

I think I can speak for a fair number of people when I say, I'm really glad that's how this story unfolded.

Now, Marty graduated a year ahead of you from Cornell, and he went to Harvard for his first year of law school. Then, after you graduated from Cornell, you were married. I'm wondering when you got married whether you received any particularly useful marriage advice?

RBG

Oh yes, the best advice I've ever received, and it came from my mother-in-law. The day we were married, we were married in Marty's home, and just before the ceremony, Mother said, "Ruth, I would like to tell you the secret of a happy marriage." "Oh, I'd be delighted to know. What is it?" "It helps every now and then to be a little deaf." So if an unkind or thoughtless word is spoken, you just tune out. You don't hear it. I have followed that advice not only in a marriage of 56 years, but also to this day in dealing with my colleagues.

ALT

Following your marriage, you were off to Fort Sill, where Marty had his military service. And during that time, you and Marty welcomed your daughter, Jane. And from there, you went together to Cambridge to study at Harvard Law School. You were a year behind Marty. How many women were there in your law school class?

RBG

There were nine women in a class of over 500. One of Berkeley Law's professors was in my first-year class, Mel Eisenberg. The number nine was a jump up from my husband's class. He was a year ahead of me, having completed his first year while I was a senior at Cornell and before his military service. His entering class had five women. Harvard didn't start admitting women to the law school until the fall of 1950. I entered in the fall of 1956.

ALT

When you look today at the makeup of women among the law student populations at law schools around the country and at a place like Berkeley, where I believe our current population is 60 percent women, does that make you happy?

RBG

Overjoyed, yes, that at long last, women are welcomed in law schools, at the bar, and on the bench.

ALT

When you were in law school, you were also a mother, and you told me before that having Jane while you were in law school was not a burden, but was actually an advantage. Can you say something about why?

RBG

1Ls tend to be consumed by their law studies.[7] My life had balance. I went to class in the morning. I wasted no time. I studied in between classes, but then at 4 o'clock, when the babysitter left, that was Jane's time. We went to the park. We played silly games. Each part of my life was a respite from the other. After an intense day at the law school, I was glad to have the child-care hours. And then when Jane went to bed, I was ready to go back to the books. I think it was appreciation that there is more to life than law school that accounts for how well I did.

ALT

You are without fail the hardest working person I have ever met, and I have often wondered whether your legendary work ethic derived from your law school years because, as many people know, Marty was diagnosed with cancer while you were in law school together. I think it's probably fair to say that you were faced with rather extraordinary circumstances with all that you had on your respective plates. How did you manage everything during that period?

RBG

When Marty was diagnosed with a virulent cancer, there were precious few known survivors. He first had extensive surgery. In those days, I would attend my classes in the morning. I had enlisted very good people to be note-takers in all of his classes. I would then go to Mass General, come home and take care of Jane.[8] After recovering from his surgery, Marty had massive daily radiation for six weeks. At that time, there was no chemotherapy. There was only radiation, and it wasn't pinpointed as mine was in 2000 and 2019. His routine was he would go to the radiation session, come home, get sick, fall asleep. He'd wake up about midnight and between the hours of midnight 'til two in the morning, he ate whatever he ingested for the day. I cooked it, mainly hamburgers. Perhaps that contributed to Marty's eagerness to get me out of the kitchen.[9] In any event, he would then go over the notes I had collected for him. And he would dictate his senior paper to me, which was on loss corporations.

ALT

A tax subject, no doubt.

RBG

And then when he was well enough, he had private tutorials. His classmates would come to our apartment and bring Marty up to speed. He attended two weeks of classes that final semester and ended up with the highest grades he'd ever gotten in law school because he had the best teachers, his own classmates. We just took each day as it came, we were determined to prevail. After those hard months, I believed that whatever came my way, I could handle it.

ALT

When you look back, was there any silver lining to Marty getting sick so early in your marriage?

RBG

Yes, and I know now from my own personal experience, if you have survived cancer, you have a zest for life that you didn't have before, you count each day as a blessing.

ALT

Now, because Marty graduated a year ahead of you and he accepted a job in New York, you and Jane moved to New York with him. And you enrolled at Columbia Law School, where you took your final year. You graduated tied for first in your class. Notwithstanding having served on the *Harvard Law Review* and the *Columbia Law Review* and graduating with such honors, finding a job was very difficult. But you were able to get a clerkship, and one of your great mentors, Professor Gerald Gunther, helped secure it. But he had to secure it under rather interesting terms. How did he do that?

RBG

I graduated from law school in 1959. There was no Title VII. There was no anti-discrimination in employment law, so employers were upfront about wanting no lady lawyers. Some of the sign-up sheets for interviews posted at Columbia said "men only." Very few firms were willing to take a chance on a woman, and no firm was ready to engage a mother. Gerry Gunther, who later became a distinguished professor at Stanford Law School, was determined to get a clerkship for me. He called every Second Circuit judge, every Eastern District of New York judge, every Southern District judge, and then he settled on one who was a Columbia College graduate and a Columbia Law School graduate, and most often took his clerks from Columbia. Gunther said, "Judge Palmieri, my recommendation for you this year is Ruth Bader Ginsburg." Judge Palmieri replied, "Her record is good, and I've had a woman clerk. So that's not a problem. But this is a difficult job, and sometimes, we have to work late at night, sometimes even on a Sunday, and I can't risk her not being there when I need her." Gunther then gave the judge an offer he couldn't refuse. He said, "Give her a chance, and if she doesn't work out, there's a young man in her class who has been engaged by a downtown firm. He will clerk for you if she doesn't do the job well." That was the carrot. The stick: "If you don't give her a chance, I will never recommend another Columbia Law student to you."

The huge challenge was to get your foot in the door, to get the first job. If you did, you usually performed it at least as well as the men, so the second job wasn't that same hurdle. I compare my experience with Justice O'Connor's. She attended Stanford Law School, and had very good grades. No one would hire her, so what did she do? She volunteered to work for a county attorney free for four months. Her proposal was, "If you think I'm worth it after four months, you can put me on the payroll." That's how she got her first job in the law. Getting the first job was daunting. I've often repeated Sandra's comment. She said, "Suppose you and I had gone to law school in days when there was no barrier to women in the legal profession. Where would we be now?" "We would be retired partners of a large law firm. But because we didn't have that path available to us, we had to find a different one, and both of us ended up on the U.S. Supreme Court."

ALT

Now, Professor Gunther must have been an incredible mentor to go to bat for you like that. I should share with the audience that he also testified at your confirmation proceedings, comparing you to the great Judge Learned Hand.[10] That's a rather nice compliment from one's former professor. And, I assume that it was with his encouragement that you transitioned ultimately to join the legal academy. As I said earlier, you were the nineteenth woman law professor in the country. Herma was the fifteenth.

I want to talk now about the terms of your appointment at Rutgers. You joined the law faculty there in 1963. This was an important year because it's the year that the Equal Pay Act became law, and so it was no longer legal to pay men and women differently for the same job. And yet you were paid differently than your male counterparts. Why was that?

RBG

The Equal Pay Act passed, but it didn't sink in. And when the good dean at Rutgers—and he was a very good dean—told me I would have to take a substantial cut in pay, I said, "I expected that." I knew that Rutgers Law School was part of a state university and didn't have a large budget. But when he told me how much the cut would be, I was taken aback. I asked how much a man who had about my same years out of law school, and similar experience after, was paid. The dean's answer, "Ruth, he has a wife and two children to support. You have a husband with a well paid job in a New York law firm." That was the way thinking was among employers in 1963. The women at Rutgers Newark, women employed at the university campus there, began an equal pay suit. The suit was settled in 1969. The lowest annual increase any woman got was $6,000, which in those days purchased a lot more than it does today. It took a while for employers, including academic employers, to appreciate first, that the Equal Pay Act was law and then, that Title VII really did prohibit gender-based discrimination.

ALT

On that note, I've wanted to ask you about what happened in your second year of teaching at Rutgers when you found yourself on a year-to-year contract. You did not yet have tenure, and you were pregnant with your second child, your son, James. There weren't a lot of women around, and there presumably weren't maternity leave policies and the sort of things we take for granted today. How did you navigate that?

RBG

I didn't tell my colleagues that I was pregnant, and for the last two months of the semester, I wore my mother-in-law's clothes. She was one size larger. Then, with contract in hand, I told them, "When I come back for the fall semester, there'll be a new member of our family." That experience led to the first gender-based discrimination cases in which I participated, claims on behalf of pregnant public school teachers. School districts maintained what was euphemistically called "maternity leave." Maternity leave was unpaid, and there was no guaranteed right of return. Women were asked to leave the classroom when their pregnancy began to show, because schools didn't want the little children to think that their teacher had swallowed a watermelon. The pregnant teachers wanted to do a day's work for a day's pay and were perfectly capable of remaining in the classroom. So it was my own experience that led me to realize discrimination on the basis of pregnancy is certainly discrimination on the basis of sex. It took a while for the Supreme Court to understand. In the first cases that came to the Court, the majority took the view that differential treatment of pregnant workers couldn't rank as sex-based discrimination. That was thought to be so because the world is divided into two categories of people. There are non-pregnant people. They include women as well as men. Then there are pregnant people, and they include only women. There's no male compara-tor, so it can't be sex-based discrimination. Well, when the Supreme Court made that mistake twice, first under the Constitution, then under Title VII, a huge lobbying campaign was launched with people from all sides of the political spectrum. Before long, Congress passed a law amending Title VII to say: Discrimination on the basis of pregnancy is discrimination on the basis of sex.

ALT

I want to talk shortly about your litigating career. But I do have a question I want to ask you first. You were teaching law, and you know the curricu-lum of the law schools well. As you look back and you think about the first-year curriculum in particular, was there any particular class that was especially helpful to you when you later litigated all those important cases?

RBG

Far and above any other class in law school, it was my first-year Civil Procedure course. I was skilled at navigating my way through the federal courts.

ALT

I had a feeling you might say that.[11]

Now you were recruited away from Rutgers to Columbia Law School in 1972, as Columbia's first tenured female law professor. That timing is important because it is the year that Title VII became applicable—finally—to higher educational institutions. By this time, you were litigating cases, you were teaching, and you were raising two children. You're litigating pathbreaking cases about gender roles, and you're doing all this at a time when I think it's fair to say, based on everything you've said and everything we know, that society wasn't especially supportive of working women. One of the leading questions I get in office hours from my students—both men and women—is, "How do you make it work? How do you find this work–life balance?" And in particular, I get a lot of questions from my students about how they can enter this extremely demanding profession and also raise a family. And so I wanted to ask you if you have any advice from your experience on this score.

RBG

My number one advice is choose a partner in life who thinks that your work is as important as his. Marty was always my biggest booster. He also wanted to be an equal partner in parenting. He had an idea that a child's personality was formed in her first year of life, so even in the days we were at Fort Sill, Marty was a very caring parent to our daughter.

ALT

Marty once said, "I have been supportive of my wife since the beginning of time, and she has been supportive of me. It's not sacrifice. It's family." And I think that's pretty special. He was also legendarily funny, and I'm sure that that kept you on your toes a little bit over the years.

RBG

Yes, Marty had a wonderful sense of humor. One typical example, when I was a brand new judge on the U.S. Court of Appeals for the D.C. Circuit, I was introduced at receptions as Judge Ginsburg. As often as not, the hand would go out to Marty, and he would reply, "She's Judge Ginsburg. I'm still hopeful." Another time, it was just after the Court decided *Bush* v. *Gore*.[12] We were attending theater in New York. When I came back from intermission, everyone stood up and applauded. Marty immediately said, "Oh, I forgot to tell you. There's a tax lawyers convention in town."[13]

ALT

Now, Marty was so important for so many reasons in your life, not the least of which is that he handed you the Tax Court sheets that led to that first case in the series of gender discrimination cases that you litigated.

RBG

It was the *Moritz* case.

ALT

Yes, *Moritz*, and that case wound up proving to be a gold mine. It was over a $600 deduction. The two of you litigated it together. Ultimately, you prevailed in the Tenth Circuit, and a lot of this story is told in a recent movie, *On the Basis of Sex*.

RBG

The script for the movie, by the way, was written by my nephew. He's in that line of work. I asked him, "Why did you pick the *Moritz* case? It wasn't heard by the Supreme Court." His reply, he wanted to tell the story of a marriage as much as the story of the development of a legal strategy.

Charles E. Moritz had an elderly mother. He took good care of her, though she was 93. He was a book salesman. In order to work, he hired a nurse to take care of his mother during the day and when he was out of town. At the time, the tax code allowed a deduction, $600—not a whole lot—to a person who took care of a child, an elderly parent, an infirm relative of any age. The deduction was available to any woman or any widowed or divorced man. Charles E. Moritz was a never married man, so he didn't fit. He argued his own case in the Tax Court. He filed a brief that was the soul of simplicity. It said, "If I were a dutiful daughter, I would get this deduction. I am a dutiful son. It should make no difference."

ALT

I once read something that Marty wrote about this—or maybe it was a speech—in which he said that it was one of the best legal briefs he ever read.[14] The case was important even though it was not heard by the Supreme Court. But the government tried to take it to the Supreme Court by petitioning for review. And the Solicitor General did something in the government's petition that was very helpful to you as you launched the Women's Rights Project at the ACLU. What was that?

RBG

Yes. Congress had already amended the law so any caregiving person could get the deduction, so there was no continuing problem. But the government urged the Supreme Court to take the case nonetheless because the Tenth Circuit decision cast a cloud of unconstitutionality on dozens of federal statutes.[15] Now, these were pre–personal computer days. But the Defense Department computer did provide a printout of every provision of the U.S. code that differentiated on the basis of sex. So there it was, right in front of us, all the laws that needed to be changed or eliminated, through legislative amendment preferably, if not, through litigation. It was our road map, a pearl beyond price, that list of federal statutes differentiating on the basis of gender. Many of the code provisions were typical of laws in force at the time. They treated men as breadwinners. Wives or widows could get benefits as dependents of male breadwinners. If a woman was a breadwinner, there would be no benefits for her spouse because women were considered only pin-money earners. Their main domain was home and family. What we needed to do was to break down that separate spheres mentality and have Congress use neutral terms, "wage-earner," not "male," and the same for childcare.

One of my favorite cases was the *Wiesenfeld* case.[16] It involved a man whose wife died in childbirth. Congress had provided benefits for a widow who had a young child in her care, but not for a widower who cared for a child. My client, Stephen Wiesenfeld, was bound and determined not to work full-time until his child was in school full-time. He thought that with social security benefits and the limited earnings he could make and still keep the social security benefits, he would have enough to take care of himself and his son. But those benefits were available only to widows, not widowers. The Supreme Court was puzzled by the case. The Court reached a unanimous judgment, but divided three ways on reasons for the judgment. Justice Brennan, who wrote for the majority, said "Stephen Wiesenfeld is experiencing the harm, but the discrimination was against his wife as wage-earner." She paid the same social security taxes as a man, but she doesn't get the same protection for her family. Other Justices thought the discrimination was against the male as parent because he wouldn't even have the opportunity to care personally for his child. He would have to work full-time to support the family. One Justice, who later became the Chief Justice, he was then Justice Rehnquist, said, "This is utterly irrational from the point of view of the baby. Why should the baby have the care of a sole surviving parent if that parent is female, but not if the parent is male?" The Court was getting the message. Congress was too, and the separate spheres mentality no longer held sway.

ALT

I was researching about you and Herma, and you wrote some years before in the foreword to your book on gender discrimination that although men historically have gained the greater share of power and prestige, they are no less trapped by their assigned roles. It was as though you foresaw that this was going to be a good path for litigation to have the Justices finally understand and see discrimination.

As you look back on your arguments before the Supreme Court in the 1970s, there are two arguments in which you spoke for over ten minutes uninterrupted. Putting aside that that would never happen at the Court today, why was that? Was it because it was hard to convince them?

RBG

I was at sea. The first argument was *Frontiero* against *Richardson*.[17] I wondered, are they just indulging me because they don't think I have anything worthwhile to say, or are they really listening? I wanted the Justices to begin to think in a new way in that argument, and I thought something attention-grabbing would help. So I quoted Sarah Grimké, a leading abolitionist and feminist. I quoted her line: "I ask no favor for our sex. All I ask of our brethren is that they take their feet off our necks."

The prevailing notion among judges was that women were favorites of the law. For example, many states didn't put women on juries, or they gave them an automatic exemption. My state, New York, had an exemption for "a woman." I tried to point out that a favor of that kind says something about how the society views women. That is, men have to serve. It's obligatory for male citizens to take part in the administration of justice. But women are expendable. Citizens have obligations as well as rights. One obligation is to vote. Another is to serve on juries. Exempting women was demeaning. It signaled that the society didn't need women's participation in the administration of justice.

Or take *Goesaert* against *Cleary*, a 1948 case.[18] During World War II, when men were off fighting in the war, women began to occupy fields that up until then had been reserved for men. One popular field for women at that time was bartending. When the war ended, the state of Michigan passed a law prohibiting women from tending bar unless the woman is the wife or the daughter of a male tavern owner. The plaintiff in the case, Goesaert, was a woman who owned a bar. Her daughter was her bartender. Michigan's law would have put mother and daughter immediately out of business. The Supreme Court opinion upholding the law described it as protective of women. Bars are unsavory places. Rowdy people congregate there. A state can spare women from that atmosphere. The Court didn't mention that the prohibition was only on the bartender who worked behind a bar. Bar maids could take the drinks right down to the rowdy men's tables and that was okay.

The mission was to get the Court to understand that what was once thought of as protection—as Justice Brennan put it so well, the pedestal on which women are thought to stand more often turns out to be a cage that confines women, keeping them from contributing to society in whatever way their talent allowed them to contribute. The objective was to show the Court that women were not favorites of the law, that they were hemmed in by the law's restrictions. Another example, women couldn't serve tables at night. Well, at night is when you get the best tips. The supposed protections were protecting men's jobs against women's competition.

ALT

You accomplished so much as an advocate, and you've also done a great deal as a Justice. When you sit down and you look at the progress that has been made on gender discrimination over the course of your lifetime and you look ahead, what work do you think remains to be done?

RBG

In the '70s, our aim was to get rid of explicit gender-based classifications in the law, and that job was almost completed by the end of the decade. What remains, and is hard to get at, is unconscious bias. My best example is the symphony orchestra. A well-known music critic for *The New York Times*, Howard Taubman, said, "Blindfold me, and I can tell you if it's a woman playing the piano." He took the blindfold test, and was all mixed up. He said a man was playing when it was a woman, or a woman when it was a man. And he came to understand that, yes, when he saw a woman seated at the piano, he had a lesser expectation of how well she would play.

A Title VII case from the '70s is also a good illustration. Suit was brought against AT&T by women disproportionately kept out of middle-management jobs. The women did as well as the men on all the criteria, save the very last one, which was called the "total person" test. In the total person test the interviewer sat down with the candidate for promotion, and that's when women [were] dropped out. Why? Not because the interviewer was hell-bent on keeping women out of those jobs, but because he felt a certain discomfort dealing with someone who was not like himself. Confronting a white male, he had a comfort level. If he is facing someone of another race or a woman, he's a bit uncomfortable. He doesn't really know how this person ticks. That discomfort results in a lower rating for the woman.

There was a similar case on unconscious bias in the European Court of Justice. It involved a certain province in Germany that had a rule for government jobs. If there are two people of roughly equal qualifications, prefer the woman. That rule was challenged as a violation of the equality provision of the Rome Treaty, the principal treaty starting the European Union. Between the lines, you could see what the Court was appreciating, that it may not be a preference for the woman. It may just be overcoming the unconscious bias she would have encountered when the employer had a choice between a woman and a man. Unconscious bias is a major problem. I'm delighted today when I attend a concert, and see women in numbers in the orchestra. Women are also emerging as conductors. In my growing up years, that was beyond imagining.

ALT

Because we are rapidly running out of time, I want to jump ahead some. Now normally, if it were just me up here, my students would complain and say, "You're going over time, Professor Tyler." I think this is one day where they might not complain if I go a little bit over.

President Carter nominated you to the D.C. Circuit in 1980, and then in 1993, while Herma Hill Kay was Dean of Berkeley Law, you took your seat on the Supreme Court. So in what little time we have left, I want to ask you about your time on the Court. You are starting your twenty-seventh term this month on the Supreme Court, and while I know that you're just getting warmed up, after twenty-six years, I wonder whether you look back and you take stock of some of the things that have happened. And in particular, I wonder whether there's one opinion that you wrote of which you're most proud.

That's a little like asking about my four grandchildren, two step-grandchildren, one great-grandchild, which one do I love the most? There are some opinions that stand out. One is the *VMI* case.[19] Marty's comment about that was, "It took you twenty years to win the *Vorchheimer* case, but you finally did." So what was the *Vorchheimer* case? There were two high schools in Philadelphia for gifted children. One was called Central High School, and the other, Girls High. Central had better math and science facilities, infinitely better playing fields. The District Court had held in favor of the plaintiff. The Court of Appeals reversed two to one so that the tally was two to two. And then the Supreme Court affirmed the Third Circuit's wrong decision by an equally divided Court.[20]

VMI was the same kind of case. The state of Virginia was making an opportunity available to men that was not available to women. I was sometimes asked, what woman would want to attend VMI and go through that rigorous training and the rat line? My reply, "I wouldn't. Probably, you wouldn't either, but there are women who want to go to VMI and meet all the qualifications. The state can't leave them out." A few years ago, I visited VMI to celebrate the twenty-first anniversary of the decision. The school is so proud of its women cadets. Some of them want to be engineers, nuclear scientists. They like being exposed to the same rigorous training as the men. They live in the same spartan quarters that the men do. The commander is pleased with the change in the school. For one thing, VMI was able to upgrade its applicant pool by including women.

Another case I love—some of my favorite opinions are dissents—is Lilly Ledbetter's case.[21] Lilly Ledbetter was an area manager at a Goodyear Tire plant. She was one of the first women hired for that position. One day, she found a slip of paper in her mailbox with a series of numbers. She immediately recognized what those numbers meant. The numbers revealed the pay the area managers received. Lilly Ledbetter saw that she was being paid less than even the young man she had trained to do the job. So she decided, "I've had it. I've heard about Title VII. I'll sue." She prevailed in the District Court, gaining a sizeable jury verdict. When her case came to the Supreme Court, the Justices ruled Lilly Ledbetter sued too late. Title VII requires that you file a complaint with the Equal Employment Opportunity

Commission within 180 days of the discriminatory incident. And Lilly Ledbetter, you've been working there year after year. You're way out of time.

What would have happened if Lilly Ledbetter had sued early on? Well, first, the employer didn't give out pay figures, so how would she know? But assuming she did, the defense inevitably would have been, she just doesn't do the job as well as the men. That's why we pay her less. But after she's working there for years, and gets good performance ratings from her employer, the defense that she doesn't do the job as well is off the page. The first woman in a field that has been dominated by men doesn't want to be seen as a troublemaker. She doesn't want to rock the boat. What about the 180-day limit? Well, every paycheck Lilly Ledbetter received incorporated the pay differential, so in my view, a suit within 180 days of her most recent paycheck would be timely. The tagline of my dissent in her case was, "The ball is now in Congress's court to correct the error into which my colleagues have fallen." In short order, with overwhelming majorities, Republicans as well as Democrats, Congress amended Title VII to adopt the paycheck theory. It was the first law President Obama signed when he took office.[22]

ALT

Justice, I could sit here and do this all day, but I suppose at some point we have to stop. And unfortunately, I think we're at time. So I wanted to close by saying thank you and by bringing someone back into the conversation who's been looming large and beautifully over us as we've spoken, Herma Hill Kay. Her legacy here at UC Berkeley is wonderful and longstanding, and this is the first of many events that will honor her and keep that legacy alive. I thought that the best way to conclude would be to bring her back into the conversation through her words, and specifically by quoting from her testimony at your confirmation proceedings.

In 1993, when then-Dean of Berkeley Law Herma Hill Kay appeared before the Senate Judiciary Committee, she said that President Clinton's choice to nominate you to the Supreme Court was "wise and inspired" and she testified that you "think deeply and choose your words with care." She continued, "I can tell you that her compassion is as deep as her mind is brilliant. In Ruth Bader Ginsburg, the President has offered the country a Justice worthy of the title."[23] I couldn't have said it better myself.

Justice, it has been such a privilege to be up here with you today, honoring Herma Hill Kay. On behalf of UC Berkeley, thank you for being with us today.

RBG

Thank you Amanda for a well-planned interview, and thanks to the audience for its patient listening.

NOTES

1. The entirety of this conversation may be viewed and/or listened to at https://www.law.berkeley.edu/news/livestream-justice-ginsburg/.

2. See Bryant Johnson, *The RBG Workout* (Houghton Mifflin Harcourt, 2017).

3. For more details on how the book came together and its reception, see Herma Hill Kay, "Claiming a Space in the Law School Curriculum: A Casebook on Sex-Based Discrimination," *Columbia Journal of Gender and the Law* 25 (2013): 54.

4. For more details on the early women law professors and Justice Ginsburg's time as a law professor, see Herma Hill Kay, "Ruth Bader Ginsburg, Professor of Law," *Columbia Law Review* 104 (2004): 2.

5. See Herma Hill Kay, *Paving the Way: The First American Women Law Professors*, Patricia A. Cain ed. (forthcoming, University of California Press).

6. Editorial by Ruth Bader, Grade 8B1, *Highway Herald*, June 1946, in Ruth Bader Ginsburg, with Mary Hartnett and Wendy W. Williams, *My Own Words* (Simon and Schuster, 2016).

7. Law school convention is to refer to first-year law students as "1Ls."

8. Justice Ginsburg is here referring to Massachusetts General Hospital.

9. Marty Ginsburg, a prominent tax lawyer and scholar, was an absolutely spectacular cook who, according to their son, James, once said: "Mommy does the thinking and Daddy does the cooking." A collection of tributes to Marty and many of his recipes may be found in the book *Chef Supreme: Martin Ginsburg—Created by the Justices' Spouses In Memoriam* (Supreme Court Historical Society, 2011).

10. Specifically, Professor Gunther testified that "[a] great judge, Learned Hand said, acts 'with patience, courage, insight, self-effacement, understanding, imagination and learning.'" He continued: "Ruth Bader Ginsburg, I am convinced, possesses the ingredients, the 'moral' qualities, Hand thought essential for greatness." Prepared Statement of Gerald Gunther, *S. HRG. 103-482, Hearings Before the Committee on the Judiciary of the United States Senate, 103rd Cong., 1st Sess., The Nomination of Ruth Bader Ginsburg, to be Associate Justice of the Supreme Court of the United States*, July 20-23, 1993 (U.S. Government Printing Office, 1994), 400.

11. As one who, like Justice Ginsburg before me, teaches the subject of Civil Procedure to first-year law students, I could not resist the opportunity with my students in the audience to ask her this question, confident in what she would answer.

12. *Bush* v. *Gore,* 531 U.S. 98 (2000).

13. What the Justice did not share here is that according to Marty, following that remark, she "smacked" him "right in the stomach, but not too hard." This, he once said, "fairly captures our nearly fifty-year happy marriage. . . ." Martin D. Ginsburg, "Introduction by Martin Ginsburg of Ruth Bader Ginsburg," September 25, 2003, reprinted in Ginsburg, *My Own Words,* 27.

14. Reflecting on the case years later, Marty wrote that Moritz's one-page submission "remains . . . the most persuasive brief I have ever read." Martin D. Ginsburg, "How the Tenth Circuit Court of Appeals Got My Wife Her Good Job," 2010, reprinted in Ginsburg, *My Own Words,* 126. Marty also described how he remembers bringing the case to his wife's attention:

> I went to the big room next door, handed the Tax Court advance sheets to my spouse, and said, "Read this." Ruth replied with a warm and friendly snarl, "I don't read tax cases." I said, "Read this one," and returned to my little room.
>
> No more than five minutes later—it was a short opinion—Ruth stepped into my little room and, with the broadest smile you can imagine, said "Let's take it!" And we did.

Id., at 128.

15. *Moritz* v. *Commissioner of Internal Revenue,* 469 F.2d 466 (C.A.10 1972), cert. denied, 412 U.S. 906 (1973). The opening brief filed by Justice Ginsburg and Marty is replicated in the next section.

16. *Weinberger* v. *Wiesenfeld,* 420 U.S. 636 (1975). A transcript of Justice Ginsburg's oral argument in *Wiesenfeld* is included in the next section.

17. *Frontiero* v. *Richardson,* 411 U.S. 677 (1973). A transcript of Justice Ginsburg's oral argument in *Frontiero* is included in the next section.

18. *Goesaert* v. *Cleary,* 335 U.S. 464 (1948).

19. *United States* v. *Virginia,* 518 U.S. 515 (1996). This case, as Justice Ginsburg's discussion notes, was about the Virginia Military Institute, known as VMI.

20. *Vorchheimer* v. *School District of Philadelphia,* 532 F.2d 880 (C.A.3 1975), affirmed by an equally divided Court, 430 U.S. 703 (1977). Justice Ginsburg was principal author of petitioner's opening brief to the Supreme Court.

21. See *Ledbetter* v. *Goodyear Tire & Rubber Co.,* 550 U.S. 618 (2007).

22. See the Lilly Ledbetter Fair Pay Act of 2009, Pub. L. No. 111-2, 123 Stat. 5.

23. Kay's remarks to the Senate Judiciary Committee are reprinted as the first document of the third section of this book and also are published in *Hearings Before the Committee on the Judiciary of the United States Senate,* 402.

RUTH BADER GINSBURG
THE ADVOCATE

What follows are materials chosen by the authors from Justice Ginsburg's time as an advocate for gender equality. The three selected cases, which Justice Ginsburg litigated and won, are among the many she handled in the 1970s as part of her work to dismantle gender discrimination in the United States. Justice Ginsburg discussed each of these cases in the conversation featured in the first section.

This section begins with the brief that Justice Ginsburg and her husband, Martin Ginsburg, filed in *Moritz* v. *Commissioner of Internal Revenue*, 469 F.2d 466 (C.A.10 1972), cert. denied, 412 U.S. 906 (1973). Charles Moritz, a never married man who cared for his mother, was denied a caregiver tax deduction that a woman in his position would have received. Representing himself in Tax Court, his brief was direct and straightforward, arguing: "If I were a dutiful daughter, I would get this deduction. I am a dutiful son. It should make no difference." Together, the Ginsburgs took over his case on appeal to the United States Court of Appeals for the Tenth Circuit, contending that the discriminatory tax deduction provision should be held unconstitutional. This brief was the first of many that Justice Ginsburg filed in a series of pathmarking gender discrimination cases throughout the 1970s. Here, the Ginsburgs assert that Mr. Moritz should prevail under existing standards, but also argue that the appellate court should move beyond those standards and apply heightened scrutiny to gender-based distinctions in the law, something courts had not yet done. Notably, the Ginsburgs also contend that upon holding the statute unconstitutional the court should not declare the provision inoperative, but instead should "declar[e] the statute equally operative upon all persons similarly situated," thereby permitting Mr. Moritz his deduction.

As Justice Ginsburg noted in the conversation featured in the first section, while she and Marty were litigating *Moritz* before the United States Court of Appeals for the Tenth Circuit, Congress amended the relevant law to permit all caregivers to claim the deduction going forward. The government nevertheless urged the Supreme Court to review Mr. Moritz's case, fearing the precedential impact of the Tenth Circuit's decision. In so doing, the government appended to its brief to the Court a list of every provision in the United States Code that differentiated on the basis of sex. As Justice Ginsburg described the list, "there it was, right in front of us, all the laws that needed to be changed or eliminated, through legislative amendment preferably, if not, through litigation. It was our road map, a pearl beyond price, that list of federal statutes differentiating on the basis of gender."

Included next are the transcripts of Justice Ginsburg's Supreme Court arguments in *Frontiero* v. *Richardson*, 411 U.S. 677 (1973), and *Weinberger* v. *Wiesenfeld*, 420 U.S. 636 (1975), two cases, following on the heels of *Moritz*, in which she again successfully challenged laws that discriminated based on gender.

In *Frontiero*, the first case Justice Ginsburg argued before the Supreme Court, she spoke uninterrupted for the entirety of her almost eleven-minute presentation. The case involved a challenge brought by Sharron Frontiero, a lieutenant in the United States Air Force, to a federal statute that granted fewer dependency benefits to male spouses of female servicepersons than to female spouses of male servicepersons. Justice Ginsburg convinced eight of the nine members of the Supreme Court that the law violated the Fifth Amendment to the United States Constitution by treating the genders unequally.

Justice William J. Brennan, Jr., authored a plurality opinion in the case on behalf of four justices. He would have applied heightened, or "strict," scrutiny to laws that differentiate on the basis of gender, the same level of scrutiny that the Supreme Court applies to laws that differentiate on the basis of race. But four concurring justices would not go so far. Justice Lewis F. Powell, Jr., wrote a concurrence maintaining that there was no reason to decide whether strict scrutiny should apply to gender-based classifications because the statute at issue was problematic under any level of scrutiny and such a decision might prove unnecessary in the event that the then-pending Equal Rights Amendment witnessed ratification. Justice Ginsburg never did convince five members of the Supreme Court that classifications based on gender should receive the same level of scrutiny as those based on race. All the same, in 1982, the Supreme Court held in *Mississippi University for Women* v. *Hogan*, 458 U.S. 718, that laws differentiating on the basis of gender are inherently suspect unless the government demonstrates an "exceedingly persuasive justification" for any distinction drawn.

Wiesenfeld proved another victory for Justice Ginsburg before the Supreme Court. Here, as in *Moritz*, Justice Ginsburg's client was a man, Stephen Wiesenfeld. His wife, Paula, had died in childbirth delivering their son, Jason Paul. In the wake of her death, Wiesenfeld wished to stay home to raise their son. When Wiesenfeld applied for social security survivor benefits on behalf of himself and Jason, citing his wife's contributions from her years of work as a teacher, he was denied the benefits that a surviving female spouse would have received. Wiesenfeld wrote a letter to the editor of his local newspaper describing his plight and asking, "I wonder if Gloria Steinem knows about this?" Once the letter came to the attention of Justice Ginsburg, she offered to represent Wiesenfeld and took on his case from the beginning. Justice Ginsburg knew that if it eventually made its way to the all-male Supreme Court, she could now put a relatable face to how gender discrimination hurts not just women, but both genders—an important part of her litigation strategy. To that end, when she argued Wiesenfeld's case before the Court, Justice Ginsburg invited her client to sit by her side at counsel's table, a rare occurrence in Supreme Court arguments.

The result was a unanimous 8-0 victory in which the Supreme Court held that the relevant social security provision was as problematic as the classification invalidated in *Frontiero*. In an opinion for the Court, Justice Brennan wrote, "such a gender-based generalization cannot suffice to justify the denigration of the efforts of women who do work and whose earnings contribute significantly to their families' support." As Justice Ginsburg noted in the conversation featured in the first section, it was in *Wiesenfeld* that she finally won a vote from then-Justice William H. Rehnquist (later Chief Justice), who concurred in the result on the basis that "it is irrational to distinguish between mothers and fathers when the sole question is whether a child of a deceased contributing worker should have the opportunity to receive the full-time attention of the only parent remaining to it."

MORITZ V. *COMMISSIONER OF INTERNAL REVENUE*, NO. 71-1127

BRIEF (1971)

United States Court of Appeals for the Tenth Circuit

CHARLES E. MORITZ,

Petitioner-Appellant

v.

COMMISSIONER OF INTERNAL REVENUE,

Respondent-Appellee

BRIEF FOR PETITIONER-APPELLANT

Ruth Bader Ginsburg
Martin D. Ginsburg
Attorneys for Petitioner-Appellant
767 Fifth Avenue
New York, New York 10022

Melvin L. Wulf, Esq.,
American Civil Liberties Union Foundation
Weil, Gotshal & Manges
Of Counsel

STATEMENT OF THE ISSUES

1.　Is the statutory classification based on the sex of the wage earner, established in section 214(a) of the Internal Revenue Code for a purpose unrelated to any biological or functional difference between the sexes, an "invidious classification" proscribed by the fifth amendment to the United States Constitution?

2.　Does the section 214(a) classification based on sex or prior marital status of a wage earner lack the constitutionally required "fair and substantial relationship" to the congressional objective that a deduction be afforded those who, in order to earn a livelihood, must incur expenses for the care of physically or mentally incapacitated dependents?

3.　Having provided an incapacitated parent dependent care deduction as a matter of "legislative grace", may Congress arbitrarily select those on whom its grace is shed, or was the Tax Court mistaken in assuming that taxpayer classifications established in a tax deduction provision need not bear a reasonable relationship to any rational legislative purpose?

4.　Upon determining that section 214(a) as written violates the constitutional mandate of the fifth amendment, may the Court, consistent with the dominant congressional purpose, remedy the defect by holding the deduction available to all taxpayers similarly situated?

STATEMENT OF THE CASE

This is an appeal from a decision and judgment of the United States Tax Court, 55 T.C. No. 14, rendered and entered October 22, 1970, holding that taxpayer-petitioner, a single man who has never married, as a matter of law is not entitled to a deduction under section 214 of the Internal Revenue Code for expenses paid for the care of his dependent invalid mother. Petitioner's taxable year in issue is 1968, and the amount of tax in controversy is $296.70 (an additional deficiency of $32.10 involving an unrelated issue was conceded by the taxpayer prior to trial).

In the proceeding below, all of the relevant facts were stipulated (Record, pp. 16-19). No facts are in dispute.

Petitioner Charles E. Moritz (the taxpayer) is single and has never been married. For the period in question, taxpayer's 89 year old mother resided with him, qualified as his dependent for all pertinent tax purposes, and was physically and mentally incapable of caring for herself. Taxpayer incurred

and paid expenses in excess of $600 for the care of his mother for the pur-
pose of enabling himself to be gainfully employed. In his 1968 Federal income
tax return, taxpayer deducted $600 for "Household help for invalid mother."
Appellee, Commissioner of Internal Revenue, disallowed the deduction.

The United States Tax Court held that, although the taxpayer qualified
in all other respects for the $600 dependent care deduction provided by
section 214(a) of the Internal Revenue Code, he was ineligible for that
deduction solely on the ground of his status as a single man who has never
been married. Concededly, the deduction for the care of an incapacitated
dependent parent would have been available had the taxpayer been an
unmarried woman, or a widowed or divorced person of either sex.

STATUTE INVOLVED

SECTION 214. EXPENSES FOR CARE OF CERTAIN DEPENDENTS.
[Internal Revenue Code of 1954]

(a) General Rule.—There shall be allowed as a deduction expenses paid
during the taxable year by a taxpayer who is a woman or widower, or
is a husband whose wife is incapacitated or is institutionalized, for the
care of one or more dependents (as defined in subsection (d)(1)), but
only if such care is for the purpose of enabling the taxpayer to be gainfully employed.

* * *

(d) Definitions. For purposes of this section—

(1) Dependent.—The term "dependent" means a person with respect
to whom the taxpayer is entitled to an exemption under section
151(e)(1)—

* * *

(B) who is physically or mentally incapable of caring for himself.

(2) Widower.—The term "widower" includes an unmarried individual
who is legally separated from his spouse under a decree of divorce
or of separate maintenance.

ARGUMENT

A.

The Fifth Amendment Due Process Clause Encompasses Guarantees of
Security from Arbitrary Treatment and of Equal Protection of the Laws;
Petitioner's Case Rests on These Fundamental Guarantees

The fifth amendment to the United States Constitution, commanding and regulating federal action and legislation, via the due process clause guarantees to every person security from arbitrary treatment and the equal protection of the laws. In this regard, the fifth amendment imposes no less an obligation upon the federal government than does the fourteenth amendment upon the states. *Shapiro v. Thompson*, 394 U.S. 618, 641-42 (1969); *Bolling v. Sharpe*, 347 U.S. 497, 499 (1954); *Hobson v. Hansen*, 269 F. Supp. 401, 497 (D.D.C. 1967), *aff'd sub nom. Smuck v. Hobson*, 408 F.2d 175 (D.C. Cir. 1969); *Simkins v. Moses H. Cone Memorial Hospital*, 323 F.2d 959, 969-70 (4th Cir. 1963) (en banc), *cert. denied*, 376 U.S. 938 (1964); Brief for the United States at 28, *Welsh v. United States*, 398 U.S. 333 (1970) (federal government's affirmation that "equal protection" notion implicit in the fifth amendment precludes Congress from acting arbitrarily or capriciously, and from engaging in invidious discrimination).

Petitioner, Charles E. Moritz, a single man who has never been married, bore the cost of caring for his invalid dependent mother in order that he might be gainfully employed. Had petitioner been a divorced man or a widower, or had he been a single woman whether or not divorced or widowed, he would have been allowed the dependent care deduction authorized by section 214(a) of the Internal Revenue Code. Solely because of his status as a never married man, he was denied that deduction by the terms of the statute. Recognizing that any individual may have an invalid parent for whom he or she must provide care, the overriding issue in this case is whether, as petitioner contends, the exclusion of the never married man from section 214(a) constitutes arbitrary and unequal treatment proscribed by the Constitution.

In determining whether a particular statute or governmental action establishes a classification violative of the constitutional guarantee that those similarly situated shall be similarly treated, the courts have developed two standards of review. See *Developments in the Law—Equal Protection*, 82 Harv. L. Rev. 1065 (1969).

In the generality of cases a test of reasonable classification has been applied: Does the classification established by the legislature bear a reasonable and just relation to the permissible objective of the legislation? Under this general test, if the purpose of the statute is a permissible one and if the statutory classification bears the required fair relationship to that purpose, the constitutional mandate will be held satisfied. *F. S. Royster Guano Co. v. Virginia*, 253 U.S. 412, 415 (1920) ("But the classification must be reasonable, not arbitrary, and must rest upon some ground of difference having a fair and substantial relation to the object of the legislation, so that all persons similarly circumstanced shall be treated alike.").

In two circumstances, however, a more stringent test is applied. When the legislative product affects "fundamental rights or interests", *e.g., Harper v. Virginia Board of Elections*, 383 U.S. 663, 667, 670 (1966) (poll tax in state elections), or when the statute classifies on a basis "inherently suspect," the courts will subject the legislation to the most rigid scrutiny. Thus, a statute distinguishing on the basis of race or ancestry embodies a "suspect" or "invidious" classification and, unless supported by the most compelling affirmative justification, will not pass constitutional muster. *McLaughlin v. Florida*, 379 U.S. 184 (1964); *Korematsu v. United States*, 323 U.S. 214, 216 (1944); *Takahashi v. Fish and Game Commission*, 334 U.S. 410 (1948); *Sei Fujii v. State*, 38 Cal. 2d 718, 730, 242 P.2d 617, 625 (1952).

Petitioner's position is two-fold: (1) the section 214(a) sex-based classification—had petitioner been a single woman rather than a single man the deduction denied him would have been allowed her—is a suspect classification for which no compelling justification can be shown; (2) without regard to the suspect or invidious nature of the classification, the line drawn by Congress, distinguishing the never married man from the widower, the divorced man, and the single woman who may or may not previously have been married, lacks the constitutionally required fair and reasonable relation to the congressional objective that a deduction be afforded those who, in order to earn a livelihood, must incur expenses for the care of physically or mentally incapacitated dependents.

B.

The Legislative History of Section 214 Confirms a Dominant Congressional Purpose to Afford the Dependent Care Deduction to Taxpayers Who, If They Are to be Gainfully Employed, Must Provide Child Care or Care for Physically or Mentally Incapacitated Dependents Other Than Children

The legislative history of section 214 establishes the dominant proper congressional purpose embodied in the statute as enacted. That purpose is pertinent to the threshold issue of constitutionality and determinative of the ultimate issue of remedy presented in this case.

Section 214 had no predecessor in the Internal Revenue Code of 1939. Responding to the recommended tax legislation segment of President Eisenhower's 1953 budget message for the fiscal year 1955, the House Ways and Means Committee in 1954 formulated and the House of Representatives passed and sent to the Senate H. R. 8300, 83d Cong., 2d Sess., containing the following early form of section 214:

SEC. 214 CHILD CARE EXPENSES.

(a) GENERAL RULE.—There shall be allowed as a deduction expenses paid during the taxable year by a taxpayer who is—

(1) a widow or widower, or

(2) a mother whose husband is incapable of self-support because mentally or physically defective, for the care during such year of a child (as defined in subsection (c)(1)), but only if such care is for the purpose of enabling the taxpayer to be gainfully employed.

(b) LIMITATIONS.—The deduction under subsection (a)

(1) —shall not exceed $600 for any taxable year;

(2) shall not apply to any amount paid to an individual with respect to whom the taxpayer is allowed for his taxable year a deduction under section 151 (relating to deductions for personal exemptions).

(c) DEFINITIONS.—For purposes of this section—

(1) CHILD DEFINED.—The term "child" means an individual who (within the meaning of section 152) is a son, stepson, daughter, or stepdaughter of the taxpayer and—

(A) who has not attained the age of 10 years;

or

(B) who has not attained the age of 16 years and who, because mentally or physically defective, is unable to attend school.

(2) WIDOW AND WIDOWER DEFINED.—The terms "widow" and "widower" include an unmarried individual who is legally separated from his spouse under a decree of divorce or an individual who is legally separated from his spouse under a decree of separate maintenance.

The Ways and Means Committee's general explanation of the provision was appropriately brief:

Child-care expenses (sec. 214)

Your committee's bill provides a new deduction for child-care expenses paid by a working widow, widower, or divorced person, or a working mother whose husband is incapacitated. The child must be below the age of 10 (or 16 if the child is physically or mentally unable to attend a regular school). The deduction is limited to actual expenses, but it may not exceed $600. The expenses must be for the purposes of permitting the taxpayer to follow a gainful employment. Expenses paid to a person who is a dependent of the taxpayer may not be deducted. An individual deducting these expenses may not use the standard deduction.

Your committee has added this deduction to the code because it recognizes that a widow or widower with young children must incur these expenses in order to earn a livelihood and that they, therefore, are comparable to an employee's business expenses.

H. R. Rep. No. 1337, 83d Cong., 2d Sess. 30 (1954).

Thus, the initial legislative conception was narrowly limited to child care—any child under 10 years of age and handicapped children under 16 years of age—and the exclusion from the class of benefited taxpayers of never married persons, women as well as men, was thus altogether explicable, although the drafters were perhaps unworldly in failing to advert to the illegitimate offspring.

After receiving written and oral testimony from a variety of sources, the Senate Finance Committee revised section 214 of H.R. 8300 to read, in pertinent part, as follows:

SEC. 214 EXPENSES FOR CARE OF CERTAIN DEPENDENTS.

(a) GENERAL RULE.—There shall be allowed as a deduction expenses paid during the taxable year by a taxpayer who is a woman or a widower for the care of one or more dependents (as defined in subsection (c)(1)), but only if such care is for the purpose of enabling the taxpayer to be gainfully employed.

* * *

(c) DEFINITIONS.—For purposes of this section—

  (1) DEPENDENT.—The term "dependent" means a person, with respect to whom the taxpayer is entitled to an exemption under section 15l(e)(1)—

    (A) who has not attained the age of 12 years and who (within the meaning of section 152) is a son, stepson, daughter, or stepdaughter of the taxpayer; or

    (B) who is physically or mentally incapable of caring for himself.

  (2) WIDOWER.—The term "widower" includes an unmarried individual who is legally separated from his spouse under a decree of divorce or of separate maintenance.

The two significant changes proposed by the Senate Finance Committee were (1) converting section 214 from merely a child care provision to one encompassing the care of incapacitated dependents of any age, and (2) enlarging the class of benefited taxpayers to include all women without regard to prior marital status. The Committee's Report stated:

> Your committee accepts the principle of the new deduction provided in the House bill but substantially liberalizes it with the following changes:

> (a) The deduction is allowed to a working woman or a widower for expenses paid for the care of any dependent who is mentally or physically incapable of caring for himself.

>   * * *

> The House bill provided this deduction because it was recognized that a widow or widower with small children must incur child-care expenses in order to earn a livelihood and that these expenses, therefore, are comparable to an employee's business expenses. Your committee's action in extending the deduction recognizes that similar financial problems may be incurred by taxpayers who, if they are to be gainfully employed, must provide care for physically or mentally incapacitated dependents other than their children.

>   S. Rep. No. 1622, 83d Cong. 2d Sess. 36 (1954).

> Your committee has revised section 214 of the House bill to provide for a deduction for all working women and for widowers for the care of certain dependents.

> This section provides a deduction (not to exceed $600 for any taxable year) for expenses of care of certain dependents which are paid for the purpose of permitting a taxpayer to be gainfully employed (including self-employed).

In order to qualify for this deduction the taxpayer must be either (1) a woman or (2) a widower. Widower is defined in the usual way as a man whose spouse has died and who has not remarried. The term also includes a married man who is legally separated from his spouse under a decree of divorce or of separate maintenance. This deduction is allowed for the care of a child who is a son, daughter, or stepchild of the taxpayer as defined in section 152 under the age of 12, or for a dependent, as defined in section 152, for whom the taxpayer is entitled to a deduction under section 151(e)(1), who is physically or mentally incapable of caring for himself.

S. Rep. No. 1622, 83d Cong., 2d Sess. 220 (1954).

The Finance Committee amendments quoted above were passed by the Senate, accepted by the Conference Committee, and enacted as part of the 1954 Code.[1]

Nothing in the legislative history of section 214 indicates why the Senate Finance Committee, when it enlarged the provision to encompass care of physically or mentally incapacitated dependents of any age, afforded the deduction to the never married single woman but not to the never married single man. The Tax Court, noting that a proposed amendment that would have afforded the deduction to *any* taxpayer was submitted to the Committee, see *Hearings before Senate Committee on Finance on H. R.* 8300, 83d Cong., 2d Sess. 1798 (1954), assumed that the Committee, by failing to accept the amendment, intended to discriminate against the never married man. In view of the thousands of pages of testimony and hundreds of amendments and suggestions for change that were presented at the Hearings on H. R. 8300, it seems far more likely that the Senate Finance Committee, when it chose not to extend the deduction without limitation to any taxpayer, simply failed to focus upon the discrimination engendered by the changes it did make in the House Bill: It changed the Bill to cover care of invalid dependent parents as well as child care, but neglected to adjust the catalogue of taxpayers to include the one class unlikely to have child care responsibilities, but as likely as all the others to have parent care responsibilities. Certainly, it is clear that the

---

1. Subsequently, section 214 was amended, in 1963 by section 1 of P.L. 88-4 and in 1964 by section 212(a) of P.L. 88-272. Except in redesignating as subsection (d) what had been subsection (c) of section 214, these later amendments do not bear upon the case at bar.

purpose of the Senate amendments was not to discriminate against the never married man, but was to afford the deduction to taxpayers who, "with small children must incur child care expenses," or "who, if they are to be gainfully employed, must provide care for physically or mentally incapacitated dependents other than their children." S. Rep. No. 1622, 83d Cong., 2d Sess. 36 (1954).

C.

The Statutory Classification Based on the Sex of the Wage Earner, Established in Section 214(a) for a Purpose Unrelated to any Biological or Functional Difference Between the Sexes, is an "Invidious Classification" Proscribed by the Fifth Amendment to the United States Constitution

Section 214(a) reflects a congressional purpose to ease the financial burden on "taxpayers who, if they are to be gainfully employed, must provide care for physically or mentally incapacitated dependents." S. Rep. No. 1622, 83d Cong., 2d Sess. 36 (1954). Thus, one of the dependents specifically envisioned by Congress was the invalid parent. Although any taxpayer may have an invalid parent, Congress did not authorize a dependent care deduction for taxpayers generally but only, in the case of unmarried persons,[2] for single women, and widowed and divorced persons of either sex.

In sum, section 214(a) draws a line solely on the basis of sex. The gainfully employed single woman who provides care for an ailing mother or father is covered; the gainfully employed bachelor who provides care for an ailing mother or father is excluded. Neither the legislative history nor common sense suggests any rational basis for the difference in treatment accorded sons and daughters by section 214(a).

A generation ago, it was the prevailing view in judicial arenas that, with minimal justification, the legislature could draw "a sharp line between the sexes," *Goesaert v. Cleary*, 335 U.S. 464, 466 (1948), just as a generation earlier, it was settled law that "separate but equal" treatment of the races was constitutionally permissible. *Plessy v. Ferguson*, 163 U.S. 537 (1896). Today, of course, a classification based on race, creed or national origin is "suspect" or "invidious" and a very heavy burden of justification is demanded

---

2. The statute provides special treatment for married taxpayers. The treatment accorded married taxpayers is not in issue in this proceeding.

of a legislature which draws such a distinction. *Loving v. Virginia*, 388 U.S. 1 (1967); *McLaughlin v. Florida*, 379 U.S. 184 (1964); *Korematsu v. United States*, 323 U.S. 214, 216 (1944). See generally *Developments in the Law— Equal Protection*, 82 Harv. L. Rev. 1065 (1969).

It is only within the last half dozen years that the light of constitutional inquiry has focused upon sex discrimination. Emerging from this fresh examination, in the context of the significant changes that have occurred in societal attitudes,[3] is a deeper appreciation of the premise underlying the "suspect classification" doctrine: Although the legislature may distinguish between individuals on the basis of their ability or need, it is presumptively impermissible to distinguish on the basis of congenital and unalterable biological traits of birth over which the individual has no control and for which he should receive neither penalty nor reward. Such conditions of birth include not only race, a matter clearly within the "suspect classification" doctrine, but include as well the sex of the individual.

When biological differences are not related to the activity in question, sex-based discrimination clashes with contemporary notions of fair and equal treatment. See *Developments in the Law—Equal Protection*, 82 Harv. L. Rev. 1065, 1174 n.61 (1969). Congress never suggested, nor could any rational person believe, that the biological differences between sons and daughters are related to the activity in question here—provision of care for an invalid parent. No longer shackled by decisions reflecting social and economic conditions or legal and political theories of an earlier era, see *Harper v. Virginia Board of Elections*, 383 U.S. 663, 669-70 (1966), both federal and state courts have viewed with keen skepticism lines drawn or sanctioned by governmental authority on the basis of sex; absent strong affirmative justification, these lines have not survived constitutional scrutiny. *Abbott v. Mines*, 411 F.2d 353 (6th Cir. 1969); *Seidenberg v. McSorleys' Old Ale House*, 317 F. Supp. 593 (S.D.N.Y. 1970), 308 F. Supp. 1253 (S.D.N.Y. 1969); *United States ex rel. Robinson v. York*, 281 F. Supp. 8 (D. Conn. 1968); *White v. Crook*, 251 F. Supp. 401 (M.D. Ala. 1966) (three

---

3. See Dahlstrom ed., The Changing Roles of Men and Women (1967); Montagu, Man's Most Dangerous Myth 181-84 (4th ed. 1964); Myrdal, An American Dilemma 1073-78 (2d ed. 1962); Watson, Social Psychology Issues and Insights 435-56 (1966); Murray & Eastwood, Jane Crow and the Law: Sex Discrimination and Title VII, 34 Geo. Wash. L. Rev. 232, 235-42 (1965).

judge court); *Owen v. Illinois Baking Corp.*, 260 F. Supp. 820 (W.D. Mich. 1966); *Kirstein v. Rector and Visitors of University of Virginia*, 309 F. Supp. 184 (E.D. Va. 1970) (three judge court); *In re Estate of Legatos*, 1 Cal. App. 3d 657, 81 Cal. Rptr. 910 (1969); *Commonwealth v. Daniel*, 430 Pa. 642, 243 A.2d 400 (1968); *Paterson Tavern & Grill Owners Assoc. v. Borough of Hawthorne*, 57 N.J. 180, 270 A.2d 628 (1970); *Matter of Shpritzer v. Lang*, 17 App. Div. 2d 285, 289, 234 N.Y.S. 2d 285, 289 (1st Dept. 1962), *aff'd*, 13 N.Y. 2d 744, 241 N.Y.S. 2d 869 (1963); *Wilson v. Hacker*, 101 N.Y.S. 2d 461 (N.Y. Sup. Ct. 1950) ("Discrimination on the ground of sex . . . must be condemned as a violation of the fundamental principles of American democracy."). See also *Mengelkoch v. Industrial Welfare Commission*, [442] F.2d [1119], 39 U.S. Law Week 2415 (9th Cir. 1971), for perceptive distinction of decisions rendered in a different societal climate and legal setting.

The trend is clearly discernible: Legislative discrimination grounded on sex, for purposes unrelated to any biological or functional difference between the sexes, ranks with legislative discrimination based on race, another condition of birth, and merits no greater judicial deference. Each exemplifies a "suspect" or "invidious" classification. While instances of discrimination against women dominate the rapidly developing case law in this area, the constitutional sword necessarily has two edges. Fair and equal treatment for women means fair and equal treatment for members of both sexes. The fundamental principles of American democracy reflected in constitutional guarantees of due process and equal protection apply to all *persons*, a class in which men and women share full membership.

D.

The Section 214(a) Classification Based on Sex or Prior Marital Status of a Wage Earner Lacks the Constitutionally Required "Fair and Substantial Relationship" to the Congressional Objective that a Deduction be Afforded Those Who, in Order to Earn a Livelihood, Must Incur Expenses for the Care of Physically or Mentally Incapacitated Dependents

The discrimination embodied in section 214(a) is patently visible. Thus, quite without regard to the qualification of a sex-based classification as "suspect", the section 214(a) discriminatory treatment of the never married man is readily assailable under the traditional constitutional standard: The classification established by the legislature must bear a reasonable and just relation to the permissible objective of the legislation. *F. S. Royster Guano Co. v. Virginia*, 253 U.S. 412, 415 (1920); *Gulf, Colorado & S. F. Ry. v. Ellis*, 165 U.S. 150, 155 (1897).

The Tax Court concluded that section 214(a) "cannot be said to be arbitrary, capricious or unreasonable," for "petitioner is treated no differently from other unmarried, past or present, males."[4] Thus, the Tax Court recognized that in section 214(a) never married men are distinguished from all other taxpayers. Although gleaning that a constitutional issue had been raised, inexplicably the Tax Court failed to make the next, and essential inquiry: Is a classification of wage earners that encompasses all single women, and all widowed and divorced persons, but which excludes single men who have never been married, reasonable in terms of the legislative purpose that a deduction be allowed "taxpayers who, if they are to be gainfully employed, must provide care for physically or mentally incapacitated dependents." S. Rep. No. 1622, 83d Cong., 2d Sess. 36 (1954). In overlooking this critical inquiry, the Tax Court ignored the clear and contrary mandate of the United States Supreme Court.

The nation's highest tribunal has soundly repudiated the contention that the demands of equal protection are met when the law applies equally to all within the statutory class:

> Judicial inquiry . . . does not end with a showing of equal application among the members of the class defined by the legislation. The courts must reach and determine the question whether the classifications drawn in a statute are reasonable in light of its purpose. . . .

McLaughlin v. Florida, 379 U.S. 184, 191 (1964). See also *Skinner v. Oklahoma ex rel. Williamson*, 316 U.S. 535, 541 (1942); *Rinaldi v. Yeager*, 384 U.S. 305, 308-309 (1966); *Seidenberg v. McSorleys' Old Ale House*, 317 F. Supp. 593, 605 (S.D.N.Y. 1970). In short, a law does not provide equal protection if it applies only to part of a larger group similarly situated in relation to the purpose of the legislation. Thus, the issue here is not

---

4. Additionally, the Tax Court appears to have grounded its determination in part upon a belief that tax legislation enjoys special insulation from constitutional attack. The infirmity of this position is discussed separately in section E of this Argument.

whether never married men differ from women, widowers and divorced men, but whether the differences between the excluded and included groups are pertinent to the subject with respect to which the classification is made. See *In re Estate of Legatos*, 1 Cal. App. 3d 657, 81 Cal. Rptr. 910 (1969) (equal protection proscribes arbitrary tax classifications).

Some rational purpose, however doubtful, might be ascribed to the section 214(a) classification if Congress had limited the deduction to expenses for the care of children.[5] Even in that event, however, it would be difficult to justify allowing a deduction to an unmarried wage earning mother, while denying a deduction to an unmarried wage earning father who has custody of his illegitimate offspring. In terms of a deduction for care of a taxpayer's parent "who is physically or mentally incapable of caring for himself", section 214(d)(1)(B), it is impossible to construct any rational basis for distinguishing dutiful daughters and once married sons from dutiful sons who have never married.[6]

It merits emphasis that, in addition to its wholly irrational distinction between single sons and daughters, the statute capriciously prefers sons who are widowed or divorced to sons who are lifelong bachelors. Had Charles E. Moritz prior to the year in issue married and divorced his housekeeper, or any other woman, the deduction here sought unquestionably would have been allowed, although that matrimonial adventure would have borne not the slightest relationship to the dependent care

---

5. Significantly, as originally introduced, H. R. 8300, 83d Cong., 2d Sess. (1954), section 214 allowed the deduction only for child care. Care of physically or mentally incapacitated dependents other than children was added to the House Bill by the Senate Finance Committee. S. Rep. No. 1622, 83d Cong. 2d Sess. 36 (1954). See section B of this Argument.

6. Contrast with the wholly irrational discrimination embodied in section 214(a), the Louisiana succession statute upheld by the United States Supreme Court in *Labine v. Vincent*, [401] U.S. [532], 39 U.S. Law Week 4344 (decided March 29, 1971). Finding that it was permissible for the Louisiana legislature to distinguish for inheritance purposes between legitimate and illegitimate children, the Justice who cast the deciding vote stressed that, "it is surely entirely reasonable for Louisiana to provide that a man who has entered into a marital relationship thereby undertakes obligations to any resulting offspring beyond those which he owes to the products of a casual liaison . . . ." (Harlan, J. concurring opinion). By parity of reasoning, it is surely entirely unreasonable for the United States to provide that an unmarried individual who has honored the obligation to support an incapacitated dependent parent is to be allowed a deduction for the expenditure if a woman or a previously married man, but disallowed the deduction if he is a man who has never been married.

expenditure here in issue. With respect to parent-dependents, there can be no basis for preferring divorced or widowed men over never married men, just as there can be no basis for preferring single daughters over single sons.

Nothing in the legislative history of section 214 offers any justification for the complete exclusion of but one group of taxpayers—never married men—from the coverage of that deduction provision. It is difficult to avoid the conclusion that the exclusion reflects no policy, but simply lack of thought on the part of Congress and the Treasury. Indeed, most persuasive confirmation of the irrationality of the legislative exclusion of single men is provided by the Treasury itself. Prior to filing his petition to the Tax Court in this case, Charles E. Moritz, who appeared *pro se* in that tribunal, in direct correspondence and through Senator Peter H. Dominick, asked the Treasury Department to comment on section 214(a). In letters (Record, pp. 9, 10) dated December 23, 1969, signed by John S. Nolan, Deputy Assistant Secretary, the Treasury responded in the following terms:

> [W]e agree with Mr. Moritz that it is difficult to distinguish, for purposes of the deduction under section 214, between a bachelor and a single man who had been married at one time.

Had Congress willfully decreed the unjustifiable discrimination embodied in section 214(a), the lack of reasonable and just relation to the proper objective of the legislation would require that this Court condemn the arbitrary classification. The arbitrary classification embodied in section 214(a) can fare no better when, as appears to be the case, it represents a thoughtless oversight on the part of Congress. See *Baker v. Carr*, 369 U.S. 186, 226 (1962); *Hobson v. Hansen*, 269 F. Supp. 401, 497 (D.D.C. 1967), *affirmed sub nom. Smuck v. Hobson*, 408 F.2d 175 (D.C. Cir. 1969).

E.

Having Provided an Incapacitated Parent Dependent Care Deduction as a Matter of "Legislative Grace", Congress May Not Arbitrarily Select Those on Whom its Grace is Shed; The Tax Court was Mistaken in Assuming that Taxpayer Classifications Established in a Deduction Provision Need Not Bear a Reasonable Relationship to any Rational Legislative Purpose

The Tax Court in significant part based its decision in favor of the Commissioner upon a belief that provisions of the Internal Revenue Code enjoy a special immunity from constitutional attack. The Tax Court stated its position in the conventional notation that "deductions are a matter of legislative grace." Content with this reference, the Tax Court did not examine the statutory classification in terms of the legislative purpose embodied in section 214(a).

Thus, the position espoused by the Tax Court is that the due process clause of the fifth amendment, which at the least requires that a statutory classification bear a reasonable and just relation to the permissible objective of the legislation, is inapplicable to federal tax legislation. The invalidity of this position can be demonstrated by hypothesizing an Internal Revenue Code provision in terms similar to section 214(a) but classifying eligible and ineligible taxpayers on the basis of race:

> There shall be allowed as a deduction expenses paid during the taxable year by a taxpayer who is a white individual for the care of one or more dependents, but only if such care is for the purpose of enabling the taxpayer to be gainfully employed.[7]

Contrary to the accepted notion of an earlier era, it is no longer held that in granting a "privilege", a legislature may establish any sort of classification it wishes. *Speiser v. Randall,* 357 U.S. 513 (1958); *Sherbert v. Verner,* 374 U.S. 398 (1963); *United States v. Seeger,* 380 U.S. 163, 188

---

7. In support of its position that Congress constitutionally may discriminate in a tax deduction provision "if all members of one class are treated alike," 55 T.C. No. 14 at p. 6, the Tax Court below mistakenly relied upon *Brushaber v. Union Pacific R.R.,* 240 U.S. 1 (1916), and *Shinder v. Commissioner,* 395 F.2d 222 (9th Cir. 1968). Neither case supports the assertion. In *Brushaber,* in which the income tax provisions of the Tariff Act of October 3, 1913, were upheld against a broad-gauged constitutional attack, the Court specifically noted that a taxing provision may be so wanting in basis for classification as to violate due process, a conception that has become far clearer in the more than half a century since that decision. See *Golden Rule Church Association,* 41 T.C. 719, 729 (1964). In *Shinder,* the taxpayer, an unmarried woman (without dependents) living in a rented apartment, attacked among other things the failure of the Internal Revenue Code to grant her "head of household" status and a deduction for that part of her rental expense allocable to the real estate taxes paid by her landlord in respect of her apartment. See 26 T.C.M. 373 (1967). The Court of Appeals properly upheld as constitutional the statutory classifications distinguishing unmarried taxpayers with dependents from those without dependents, and home owners from those who, as tenants, are not directly liable for state property taxes.

(1965) (concurring opinion); *Shapiro v. Thompson*, 394 U.S. 618, 627 n.6 (1969); Van Alstyne, *The Demise of the Right-Privilege Distinction in Constitutional Law*, 81 Harv. L. Rev. 1439, 1461 (1968) ("A minimum demand of uniformly reasonable rules in the management of public largess is surely an unexceptionable requirement of constitutional government.").

It is today clear that Congress, having provided the privilege of a tax deduction, may not arbitrarily select those who shall and shall not enjoy its benefits. An arbitrary classification bearing no discernible relationship to an appropriate legislative purpose is no less subject to constitutional review when found in a tax deduction provision than when found in other "benefit" provisions. See *In re Estate of Legatos*, 1 Cal. App. 3d 657, 81 Cal. Rptr. 910 (1969) (inheritance tax on certain property when devised by husband to wife, but not when devised by wife to husband, violates equal protection).

The Tax Court on another day better recognized the issue: "Although tax benefits such as exemption may be matters of legislative grace [citations omitted], nevertheless, a denial of such benefits granted to others of essentially the same class may well rise to the level of an unconstitutional discrimination." *Golden Rule Church Association*, 41 T.C. 719, 729 (1964).

That deductions are "a matter of legislative grace" is unquestioned; Congress was not obliged to provide a dependent care deduction anymore than it was obliged to provide any other deduction made available in the Internal Revenue Code. Nor is this correlative proposition subject to doubt: Given a rationally drawn deduction provision, the taxpayer must show that his facts bring his case within the terms of the statute. *New Colonial Ice Co. v. Helvering*, 292 U.S. 435 (1934); *Brown v. Helvering*, 291 U.S. 193 (1934); *Burnet v. Thompson Oil & Gas Co.*, 283 U.S. 301 (1931). But when the statute as written embodies an unconstitutional discrimination, it cannot stand without modification; the benefit it confers must be either expunged as to all taxpayers similarly situated, or extended to cover all taxpayers similarly situated. It is abundantly clear that bachelors with invalid parents, single women with invalid parents, and widowed and divorced persons with invalid parents are similarly, indeed identically, situated with respect to the matter here in issue. If bachelors are included in the 214(a) catalogue, then concededly the stipulated facts entitle petitioner to the deduction.

The ultimate question for this Court, and the issue to which we next turn, concerns the remedy for the unconstitutional exclusion of the never married man.

F.

Upon Determining that Section 214(a) as Written Violates the Constitutional Mandate of the Fifth Amendment, the Court May, Consistent with the Dominant Congressional Purpose, Remedy the Defect by Holding the Deduction Available to all Taxpayers Similarly Situated

When a statute denies equal protection by making an unconstitutional classification, the court may remedy the defect either by declaring the statute equally operative upon all persons similarly situated, or by declaring the statute inoperative as to all of them. *Skinner v. Oklahoma ex rel. Williamson*, 316 U.S. 535 (1942). With respect to section 214(a), therefore, upon determining that the statute as written denies equal protection to never married men, this Court, to remedy the defect, must either (1) extend the dependent care deduction to never married men or (2) declare the provision void in its entirety. In deciding whether the legislation is to be extended or the statute invalidated, the Court must be responsive to the dominant proper legislative purpose embodied in section 214(a).

In enacting section 214(a) it was the dominant intent of Congress to afford a deduction to "taxpayers who, if they are to be gainfully employed, must provide care for physically or mentally incapacitated dependents," or "must incur child-care expenses in order to earn a livelihood," expenses which, "therefore, are comparable to an employee's business expenses." S. Rep. No. 1622, 83d Cong. 2d Sess. 36 (1954). It is plain that Congress, had it been apprised in 1954 of the constitutional invalidity of the statutory classification, would have opened the class to never married men, in preference to withdrawing the deduction from women, widowers and divorced men. The Treasury Department has confessed its inability "to distinguish, for purposes of the deduction under section 214, between a bachelor and a single man who had been married at one time." (Record, p. 10.) Clearly, in terms of the dominant and proper legislative purpose, the appropriate response of this Court must be to extend section 214(a) to encompass the never married man; this Court would disserve the intent of Congress were it to invalidate the statute.[8]

Directly in point is the decision of the Supreme Court in *Levy v. Louisiana*, 391 U.S. 68 (1968). The statute there in controversy barred illegitimate children but not legitimate children from recovering in tort for the wrongful death of their mother. The Court found the exclusion of illegitimate offspring in this context an unconstitutional denial of equal protection. Its remedy was not withdrawal from legitimate children of the statutory right to recover, but rather extension of that right to illegitimate children as well.

In *Levy v. Louisiana*, it was apparent that the legislature was not so intent upon denying protection to illegitimate children that it would prefer the wrongful death statute to be totally void. Similarly, the question here raised answers itself. Congress was not so intent upon denying a deduction to bachelors with invalid parents that it would prefer invalidation of section 214 to adjustment of the statute to meet the constitutional demand. In this instance of legislative inadvertence to the equal protection requirement, it is not even arguable that Congress would want section 214 to succumb. Respondent, we believe, will concur in the view that Congress would want section 214 to survive. Accord, *Monica v. Jordan*, Civ. Action No. 32-69, D.N.J. January 27, 1970; *Schmoll v. Creecy*, 54 N.J. 194, 254 A.2d 525, 529-30 (1969). See also *Owen v. Illinois Baking Corp.*, 260 F. Supp. 820 (W.D. Mich. 1966) (constitutionally infirm one-way consortium rule cured by extending the right to wives rather than removing it from husbands); *Simkins v. Moses H. Cone Memorial Hospital*, 323 F.2d 959, 969 (4th Cir. 1963) (en banc), *cert. denied*, 376 U.S. 938 (1964) (unconstitutional racially discriminatory provision pruned and remainder of statute declared effective); *Yale & Towne Mfg. Co. v. Travis*, 262 Fed. 576 (S.D.N.Y. 1919), *aff'd*, 252 U.S. 60 (1920) (tax exemptions granted by statute only to state citizens must be extended to citizens of other states); *Burrow v. Kapfhammer*, 284 Ky. 753, 145 S.W.2d 1067 (1940) (plaintiff added to exempt class to cure unconstitutional exclusion), noted in 54 Harv. L. Rev. 1078 (1941); *Quong Ham Wah Co. v. Industrial Accident*

---

8. The Internal Revenue Code contains a comprehensive separability clause, section 7852(a).

Commission, 184 Cal. 26, 192 P. 1021 (1920), *appeal dismissed*, 255 U.S. 445 (1921) (workmen's compensation benefits extended to non-residents to cure constitutional infirmity); *Note*, 55 Harv. L. Rev. 1030 (1942).

CONCLUSION

For the reasons stated, petitioner respectfully requests that section 214(a) of the Internal Revenue Code of 1954 be held to afford the dependent care deduction to a taxpayer who is a single man who has never been married, and that the judgment of the Tax Court below be reversed and judgment entered for petitioner, with costs.

Respectfully submitted,
Ruth Bader Ginsburg
Martin D. Ginsburg
Attorneys for Petitioner-Appellant

Melvin L. Wulf, Esq.,
American Civil Liberties Union Foundation
Weil, Gotshal & Manges
Of Counsel

FRONTIERO V. RICHARDSON, NO. 71-1694

ORAL ARGUMENT

Supreme Court of the United States
(January 17, 1973)

(17:12-28:10)

CHIEF JUSTICE WARREN E. BURGER

Mrs. Ginsburg.

RUTH BADER GINSBURG

Mr. Chief Justice and may it please the Court.

Amicus views this case as kin to *Reed* v. *Reed*, 404 U.S.[1] The legislative judgment in both derives from the same stereotype.

The man is, or should be, the independent partner in a marital unit.

The woman, with an occasional exception, is dependent, sheltered from bread-winning experience.

Appellees stated in answer to interrogatories in this case that they remained totally uninformed on the application of this stereotype to service families—that is, they do not know whether the proportion of wage-earning wives of servicemen is small-, large-, or middle-sized.

What is known is that by employing the sex criterion, identically situated persons are treated differently—the married serviceman gets benefits for himself, as well as his spouse, regardless of her income; the married servicewoman is denied medical care for her spouse and quarter's allowance for herself as well as her spouse even if, as in this case, she supplies over two-thirds the support of the marital unit.

For these reasons, amicus believes that the sex-related means employed by Congress fails to meet the rationality standard. It does not have a fair and substantial relationship to the legislative objective so that all similarly circumstanced persons shall be treated alike.

Nonetheless, amicus urges the Court to recognize in this case what it has in others—that it writes not only for this case and this day alone, but for this type of case.

As is apparent from the decisions cited at pages 27 to 34 of our brief, in lower federal as well as state courts, the standard of review in sex discrimination cases is, to say the least, confused.

A few courts have ranked sex as a suspect criterion.

Others, including apparently the court below in this case, seem to regard the *Reed* decision as a direction to apply minimal scrutiny, and there are various shades between.

The result is that in many instances, the same or similar issues are decided differently depending upon the court's view of the stringency of review appropriate.

To provide the guidance so badly needed and because recognition is long overdue, amicus urges the Court to declare sex a suspect criterion.

This would not be quite the giant step appellees suggest.

As Professor Gunther observed in an analysis of last Term's equal protection decisions published in the November 1972 *Harvard Law Review*,[2] it appears that in *Reed*, some special suspicion of sex as a classifying factor entered into the Court's analysis.

Appellees concede that the principle ingredient invoking strict scrutiny is present in the sex criterion.

Sex, like race, is a visible, immutable characteristic bearing no necessary relationship to ability.

Sex, like race, has been made the basis for unjustified, or at least unproved, assumptions concerning an individual's potential to perform or to contribute to society.

But, appellees point out that although the essential ingredient rendering a classification suspect is present, sex-based distinctions, unlike racial distinctions, do not have an especially disfavored constitutional history.

It is clear that the core purpose of the Fourteenth Amendment was to eliminate invidious racial discrimination.

But why did the framers of the Fourteenth Amendment regard racial discrimination as odious?

Because a person's skin color bears no necessary relationship to ability.

Similarly, as appellees concede, a person's sex bears no necessary relationship to ability.

Moreover, national origin and alienage have been recognized as suspect classifications, although the newcomer to our shores was not the paramount concern of the nation when the Fourteenth Amendment was adopted.

But the main thrust of the argument against recognition of sex as a suspect criterion centers on two points.

First, women are a majority.

Second, legislative classification by sex does not, it is asserted, imply the inferiority of women.

With respect to the numbers argument, the numerical majority was denied even the right to vote until 1920.

Women today face discrimination in employment as pervasive, and more subtle, than discrimination encountered by minority groups.

In vocational and higher education, women continue to face restrictive quotas no longer operative with respect to other population groups.

Their absence is conspicuous in federal and state legislative, executive, and judicial Chambers, in higher civil service positions, and in appointed posts in federal, state, and local government.

Surely, no one would suggest that race is not a suspect criterion in the District of Columbia because the black population here outnumbers the white.

Moreover, as Mr. Justice Douglas has pointed out most recently in *Hadley* against *Alabama*, 41 *Law Week* 3205,[3] equal protection and due process of law apply to the majority as well as to the minorities.

Do the sex classifications listed by appellees imply a judgment of inferiority?

Even the court below suggested that they do.

That court said it would be remiss, if it failed to notice lurking in the background, the subtle injury inflicted on servicewomen, the indignity of being treated differently so many of them feel.

Sex classifications do stigmatize when, as in *Goesaert* against *Cleary*, 335 U.S.,[4] they exclude women from an occupation thought more appropriate to men.

The sex criterion stigmatizes when it is used to limit hours of work for women only.

Hours regulations of the kind involved in *Muller* against *Oregon*,[5] though perhaps reasonable on the turn of the century conditions, today protect women from competing for extra remuneration, higher paying jobs, promotions.

The sex criterion stigmatizes when as in *Hoyt* against *Florida*, 368 U.S,[6] it assumes that all women are preoccupied with home and children and therefore should be spared the basic civic responsibility of serving on a jury.

These distinctions have a common effect.

They help keep woman in her place, a place inferior to that occupied by men in our society.

Appellees recognize that there is doubt as to the contemporary validity of the theory that sex classifications do not brand the female sex as inferior.

But they advocate a hold-the-line position by this Court unless and until the Equal Rights Amendment comes into force.

Absent the Equal Rights Amendment, appellees assert, no close scrutiny of sex-based classifications is warranted.

This Court should stand pat on legislation of the kind involved in this case—legislation making a distinction servicewomen regard as the most gross inequity, the greatest irritant, and the most discriminatory provision relating to women in the military service.

But this Court has recognized that the notion of what constitutes equal protection does change.

Proponents as well as opponents of the Equal Rights Amendment believe that clarification of the application of equal protection to the sex criterion is needed and should come from this Court.

Proponents believe that appropriate interpretation of the Fifth and Fourteenth Amendments would secure equal rights and responsibilities for men and women.

But they also stressed that such interpretation was not yet discernible, and in any event the Amendment would serve an important function in removing even the slightest doubt that equal rights for men and women is fundamental constitutional principle.

In asking the Court to declare sex a suspect criterion, amicus urges a position forcibly stated in 1837 by Sarah Grimké, noted abolitionist and advocate of equal rights for men and women.

She spoke not elegantly, but with unmistakable clarity.

She said, "I ask no favor for my sex. All I ask of our brethren is that they take their feet off our necks."

In conclusion, amicus joins appellants in requesting that this Court reverse the judgment entered below and remand the case with instructions to grant the relief requested in appellants' complaint.

Thank you.

CHIEF JUSTICE WARREN E. BURGER

Thank you, Mrs. Ginsburg.

NOTES

1. The reference is to *Reed* v. *Reed*, 404 U.S. 71 (1971) (holding unconstitutional Idaho Code prescription that among multiple persons claiming the right to administer a decedent's estate "males must be preferred to females").

2. The reference is to Gerald Gunther, "Foreword: In Search of Evolving Doctrine on a Changing Court: A Model for a Newer Equal Protection," *Harvard Law Review* 86 (1972): 1.

3. The reference is to *Hadley* v. *Alabama*, 409 U.S. 937 (1972) (Douglas, J., dissenting from denial of certiorari); see id. at 937-938 (observing that the case presented the question whether "a State can give more time for filing of a transcript for a person without funds than for a person of wealth" and arguing that "a State may not grant appellate review in such a way as to discriminate between those appellants based on who are wealthy and those who are poor").

4. The reference is to *Goesaert* v. *Cleary*, 335 U.S. 464 (1948) (rejecting challenge of female tavern owner and her daughter to Michigan law denying bartender licenses to females, except for wives and daughters of male tavern owners).

5. The reference is to *Muller* v. *Oregon*, 208 U.S. 412 (1908) (upholding a state law limiting the hours of women laborers).

6. The reference is to *Hoyt* v. *Florida*, 368 U.S. 57 (1961) (upholding Florida system of jury selection in which men were automatically placed on jury rolls, but women were placed only if they expressed an affirmative desire to serve).

WEINBERGER V. WIESENFELD, NO. 73-1892

ORAL ARGUMENT

Supreme Court of the United States (January 20, 1975)

(23:12-49:27)

CHIEF JUSTICE WARREN E. BURGER

Mrs. Ginsburg.

RUTH BADER GINSBURG

Mr. Chief Justice and may it please the Court.

Steven Wiesenfeld's case concerns the entitlement of a female wage earner—a female wage earner's family—to social insurance of the same quality as that accorded to the family of a male wage earner.

Four prime facts of the Wiesenfeld family's life situation bear special emphasis.

Paula Wiesenfeld, the deceased insured worker, was gainfully employed at all times during the seven years immediately preceding her death.

Throughout this period, maximum contributions were deducted from her salary and paid to Social Security.

During Paula's marriage to Steven Wiesenfeld, both were employed.

Neither was attending school and Paula was the family's principal income earner.

In 1972, Paula died giving birth to her son Jason Paul, leaving the child's father, Steven Wiesenfeld, with the sole responsibility for the care of Jason Paul.

For the eight months immediately following his wife's death and for all but a seven-month period thereafter, Steven Wiesenfeld did not engage in substantial gainful employment.

Instead, he devoted himself to the care of the infant, Jason Paul.

At issue is the constitutionality of the gender line drawn by 42 U.S.C. 402(g), the child-in-care provision of the Social Security Act.

Congress established this child-in-care insurance in 1939, as part of that year's conversion of Social Security from a system that insured only the worker to a system that provided a family basis of coverage.

The specific purpose of 402(g) was to protect families of deceased insured workers, by supplementing the child's benefit provided in 42 U.S.C. 402(d).

Where the deceased insured worker is male, the family is afforded the full measure of protection, a child's benefit under 402(d) and a child-in-care benefit under 402(g).

Where the deceased worker is female, family protection is subject to a fifty percent discount.

A child-in-care benefit for survivors of a female insured worker is absolutely excluded, even though as here the deceased mother was the family's principal bread winner.

This absolute exclusion, based on gender *per se*, operates to the disadvantage of female workers, their surviving spouses, and their children.

It denies the female worker social insurance family coverage of the same quality as the coverage available under the account of a male worker.

It denies the surviving spouse of the female worker the opportunity to care personally for his child, an opportunity afforded the surviving spouse of a male worker, and it denies the motherless child an opportunity for parental care afforded the fatherless child.

It is appellee's position that this three-fold discrimination violates the constitutional rights of Paula, Steven, and Jason Paul Wiesenfeld to the equal protection of the laws guaranteed them with respect to federal legislation by the Fifth Amendment.

The care with which the judiciary should assess gender lines drawn by legislation is currently a matter of widespread uncertainty.

The District of Columbia Court of Appeals recently observed in *Waldie* v. *Schlesinger*, decided November 20, 1974,[1] precedent is still evolving, and existing decisions of this Court are variously interpreted by the lower courts.

Appellant had urged in his brief, that it would be sufficient if any rationality can be conceived for the overt sex discrimination operating against the Wiesenfeld family.

But this Court acknowledged in *Reed* v. *Reed*, 404 U.S.,[2] that the legislative objective there in question, reducing probate court workloads, did not lack legitimacy.

Yet, in light of the differential, based on gender *per se*, the Court required a more substantial relationship between legislative ends and means so that men and women similarly circumstanced would be treated alike.

Again, in the Court's eight-to-one judgment in *Frontiero* v. *Richardson*, 411 U.S.,[3] requiring the same fringe benefits for married men and women in the military, the Court evidenced a concern to analyze gender classifications with a view to the modern world and to be wary of gross, archaic, and overbroad generalizations.

As in the case at bar, in *Frontiero*, the underlying assumption was wives are typically dependent, husbands are not.

Hence, the statutory scheme in this case, as this scheme in *Frontiero*, favors one type of family unit over another and in both cases, the basis for the distinction is that in the favored unit, the husband's employment attracts the benefit in question.

Where the bread winner is male, the family gets more, and where the bread winner is female, the family gets less.

Kahn v. *Shevin*, 416 U.S.,[4] and *Schlesinger* v. *Ballard*,[5] this Court's most recent expression, are viewed by some as reestablishing a slack or a cursory review standard, at least when the defender of discrimination packages his argument with a protective or remedial label.

Kahn approved Florida's fifteen dollar real property tax saving for widows.

The decision reflects this Court's consistent deference to State policy in areas of local concern such as State tax systems, domestic relations, zoning, disposition of property within a State's borders.

By contrast, national workers' insurance, and no issue of local concern, is in question here.

The differential in *Schlesinger* v. *Ballard*, this Court pointed out, did not reflect archaic, overbroad generalizations of the kind involved in *Frontiero* or in the instant case.

Indeed, there might have been a certain irony to a ruling in Lieutenant Ballard's favor.

To this day, women seeking careers in the uniformed services are barred by federal statute and regulations from enlistment training and promotion opportunities open to men.

The Court's majority thought it a mismatch for federal law to mandate unequal treatment of women officers, denial to them of training and promotion opportunities open to men—a denial not challenged by Lieutenant Ballard—but to ignore that anterior discrimination for promotion and tenure purposes.

Perhaps most significantly, *Kahn* and *Ballard* are among the very few situations where a discriminatory advantage accorded some women is not readily perceived as a double-edged sword, a weapon that strikes directly against women who choose to be wives and mothers and at the same time to participate as full and equal individuals in a work-centered world.

But there could not be a clearer case than this one of the double-edged sword in operation of differential treatment accorded similarly situated persons based grossly and solely on gender.

Paula Wiesenfeld, in fact the principal wage earner, is treated as though her years of work were of only secondary value to her family.

Steven Wiesenfeld, in fact the nurturing parent, is treated as though he did not perform that function. And Jason Paul, a motherless infant with the father able and willing to provide care for him personally, is treated as an infant not entitled to the personal care of his sole surviving parent.

The line drawn is absolute, not merely a more onerous test for one sex than the other as in *Frontiero* and in *Stanley* v. *Illinois*, 405 U.S.[6]

And the shut-out is more extreme than it was in *Reed*, where a woman could qualify as administrator, if the man who opposed her were less closely related to the decedent.

This case, more than any other yet heard by this Court, illustrates the critical importance of careful judicial assessment of law-reinforced sex role pigeon-holing defended as a remedy.

For on any degree of scrutiny that is more than cursory, 402(g)'s conclusive presumption, automatically and irrebuttably ranking husband principal bread winner, displays the pattern Justice Brennan identified in *Frontiero*. In practical effect, laws of this quality help to keep women not on a pedestal, but in a cage.

They reinforce—not remedy—women's inferior position in the labor force.

Appellant has pointed out that women do not earn as much as men and urges that 402(g) responds to this condition by rectifying past and present economic discrimination against women.

This attempt to wrap a remedial rationale around a 1939 statute, originating in and reinforcing traditional sex-based assumptions, should attract strong suspicion.

In fact, Congress had in view male breadwinners, male heads of household, and the women and children dependent upon them.

Its attention to the families of insured male workers, their wives, and children is expressed in a scheme that heaps further disadvantage on the woman worker.

Far from rectifying economic discrimination against women, the scheme conspicuously discriminates against women workers by discounting the value to their family of their gainful employment.

And, it intrudes on private decision making in an area in which the law should maintain strict neutrality, for when federal law provides a family benefit based on a husband's gainful employment but absolutely bars that benefit based on a wife's gainful employment, the impact is to encourage the traditional division of labor between man and woman to underscore twin assumptions—first, that labor for pay including attendant benefits is the prerogative of men; and second, that women, but not men, appropriately reduce their contributions in the working life to care for children.

On another day, the pernicious impact of gender lines, like the one drawn by 402(g), was precisely and accurately discerned by appellant, in common with every government agency genuinely determined to break down artificial barriers and hindrances to women's economic advancement.

Appellant has instructed that employer's fringe benefit and pension schemes must not presume, as 402(g) does, that husband is head of household or principal wage earner.

It is surely irrational to condemn this sex line as discriminating against women when it appears in an employer's pension scheme, while asserting that it rectifies such discrimination when it appears in workers' social insurance.

JUSTICE POTTER STEWART

You say the appellant has taken these inconsistent positions.
I assume, he was, it wasn't just his idea . . .

RUTH BADER GINSBURG

He was . . .

JUSTICE POTTER STEWART

. . . promulgating that for private pension schemes, but that he was carrying out his understanding of a federal statute.

RUTH BADER GINSBURG

He was carrying out inconsistent congressional commands, guidelines that he issued pursuant to Title IX of the Education Amendments of 1972 . . .

JUSTICE POTTER STEWART

Right.

RUTH BADER GINSBURG

. . . forbid recipients of federal money from making distinctions of this kind.

In sum, the prime generator of discrimination accounted by women in the economic sector is the pervasive attitude, now lacking functional justification, that pairs women with children, men with work.

This attitude is shored up and reinforced by laws of the 402(g) variety, laws that tell a woman her employment is less valuable to and supportive of the family than the employment of a male worker.

Surely, Paula Wiesenfeld would find unfathomable this attempt to cast the compensatory cloak over the denial to her family of benefits available to the family of a male insured.

Nor does appellant's rationalization for discrimination even attempt to explain why Jason Paul, child of a fully insured deceased worker, can have the personal care of his sole surviving parent only if the deceased wage earning parent was male.

Appellant has asserted that providing child-in-care benefits under a female worker's account would involve fiscal considerations.

The amount involved is considerably less than was indicated some moments ago.

He estimates the cost for this particular benefit to be 0.01 percent of taxable payroll in the appendix at 16, and other differentials are not now before this Court.

At the same time, he maintains . . .

JUSTICE POTTER STEWART

Are you familiar, Mrs. Ginsburg, with the little chart on the top of page 15 on the appendix?

RUTH BADER GINSBURG

Yes, I am.

JUSTICE POTTER STEWART

Could you tell us which one of these are we talking about?

RUTH BADER GINSBURG

We are talking about . . .

JUSTICE POTTER STEWART

Which number?
Three?

RUTH BADER GINSBURG

We are talking about three, that's right.
The number of persons affected—fifteen thousand, estimated benefit . . .

JUSTICE POTTER STEWART

Twenty million.

RUTH BADER GINSBURG

Twenty million, right, and that is the only one we're talking about in this case.

JUSTICE POTTER STEWART

And the, well . . .

RUTH BADER GINSBURG

Of course, there is a somewhat inconsistent argument made and that is that the bulk of widowed fathers would not qualify for child-in-care benefits in any event according to appellant, because unlike Stephen Wiesenfeld, they would not devote themselves to childcare, but rather to gainful employment.

Budgetary considerations . . .

JUSTICE POTTER STEWART

And the children have to be under what, eighteen?

RUTH BADER GINSBURG

Yes.

A child has to be a child entitled to child's benefits under the Act.

JUSTICE POTTER STEWART

Which means, among other things, that he is under eighteen?

RUTH BADER GINSBURG

Yes.

Budgetary considerations to justify invidious discrimination should fare no better in this case than such considerations fared in cases in which relatively larger cost savings were involved.

For example, *New Jersey Welfare Rights Organization* against *Cahill*, 411 U.S.,[7] summarily reversing 349 Federal Supplement.

CHIEF JUSTICE WARREN E. BURGER

What is the justification for benefits for, with respect to children, persons under age eighteen as distinguished from having a line at twenty-one or twenty-four or some other age?

RUTH BADER GINSBURG

I don't know why the age line was set, but it's for all benefit purposes under the Social Security Act. I think a distinction is made if a child is attending school after eighteen, but I'm not certain of that.

CHIEF JUSTICE WARREN E. BURGER

But you don't need a babysitter for . . .

RUTH BADER GINSBURG

No, you certainly don't.

CHIEF JUSTICE WARREN E. BURGER

Twelve, fourteen, sixteen, and eighteen year-old people, do you?

RUTH BADER GINSBURG

That's right.

And whether that Congress has gone too far in that direction is not of concern here.

Certainly, it has not gone too far when it considers that an infant such as Jason Paul Wiesenfeld might benefit from the personal care of a parent.

CHIEF JUSTICE WARREN E. BURGER

Well, is there any possibility that the reasoning for his claim depends somewhat on this age factor?

RUTH BADER GINSBURG

The reasoning for?

CHIEF JUSTICE WARREN E. BURGER

The justification?

If the justification is not warranted would that enter into it?

RUTH BADER GINSBURG

Presumably, the greatest need is for very young children, preschool children, and in many cases, the sole surviving parent, male or female, may not avail herself, as the statute now stands, of this benefit once the child gets beyond preschool age or school age.

Remember that this is not a benefit that is paid automatically no matter what.

There is an income limitation.

Once you earn beyond—it was twenty-four hundred dollars—one dollar of benefit is removed for every two dollars earned. So the parent who receives this benefit must be performing that function, must be performing the childcare function.

CHIEF JUSTICE WARREN E. BURGER

I suppose we're not confronted with that age problem unless a nineteen-year-old brings an equal protection claim of some kind?

RUTH BADER GINSBURG

Well, with eighteen years as the voting age now, I think that that is probably unlikely.

But in any event, comparing the cost analysis here with the *New Jersey Welfare Rights Organization* case, that case involved a wholly state-funded program for aid to families of the working poor.

This Court declared unconstitutional limitation of benefits under that program to families with wed parents.

Unlike *New Jersey Welfare Rights Organization*, the case at bar presents no issue of federal deference arguably due to state family law policy or any other local concern.

And surely, leeway for cost saving is no broader in federal workers' insurance than it is in a wholly state-financed and -operated welfare program, a program funded by general state revenues, rather than by contributions of insured workers and their employers.

Budgetary policy, like administrative convenience, simply cannot provide a fair and substantial basis for a scheme that establishes two classes of insured workers, both subject to the same contribution work rate—male workers, whose families receive full protection, and female workers, whose families receive diminished protection.

Finally, the appropriate remedy is correctly specified in the judgment below.

That judgment declares the gender line at issue unconstitutional because it discriminates in violation of the Fifth Amendment against gainfully employed women such as Paula Wiesenfeld as well as against men and children who have lost their wives and mothers.

The judgment enjoins enforcement of the statute insofar as it discriminates on the basis of sex.

Extension of child-in-care benefits under Paula Wiesenfeld's account is unquestionably the course consistent with the dominant congressional purpose to insure the family of deceased workers and the express congressional concern to ameliorate the plight of the deceased worker's child by facilitating a close relationship with the sole surviving parent.

Unequal treatment of male and female workers surely is not a vital part of the congressional plan.

Withdrawal of benefits from female parents who now receive them would conflict with the primary statutory objectives to compensate the family unit for the loss of the insured individual and to facilitate parental care of the child.

Under the circumstances, extension of benefits to the surviving spouse of female insured workers—to the father who devotes himself to child rearing—is the only suitable remedy.

It accords with the express remedial preference of Congress in all recent measures of eliminating gender base differentials, for example, 5 U.S.C. 7152, cited at pages 39 to 40 of our brief, and with this Court's precedent in such cases as *U.S. Department of Agriculture* v. *Moreno*, 413 U.S.,[8] *New Jersey Welfare Rights Organization* against *Cahill*, 411 U.S., and *Frontiero* v. *Richardson*, 411 U.S.

I did want to comment very briefly on the point made with respect to women receiving Social Security benefits that exceed the amount of their contribution.

The reason for this, the prime reason of course, is that women live longer than men.

Most benefits are paid to retirement age beneficiaries and women happened to be fifty-eight percent of the population of persons over sixty-five.

That increases in time.

They're about fifty-four and a half percent of the sixty-five-year-olds, fifty-eight and a half percent of the seventy-five-year-olds, and about sixty-four and a half percent of the eighty-five-year-olds.

But the critical point here is that payments to the elderly are based on the individual's life span, not on his or her sex.

So, that if a man should live to be 100, he will continue to receive benefits and he won't be told, "Well, too bad, you should have died earlier, only women receive payments for that length of time."

In sum, appellee respectfully requests that the judgment below be affirmed, thereby establishing that under this nation's fundamental law, the woman worker's national social insurance is no less valuable to her family than is the social insurance of the working man.

CHIEF JUSTICE WARREN E. BURGER

Thank you, Mrs. Ginsburg.

NOTES

1. The reference is to *Waldie* v. *Schlesinger*, 509 F.2d 508 (C.A.D.C. 1974). In *Waldie*, the United States Court of Appeals for the District of Columbia Circuit had recently remanded for a full trial a case challenging the exclusion of women from the United States Air Force Academy and the United States Naval Academy on equal protection grounds. Writing for the appellate panel, Judge J. Skelly Wright remarked upon the confusion in the lower courts as to the appropriate level of scrutiny applicable to gender-based distinctions. Following *Waldie*, Congress passed, and President Ford signed, legislation opening up the academies to women, thereby mooting the case. See Pub. L. No. 94-106, 89 Stat. 531 (1975).

2. The reference is to *Reed* v. *Reed*, 404 U.S. 71 (1971) (holding unconstitutional Idaho Code prescription that among multiple persons claiming the right to administer a decedent's estate "males must be preferred to females").

3. The reference is to *Frontiero* v. *Richardson*, 411 U.S. 677 (1973) (holding unconstitutional statute that granted fewer dependency benefits to male spouses of female servicepersons than to female spouses of male servicepersons).

4. The reference is to *Kahn* v. *Shevin*, 416 U.S. 351 (1974) (upholding a Florida real estate tax exemption for widows against equal protection challenge).

5. The reference is to *Schlesinger* v. *Ballard*, 419 U.S. 498 (1975) (upholding against constitutional challenge Navy policy that accorded females a longer period than males to attain promotion on the basis that the policy redressed the lack of full opportunities for promotion being offered to females in the Navy).

6. The reference is to *Stanley* v. *Illinois*, 405 U.S. 645 (1972) (holding unconstitutional a state's scheme that did not offer an unmarried father a hearing to prove

fitness to take custody of his children following their mother's death when it offered such an opportunity to the unmarried mothers and married or divorced fathers of children born in wedlock).

7. The reference is to *New Jersey Welfare Rights Organization* v. *Cahill,* 411 U.S. 619 (1973) (holding that state benefit program that in effect denied to children born out of wedlock benefits granted to children born to married parents violates equal protection).

8. The reference is to *U.S. Department of Agriculture* v. *Moreno,* 413 U.S. 528 (1973) (holding unconstitutional federal law that rendered ineligible for food stamps households containing individuals unrelated to other members of the household).

RUTH BADER GINSBURG,
ASSOCIATE JUSTICE,
SUPREME COURT
OF THE UNITED STATES

What follows are materials assembled from Justice Ginsburg's confirmation proceedings and her service on the Supreme Court of the United States. This section begins with the testimony of Justice Ginsburg's friend and longtime co-author, then-Berkeley Law Dean Herma Hill Kay, before the Senate Judiciary Committee during Justice Ginsburg's 1993 confirmation proceedings. Kay chronicles Justice Ginsburg's exceptional career as a scholar and advocate and testifies that "[i]n Ruth Bader Ginsburg, the President has offered the country a Justice worthy of the title."

Next, Justice Ginsburg has chosen her four favorite opinions that she wrote during her time on the Supreme Court: her decision on behalf of the Court in *United States* v. *Virginia*, 518 U.S. 515 (1996) (the Virginia Military Institute, or *VMI* case), and her dissents in *Ledbetter* v. *Goodyear Tire & Rubber Co.*, 550 U.S. 618 (2007), *Shelby County* v. *Holder*, 570 U.S. 529 (2013), and *Burwell* v. *Hobby Lobby Stores, Inc.*, 573 U.S. 682 (2014).

In the Herma Hill Kay Memorial Lecture conversation reproduced in the first section, Justice Ginsburg was reluctant to name a favorite opinion. "That's a little like asking about my four grandchildren, two step-grandchildren, one great-grandchild, which one do I love the most?" All the same, she did reference and discuss her opinions in *VMI* and *Ledbetter*. She adds here two additional dissents drawn from her twenty-seven years of service on the Supreme Court. Also included are the statements Justice Ginsburg read from the bench when the Court announced the decisions in the four cases. It is rare for a dissenting justice to read a summary of their opinion from the bench, so Justice Ginsburg's decision to do so in these cases is significant, revealing she believed her colleagues in the relevant majorities had not just erred, but, as she writes in her *Shelby County* dissent, "err[ed] egregiously." Justice Ginsburg once said in an interview when asked about her dissents, "I will not live to see what becomes of them, but I remain hopeful."

ON THE NOMINATION OF RUTH BADER GINSBURG, TO BE ASSOCIATE JUSTICE OF THE SUPREME COURT OF THE UNITED STATES

HEARINGS BEFORE THE COMMITTEE ON THE JUDICIARY, UNITED STATES SENATE, ONE HUNDRED THIRD CONGRESS, FIRST SESSION (JULY 1993)

Prepared Statement of Herma Hill Kay

Senator Biden, Members of the Judiciary Committee, it gives me great pleasure to be here and participate in your deliberations as you prepare to recommend to the Senate the advice it should give President Clinton on his nomination of Judge Ruth Bader Ginsburg to the United States Supreme Court.

President Clinton's choice of Judge Ginsburg is wise and inspired, sound and practical. In Judge Ginsburg, the President has found a constitutional scholar who knows from her own experience what it means to be excluded despite outstanding credentials solely because of sex. In the early 1970s, she brought that experience—and her flawless logic—to the bar of the United States Supreme Court, where she will soon take her seat. In case after case, she hammered home the point that for the law to assign pre-existing roles to women and men is limiting to both sexes and forbidden by the equal protection clause. It is a point that—at present, twenty years later—many regard as self-evident. But the High Court seemed unable to grasp that point before Ginsburg's advocacy, instead taking as its starting position the belief that a legislative distinction drawn on the basis of sex was a rational classification that passed constitutional muster.

Ruth Bader Ginsburg's strategy of written and oral advocacy to help the nine men then sitting on the Supreme Court understand the irrationality of sex-based distinctions was one of patient instruction. She chose cases in which the law's unequal treatment of men and women was evident and the consequent need for a broader interpretation of the equal protection clause clearly established and readily accepted. The result is that her cases are now constitutional classics: *Reed* v. *Reed*, 1971: A mother can administer a deceased child's estate as capably as a father. *Frontiero* v. *Richardson*, 1973: A servicewoman's Air Force pay earns the same fringe benefits for her "dependent" spouse that a serviceman's pay provides for his "dependent" spouse. *Weinberger* v. *Wiesenfeld*, 1975: A widowed father is entitled to the same insurance benefits available to a widowed mother to help him care for his infant son after his wife's death. *Califano* v. *Goldfarb*, 1977: A deceased wife's earned income provides the same survivor's benefits to her widowed husband that a deceased husband's widow would receive.

These are some of the legal propositions that Judge Ginsburg established as an advocate, and she used them to help the Court forge a new understanding of the equal protection of the laws. It was Ruth Bader Ginsburg's voice, raised in oral argument before the United States Supreme Court, that opened new opportunities for the women of this country. She was in the forefront of the creation of legal precedents that advocates who followed her have used, time and time again, to build a strong edifice against discrimination that now protects many groups. She left her enduring mark on the Constitution even before taking her place on the Supreme Court.

I speak today not only as an academic observer of Judge Ginsburg's work, but also as her co-author and friend. I have had the privilege of working with her on our casebook on *Sex-Based Discrimination*, published in 1974. She and I are both among the first twenty full-time women law professors in the country. We continue to serve together on the Council of the American Law Institute. From those vantage-points, I can say that hers is a courageous intellect, and that she is as steadfast and loyal a colleague and friend as anyone could wish. Her standards are exacting: she produces the best and most precise work and she expects the same from others. As this confirmation process has shown the nation, she thinks deeply and chooses her words with care. But I can tell you that her compassion is as deep as her mind is brilliant. In Ruth Bader Ginsburg, the President has offered the country a Justice worthy of the title. I urge this Committee to recommend that the Senate give its enthusiastic consent to her appointment to the United States Supreme Court.

UNITED STATES V. VIRGINIA
(1996)

In the decision that follows, *United States* v. *Virginia*, the Supreme Court confronted the argument that the admissions policy of the Virginia Military Institute (VMI) excluding female applicants violated the Equal Protection Clause of the Fourteenth Amendment to the United States Constitution. Founded in 1839, VMI's mission is to produce "citizen-soldiers" prepared for leadership in civilian life and in military service. When the United States government sued the Commonwealth of Virginia challenging the exclusionary admissions policy, the State proposed creating the Virginia Women's Institute for Leadership, a parallel program for women chartered with the same mission to produce "citizen-soldiers."

In her opinion on behalf of the Court, Justice Ginsburg writes that the case asks the Court to decide "whether the Commonwealth can constitutionally deny to women who have the will and capacity, the training and attendant opportunities that VMI uniquely affords." Holding the admissions policy to be constitutionally problematic, Justice Ginsburg invokes the standard announced by the Court in *Mississippi University for Women* v. *Hogan*, 458 U.S. 718 (1982), to conclude that Virginia had failed to demonstrate an "exceedingly persuasive justification" for its exclusionary policy. Her opinion likewise holds that Virginia's proposed new institution for female cadets could not offer the same opportunities or benefits of VMI's unique and storied program. Finally, Justice Ginsburg observes, "There is no reason to believe that the admission of women capable of all the activities required of VMI cadets would destroy the Institute rather than enhance its capacity to serve the 'more perfect Union.'"

Although he did not sign on to her opinion, Chief Justice William H. Rehnquist concurred in the judgment, agreeing with the Court's holding. This left Justice Antonin Scalia as the lone dissenter. In Justice Scalia's view, the Court had raised the level of scrutiny applied to gender classifications beyond what the Court's earlier precedents supported. Further, he believed that VMI had demonstrated that its "all-male composition" was "essential to th[e] institution's character." Justice Ginsburg's responses to the dissent may be found in her opinion for the Court.

The statement Justice Ginsburg read from the bench on the day the Court announced the VMI decision, along with her opinion for the Court, follow.

UNITED STATES V. VIRGINIA, NO. 94-1941

VIRGINIA V. UNITED STATES, NO. 94-2107

BENCH ANNOUNCEMENT

Supreme Court of the United States (June 26, 1996)

This case concerns an incomparable military college, the Virginia Military Institute (VMI), the sole single-sex school among Virginia's public institutions of higher learning. Since its founding in 1839, VMI has produced civilian and military leaders for the Commonwealth and the Nation. The school's unique program and unparalleled record as a leadership training ground has led some women to seek admission. The United States, on behalf of women capable of all the activities required of VMI cadets, instituted this lawsuit in 1990, maintaining that under the Equal Protection Clause of the Fourteenth Amendment to the U.S. Constitution, Virginia may not reserve exclusively to men the educational opportunities that VMI, and no other Virginia school, affords.

The case has had a long history in court. In the first round, the District Court ruled against the United States, reasoning that the all-male VMI served the State's policy of affording diverse educational programs. The Fourth Circuit vacated that judgment, concluding that a diversity policy serving to "favor one gender" did not constitute equal protection.

In the second round, the lower courts considered, and found satisfactory, the remedy Virginia proposed: a program for women, called the Virginia Women's Institute for Leadership (VWIL) at a private women's

105

college, Mary Baldwin College. A VWIL degree, the Fourth Circuit said, would not carry the historical benefit and prestige of a VMI degree, and the two programs differed markedly in methodology—VMI's is rigorously "adversative," VWIL's would be "cooperative." But overall, the lower courts concluded, the schools were "sufficiently comparable" to meet the demand of equal protection.

We reverse that determination. Our reasoning centers on the essence of the complaint of the United States, and on facts that are undisputed: Some women, at least, can meet the physical standards VMI imposes on men, are capable of all the activities required of VMI cadets, prefer VMI's methodology over VWIL's, could be educated using VMI's methodology, and would want to attend VMI if they had the chance.

With recruitment, the District Court recognized, VMI could "achieve at least 10% female enrollment"—a number, the District Court said, "suffi-cient . . . to provide female cadets with a positive educational experience." If most women would not choose VMI's adversative method, many men, too, would not want to be educated in VMI's environment. The question before us, however, is not whether women or men should be *forced* to attend VMI. Rather, the question is whether Virginia can constitutionally deny to women who have the will and capacity, the training and attendant opportunities VMI uniquely affords—training and opportunities VWIL does not supply.

To answer that question we must have a measuring rod—what lawyers call a standard of review. In a nutshell, this is the standard our precedent establishes: Defenders of sex-based government action must demonstrate an "exceedingly persuasive justification" for that action. To make that demonstration, the defender of a gender line in the law must show, "at least, that the [challenged] classification serves important governmental objectives and that [any] discriminatory means employed [is] substan-tially related to the achievement of those objectives." The heightened review standard applicable to sex-based classifications does not make sex a proscribed classification, but it does mark as presumptively invalid—incompatible with equal protection—a law or official policy that denies to women, simply because they are women, equal opportunity to aspire, achieve, participate in and contribute to society based upon what they can do.

Under this exacting standard, reliance on overbroad generalizations, typically male or typically female "tendencies," estimates about the way most women (or most men) are, will not suffice to deny opportunity to women whose talent and capacity place them outside the average description. As this Court said in *Mississippi University for Women* v. *Hogan* some 14 years ago, state actors may not close entrance gates based on "fixed notions concerning the roles and abilities of males and females."

A remedial decree must cure the constitutional violation—in this case, the categorical exclusion of women from an extraordinary educational/ leadership-development opportunity afforded men. To cure that violation, and to afford genuinely equal protection, women seeking and fit for a VMI-quality education cannot be offered anything less. We therefore reverse the Fourth Circuit's judgment, and remand the case for proceedings consistent with this opinion.

The Chief Justice has filed an opinion concurring in the judgment. Justice Scalia has filed a dissenting opinion. Justice Thomas took no part in the consideration or decision of the case.

UNITED STATES V. VIRGINIA, 518 U.S. 515

MAJORITY OPINION

Supreme Court of the United States

UNITED STATES, Petitioner,

v.

VIRGINIA et al.

VIRGINIA, et al., Petitioners,

v.

UNITED STATES.

Nos. 94-1941, 94-2107.

Argued Jan. 17, 1996.

Decided June 26, 1996.

Justice GINSBURG delivered the opinion of the Court.

Virginia's public institutions of higher learning include an incomparable military college, Virginia Military Institute (VMI). The United States maintains that the Constitution's equal protection guarantee precludes Virginia from reserving exclusively to men the unique educational opportunities VMI affords. We agree.

I

Founded in 1839, VMI is today the sole single-sex school among Virginia's 15 public institutions of higher learning. VMI's distinctive mission is to produce "citizen-soldiers," men prepared for leadership in civilian life and in military service. VMI pursues this mission through pervasive training of a kind not available anywhere else in Virginia. Assigning prime place to character development, VMI uses an "adversative method" modeled on English public schools and once characteristic of military instruction. VMI constantly endeavors to instill physical and mental discipline in its cadets and impart to them a strong moral code. The school's graduates leave VMI with heightened comprehension of their capacity to deal with duress and stress, and a large sense of accomplishment for completing the hazardous course.

VMI has notably succeeded in its mission to produce leaders; among its alumni are military generals, Members of Congress, and business executives. The school's alumni overwhelmingly perceive that their VMI training helped them to realize their personal goals. VMI's endowment reflects the loyalty of its graduates; VMI has the largest per-student endowment of all public undergraduate institutions in the Nation.

Neither the goal of producing citizen-soldiers nor VMI's implementing methodology is inherently unsuitable to women. And the school's impressive record in producing leaders has made admission desirable to some women. Nevertheless, Virginia has elected to preserve exclusively for men the advantages and opportunities a VMI education affords.

II

A

From its establishment in 1839 as one of the Nation's first state military colleges, see 1839 Va. Acts, ch. 20, VMI has remained financially supported by Virginia and "subject to the control of the [Virginia] General Assembly," Va. Code Ann. § 23–92 (1993). First southern college to teach engineering and industrial chemistry, see H. Wise, Drawing Out the Man: The VMI Story 13 (1978) (The VMI Story), VMI once provided teachers for the Commonwealth's schools, see 1842 Va. Acts, ch. 24, § 2 (requiring every cadet to teach in one of the Commonwealth's schools for a 2–year period).[1] Civil War strife threatened the school's vitality, but a resourceful superintendent regained legislative support by highlighting "VMI's great potential[,] through its technical know-how," to advance Virginia's postwar recovery. The VMI Story 47.

VMI today enrolls about 1,300 men as cadets.[2] Its academic offerings in the liberal arts, sciences, and engineering are also available at other public colleges and universities in Virginia. But VMI's mission is special. It is the mission of the school

"'to produce educated and honorable men, prepared for the varied work of civil life, imbued with love of learning, confident in the functions and attitudes of leadership, possessing a high sense of public service, advocates of the American democracy and free enterprise system, and ready as citizen-soldiers to defend their country in time of national peril.'" 766 F. Supp. 1407, 1425 (W.D.Va. 1991) (quoting Mission Study Committee of the VMI Board of Visitors, Report, May 16, 1986).

---

1. During the Civil War, school teaching became a field dominated by women. See A. Scott, The Southern Lady: From Pedestal to Politics, 1830–1930, p. 82 (1970).

2. Historically, most of Virginia's public colleges and universities were single sex; by the mid-1970's, however, all except VMI had become coeducational. 766 F. Supp. 1407, 1418–1419 (W.D.Va. 1991). For example, Virginia's legislature incorporated Farmville Female Seminary Association in 1839, the year VMI opened. 1839 Va. Acts, ch. 167. Originally providing instruction in "English, Latin, Greek, French, and piano" in a "home atmosphere," R. Sprague, Longwood College: A History 7–8, 15 (1989) (Longwood College), Farmville Female Seminary became a public institution in 1884 with a mission to train "white female teachers for public schools," 1884 Va. Acts, ch. 311. The school became Longwood College in 1949, Longwood College 136, and introduced coeducation in 1976, *id.*, at 133.

In contrast to the federal service academies, institutions maintained "to prepare cadets for career service in the armed forces," VMI's program "is directed at preparation for both military and civilian life"; "[o]nly about 15% of VMI cadets enter career military service." 766 F. Supp., at 1432.

VMI produces its "citizen-soldiers" through "an adversative, or doubting, model of education" which features "[p]hysical rigor, mental stress, absolute equality of treatment, absence of privacy, minute regulation of behavior, and indoctrination in desirable values." *Id.*, at 1421. As one Commandant of Cadets described it, the adversative method "'dissects the young student,'" and makes him aware of his "'limits and capabilities,'" so that he knows "'how far he can go with his anger, ... how much he can take under stress, ... exactly what he can do when he is physically exhausted.'" *Id.*, at 1421–1422 (quoting Col. N. Bissell).

VMI cadets live in spartan barracks where surveillance is constant and privacy nonexistent; they wear uniforms, eat together in the mess hall, and regularly participate in drills. *Id.*, at 1424, 1432. Entering students are incessantly exposed to the rat line, "an extreme form of the adversative model," comparable in intensity to Marine Corps boot camp. *Id.*, at 1422. Tormenting and punishing, the rat line bonds new cadets to their fellow sufferers and, when they have completed the 7–month experience, to their former tormentors. *Ibid.*

VMI's "adversative model" is further characterized by a hierarchical "class system" of privileges and responsibilities, a "dyke system" for assigning a senior class mentor to each entering class "rat," and a stringently enforced "honor code," which prescribes that a cadet "'does not lie, cheat, steal nor tolerate those who do.'" *Id.*, at 1422–1423.

VMI attracts some applicants because of its reputation as an extraordinarily challenging military school, and "because its alumni are exceptionally close to the school." *Id.*, at 1421. "[W]omen have no opportunity anywhere to gain the benefits of [the system of education at VMI]." *Ibid.*

B

In 1990, prompted by a complaint filed with the Attorney General by a female high-school student seeking admission to VMI, the United States sued the Commonwealth of Virginia and VMI, alleging that VMI's exclusively male admission policy violated the Equal Protection Clause of the

Justice Ruth Bader Ginsburg and Professor Herma Hill Kay together following Kay's recognition with the American Association of Law Schools' Ruth Bader Ginsburg Lifetime Achievement Award, 2015. (Courtesy Amanda L. Tyler)

Justice Ruth Bader Ginsburg and Professor Amanda Tyler in conversation during the inaugural Herma Hill Kay Memorial Lecture at the University of California, Berkeley, October 21, 2019. (*Both images this page:* Courtesy of the University of California, Berkeley School of Law)

Justice Ruth Bader Ginsburg on stage at the inaugural Herma Hill Kay Memorial Lecture.

Justice Ruth Bader Ginsburg and Professor Amanda Tyler following their conversation at the inaugural Herma Hill Kay Memorial Lecture at the University of California, Berkeley, October 21, 2019. (Used with permission of Associated Press Photo/Jeff Chiu)

Ruth Bader and Martin Ginsburg together at his home following their engagement party, which was held at the Persian Room of the Plaza Hotel in New York City, December 27, 1953. (Courtesy of Justice Ginsburg's personal collection)

Volume 71 of the *Harvard Law Review*, 1957–1958. Ruth Bader Ginsburg (far right, fourth row from bottom) was one of only two female members. (Harvard Law School Library, Historical and Special Collections)

Martin Ginsburg, Jane Ginsburg, and Ruth Bader Ginsburg, 1958. (Courtesy of the Collection of the Supreme Court of the United States)

Professor Ruth Bader Ginsburg at Rutgers Law School, 1969. (Courtesy of Rutgers Law School, Rutgers, the State University of New Jersey)

Ruth Bader Ginsburg, Supreme Court Justice Thurgood Marshall, and Judge Clifford Wallace judge the moot court competition at the University of California, Berkeley School of Law. They are joined by student organizer Kathleen Tuttle, 1978. (Courtesy of the University of California, Berkeley School of Law)

Ruth Bader Ginsburg on the steps of the Supreme Court following oral arguments in *Duren* v. *Missouri*, the last case she argued before the Court, November 1, 1978. Son James Ginsburg is on right, and brother-in-law and nephew Ed and David Stiepleman on left. (Courtesy of Justice Ginsburg's personal collection)

Judge Ruth Bader Ginsburg smiles at her husband, Martin Ginsburg, and son, James Ginsburg, during her Supreme Court confirmation hearings, 1993. (Used with permission of Associated Press Photo/John Duricka)

Judge Ruth Bader Ginsburg puts up her fists in mock anticipation of a fight during her Supreme Court confirmation hearings, 1993. (Used with permission of www.Newsweek.com/Larry Downing)

Justice Ruth Bader Ginsburg with husband Martin Ginsburg, children Jane and James Ginsburg, son-in-law George Spera, and grandchildren Clara and Paul Spera on the occasion of her Investiture Ceremony at the Supreme Court, 1993. (Courtesy of the Collection of the Supreme Court of the United States)

Justice Ruth Bader Ginsburg in her Supreme Court chambers, as photographed by Nancy Lee Katz, 1994. (Courtesy Michael S. Sachs)

Justice Ruth Bader Ginsburg and Martin Ginsburg, as photographed by Mariana Cook, 1998. (Courtesy Mariana Cook)

Ruth Bader Ginsburg and Martin Ginsburg embrace, 2003. (Photo copyright Lynn Saville, 2003, all rights reserved)

Justices Ruth Bader Ginsburg and Antonin Scalia in costume with members of the cast of *Ariadne auf Naxos* following a performance at the Washington National Opera in which they appeared as extras, 1994. (Used with permission of Associated Press Photo/Stephen R. Brown)

Professor Amanda Tyler and Justice Ruth Bader Ginsburg together before Justice Ginsburg offered remarks on the legacy of Chief Justice William H. Rehnquist at the George Washington University Law School, 2005. (Courtesy Amanda L. Tyler)

Justice Ruth Bader Ginsburg stands on the emptied stage at the San Francisco War Memorial Opera House during a cast party following a performance of *Dolores Claiborne* by the San Francisco Opera, 2013. A lover of opera, Justice Ginsburg once said, "If I had any talent in the world, any talent that God could give me, I would be a great diva." Photo by Drew Altizer (Courtesy Drew Altizer)

Justices Sandra Day O'Connor (Ret.), Sonia Sotomayor, Ruth Bader Ginsburg, and Elena Kagan on the occasion of Justice Kagan's Investiture Ceremony at the Supreme Court, 2010. (Courtesy of the Collection of the Supreme Court of the United States)

Justice Ruth Bader Ginsburg and former law clerk Lisa Beattie Frelinghuysen with female cadets during a visit to the Virginia Military Institute, 2017. Photo by Kevin Remington (Courtesy Kevin Remington)

The casket of Justice Ruth Bader Ginsburg arrives at the Supreme Court while her law clerks serve as honorary pallbearers, September 23, 2020. (Used with permission of the *New York Times*/Doug Mills)

A child pays respects while Justice Ruth Bader Ginsburg lies in repose under the portico at the top of the west entrance steps to the Supreme Court, September 23, 2020. (Used with permission of Associated Press Photo/Alex Brandon, pool)

Justice Ruth Bader Ginsburg lies in state in the Statuary Hall of the United States Capitol, the first woman and first Jewish person ever to be so honored, September 25, 2020. (Used with permission of Associated Press Photo/Chip Somodevilla, pool)

Associate Justice Ruth Bader Ginsburg, official Supreme Court portrait, 2016. (Courtesy of the Collection of the Supreme Court of the United States)

Fourteenth Amendment. *Id.*, at 1408.[3] Trial of the action consumed six days and involved an array of expert witnesses on each side. *Ibid.*

In the two years preceding the lawsuit, the District Court noted, VMI had received inquiries from 347 women, but had responded to none of them. *Id.*, at 1436. "[S]ome women, at least," the court said, "would want to attend the school if they had the opportunity." *Id.*, at 1414. The court further recognized that, with recruitment, VMI could "achieve at least 10% female enrollment"—"a sufficient 'critical mass' to provide the female cadets with a positive educational experience." *Id.*, at 1437–1438. And it was also established that "some women are capable of all of the individual activities required of VMI cadets." *Id.*, at 1412. In addition, experts agreed that if VMI admitted women, "the VMI ROTC experience would become a better training program from the perspective of the armed forces, because it would provide training in dealing with a mixed-gender army." *Id.*, at 1441.

The District Court ruled in favor of VMI, however, and rejected the equal protection challenge pressed by the United States. That court correctly recognized that *Mississippi Univ. for Women* v. *Hogan,* 458 U.S. 718 (1982), was the closest guide. 766 F. Supp., at 1410. There, this Court underscored that a party seeking to uphold government action based on sex must establish an "exceedingly persuasive justification" for the classification. *Mississippi Univ. for Women,* 458 U.S., at 724 (internal quotation marks omitted). To succeed, the defender of the challenged action must show "at least that the classification serves important governmental objectives and that the discriminatory means employed are substantially related to the achievement of those objectives." *Ibid.* (internal quotation marks omitted).

The District Court reasoned that education in "a single-gender environment, be it male or female," yields substantial benefits. 766 F. Supp., at 1415. VMI's school for men brought diversity to an otherwise coeducational Virginia system, and that diversity was "enhanced by VMI's unique method of instruction." *Ibid.* If single-gender education for males ranks as an important governmental objective, it becomes obvious, the District

---

3. The District Court allowed the VMI Foundation and the VMI Alumni Association to intervene as defendants. 766 F. Supp., at 1408.

Court concluded, that the *only* means of achieving the objective "is to exclude women from the all-male institution—VMI." *Ibid.*

"Women are [indeed] denied a unique educational opportunity that is available only at VMI," the District Court acknowledged. *Id.*, at 1432. But "[VMI's] single-sex status would be lost, and some aspects of the [school's] distinctive method would be altered," if women were admitted, *id.*, at 1413: "Allowance for personal privacy would have to be made," *id.*, at 1412; "[p]hysical education requirements would have to be altered, at least for the women," *id.*, at 1413; the adversative environment could not survive unmodified, *id.*, at 1412–1413. Thus, "sufficient constitutional justification" had been shown, the District Court held, "for continuing [VMI's] single-sex policy." *Id.*, at 1413.

The Court of Appeals for the Fourth Circuit disagreed and vacated the District Court's judgment. The appellate court held: "The Commonwealth of Virginia has not . . . advanced any state policy by which it can justify its determination, under an announced policy of diversity, to afford VMI's unique type of program to men and not to women." 976 F.2d 890, 892 (1992).

The appeals court greeted with skepticism Virginia's assertion that it offers single-sex education at VMI as a facet of the Commonwealth's overarching and undisputed policy to advance "autonomy and diversity." The court underscored Virginia's nondiscrimination commitment: "'[I]t is extremely important that [colleges and universities] deal with faculty, staff, and students *without regard to sex, race, or ethnic origin.*'" *Id.*, at 899 (quoting 1990 Report of the Virginia Commission on the University of the 21st Century). "That statement," the Court of Appeals said, "is the only explicit one that we have found in the record in which the Commonwealth has expressed itself with respect to gender distinctions." 976 F.2d, at 899. Furthermore, the appeals court observed, in urging "diversity" to justify an all-male VMI, the Commonwealth had supplied "no explanation for the movement away from [single-sex education] in Virginia by public colleges and universities." *Ibid.* In short, the court concluded, "[a] policy of diversity which aims to provide an array of educational opportunities, including single-gender institutions, must do more than favor one gender." *Ibid.*

The parties agreed that "*some* women can meet the physical standards now imposed on men," *id.*, at 896, and the court was satisfied that "neither the goal of producing citizen soldiers nor VMI's implementing methodology is inherently unsuitable to women," *id.*, at 899. The Court of Appeals, however, accepted the District Court's finding that "at least these three aspects of VMI's program—physical training, the absence of privacy, and the adversative approach—would be materially affected by coeducation." *Id.*, at 896–897. Remanding the case, the appeals court assigned to Virginia, in the first instance, responsibility for selecting a remedial course. The court suggested these options for the Commonwealth: Admit women to VMI; establish parallel institutions or programs; or abandon state support, leaving VMI free to pursue its policies as a private institution. *Id.*, at 900. In May 1993, this Court denied certiorari. See 508 U.S. 946; see also *ibid.* (opinion of SCALIA, J., noting the interlocutory posture of the litigation).

C

In response to the Fourth Circuit's ruling, Virginia proposed a parallel program for women: Virginia Women's Institute for Leadership (VWIL). The 4-year, state-sponsored undergraduate program would be located at Mary Baldwin College, a private liberal arts school for women, and would be open, initially, to about 25 to 30 students. Although VWIL would share VMI's mission—to produce "citizen-soldiers"—the VWIL program would differ, as does Mary Baldwin College, from VMI in academic offerings, methods of education, and financial resources. See 852 F. Supp. 471, 476–477 (W.D.Va. 1994).

The average combined SAT score of entrants at Mary Baldwin is about 100 points lower than the score for VMI freshmen. See *id.*, at 501. Mary Baldwin's faculty holds "significantly fewer Ph.D.'s than the faculty at VMI," *id.*, at 502, and receives significantly lower salaries, see Tr. 158 (testimony of James Lott, Dean of Mary Baldwin College), reprinted in 2 App. in Nos. 94–1667 and 94–1717 (CA4) (hereinafter Tr.). While VMI offers degrees in liberal arts, the sciences, and engineering, Mary Baldwin, at the time of trial, offered only bachelor of arts degrees. See 852 F. Supp., at 503. A VWIL student seeking to earn an engineering degree could gain one, without public support, by attending Washington University in St. Louis, Missouri, for two years, paying the required private tuition. See *ibid.*

Experts in educating women at the college level composed the Task Force charged with designing the VWIL program; Task Force members were drawn from Mary Baldwin's own faculty and staff. *Id.*, at 476. Training its attention on methods of instruction appropriate for "most women," the Task Force determined that a military model would be "wholly inappropriate" for VWIL. *Ibid.;* see 44 F.3d 1229, 1233 (C.A.4 1995).

VWIL students would participate in ROTC programs and a newly established, "largely ceremonial" Virginia Corps of Cadets, *id.*, at 1234, but the VWIL House would not have a military format, 852 F. Supp., at 477, and VWIL would not require its students to eat meals together or to wear uniforms during the schoolday, *id.*, at 495. In lieu of VMI's adversative method, the VWIL Task Force favored "a cooperative method which reinforces self-esteem." *Id.*, at 476. In addition to the standard bachelor of arts program offered at Mary Baldwin, VWIL students would take courses in leadership, complete an off-campus leadership externship, participate in community service projects, and assist in arranging a speaker series. See 44 F.3d, at 1234.

Virginia represented that it will provide equal financial support for in-state VWIL students and VMI cadets, 852 F. Supp., at 483, and the VMI Foundation agreed to supply a $5.4625 million endowment for the VWIL program, *id.*, at 499. Mary Baldwin's own endowment is about $19 million; VMI's is $131 million. *Id.*, at 503. Mary Baldwin will add $35 million to its endowment based on future commitments; VMI will add $220 million. *Ibid.* The VMI Alumni Association has developed a network of employers interested in hiring VMI graduates. The Association has agreed to open its network to VWIL graduates, *id.*, at 499, but those graduates will not have the advantage afforded by a VMI degree.

D

Virginia returned to the District Court seeking approval of its proposed remedial plan, and the court decided the plan met the requirements of the Equal Protection Clause. *Id.*, at 473. The District Court again acknowledged evidentiary support for these determinations: "[T]he VMI methodology could be used to educate women and, in fact, some women . . . may prefer the VMI methodology to the VWIL methodology." *Id.*, at 481. But the "controlling legal principles," the District Court decided, "do not require the Commonwealth to provide a mirror image VMI for women." *Ibid.* The court anticipated that the two schools would "achieve substantially similar outcomes." *Ibid.* It concluded: "If VMI marches to the beat of a drum, then Mary Baldwin marches to the melody of a fife and when the march is over, both will have arrived at the same destination." *Id.*, at 484.

A divided Court of Appeals affirmed the District Court's judgment. 44 F.3d 1229 (C.A.4 1995). This time, the appellate court determined to give "greater scrutiny to the selection of means than to the [Commonwealth's] proffered objective." *Id.*, at 1236. The official objective or purpose, the court said, should be reviewed deferentially. *Ibid.* Respect for the "legislative will," the court reasoned, meant that the judiciary should take a "cautious approach," inquiring into the "legitima[cy]" of the governmental objective and refusing approval for any purpose revealed to be "pernicious." *Ibid.*

"[P]roviding the option of a single-gender college education may be considered a legitimate and important aspect of a public system of higher education," the appeals court observed, *id.*, at 1238; that objective, the court added, is "not pernicious," *id.*, at 1239. Moreover, the court continued, the adversative method vital to a VMI education "has never been tolerated in a sexually heterogeneous environment." *Ibid.* The method itself "was not designed to exclude women," the court noted, but women could not be accommodated in the VMI program, the court believed, for female participation in VMI's adversative training "would destroy . . . any sense of decency that still permeates the relationship between the sexes." *Ibid.*

Having determined, deferentially, the legitimacy of Virginia's purpose, the court considered the question of means. Exclusion of "men at Mary Baldwin College and women at VMI," the court said, was essential to Virginia's purpose, for without such exclusion, the Commonwealth could not "accomplish [its] objective of providing single-gender education." *Ibid.*

The court recognized that, as it analyzed the case, means merged into end, and the merger risked "bypass[ing] any equal protection scrutiny." *Id.*, at 1237. The court therefore added another inquiry, a decisive test it called "substantive comparability." *Ibid.* The key question, the court said, was whether men at VMI and women at VWIL would obtain "substantively comparable benefits at their institution or through other means offered by the [S]tate." *Ibid.* Although the appeals court recognized that the VWIL degree "lacks the historical benefit and prestige" of a VMI degree, it nevertheless found the educational opportunities at the two schools "sufficiently comparable." *Id.*, at 1241.

Senior Circuit Judge Phillips dissented. The court, in his judgment, had not held Virginia to the burden of showing an "'exceedingly persuasive [justification]'" for the Commonwealth's action. *Id.*, at 1247 (quoting *Mississippi Univ. for Women*, 458 U.S., at 724). In Judge Phillips' view, the court had accepted "rationalizations compelled by the exigencies of this litigation," and had not confronted the Commonwealth's "actual overriding purpose." 44 F.3d, at 1247. That purpose, Judge Phillips said, was clear from the historical record; it was "not to create a new type of educational opportunity for women, . . . nor to further diversify the Commonwealth's higher education system[,] . . . but [was] simply . . . to allow VMI to continue to exclude women in order to preserve its historic character and mission." *Ibid.*

Judge Phillips suggested that the Commonwealth would satisfy the Constitution's equal protection requirement if it "simultaneously opened single-gender undergraduate institutions having substantially comparable curricular and extra-curricular programs, funding, physical plant, administration and support services, and faculty and library resources." *Id.*, at 1250. But he thought it evident that the proposed VWIL program, in comparison to VMI, fell "far short . . . from providing substantially equal tangible and intangible educational benefits to men and women." *Ibid.*

The Fourth Circuit denied rehearing en banc. 52 F.3d 90 (1995). Circuit Judge Motz, joined by Circuit Judges Hall, Murnaghan, and Michael, filed a dissenting opinion.[4] Judge Motz agreed with Judge Phillips that Virginia had not shown an "'exceedingly persuasive justification'" for the disparate opportunities the Commonwealth supported. *Id.*, at 92 (quoting *Mississippi Univ. for Women*, 458 U.S., at 724). She asked: "[H]ow can a degree from a yet to be implemented supplemental program at Mary Baldwin be held 'substantively comparable' to a degree from a venerable Virginia military institution that was established more than 150 years ago?" 52 F.3d, at 93. "Women need not be guaranteed equal 'results,'" Judge Motz said, "but the Equal Protection Clause does require equal opportunity . . . [and] that opportunity is being denied here." *Ibid.*

---

4. Six judges voted to rehear the case en banc, four voted against rehearing, and three were recused. The Fourth Circuit's local Rule permits rehearing en banc only on the vote of a majority of the Circuit's judges in regular active service (currently 13) without regard to recusals. See 52 F.3d, at 91, and n. 1.

III

The cross-petitions in this suit present two ultimate issues. First, does Virginia's exclusion of women from the educational opportunities provided by VMI—extraordinary opportunities for military training and civilian leadership development—deny to women "capable of all of the individual activities required of VMI cadets," 766 F. Supp., at 1412, the equal protection of the laws guaranteed by the Fourteenth Amendment? Second, if VMI's "unique" situation, *id.*, at 1413—as Virginia's sole single-sex public institution of higher education—offends the Constitution's equal protection principle, what is the remedial requirement?

IV

We note, once again, the core instruction of this Court's pathmarking decisions in *J.E.B.* v. *Alabama ex rel. T. B.*, 511 U.S. 127, 136–137, and n. 6 (1994), and *Mississippi Univ. for Women*, 458 U.S., at 724 (internal quotation marks omitted): Parties who seek to defend gender-based government action must demonstrate an "exceedingly persuasive justification" for that action.

Today's skeptical scrutiny of official action denying rights or opportunities based on sex responds to volumes of history. As a plurality of this Court acknowledged a generation ago, "our Nation has had a long and unfortunate history of sex discrimination." *Frontiero* v. *Richardson*, 411 U.S. 677, 684 (1973). Through a century plus three decades and more of that history, women did not count among voters composing "We the People";[5] not until 1920 did women gain a constitutional right to the franchise. *Id.*, at 685. And for a half century thereafter, it remained the prevailing doctrine that government, both federal and state, could withhold from women opportunities accorded men so long as any "basis in reason" could be conceived for

---

5. As Thomas Jefferson stated the view prevailing when the Constitution was new:

"Were our State a pure democracy . . . there would yet be excluded from their deliberations . . . [w]omen, who, to prevent depravation of morals and ambiguity of issue, could not mix promiscuously in the public meetings of men." Letter from Thomas Jefferson to Samuel Kercheval (Sept. 5, 1816), in 10 Writings of Thomas Jefferson 45–46, n. 1 (P. Ford ed. 1899).

the discrimination. See, *e.g.*, *Goesaert* v. *Cleary*, 335 U.S. 464, 467 (1948) (rejecting challenge of female tavern owner and her daughter to Michigan law denying bartender licenses to females—except for wives and daughters of male tavern owners; Court would not "give ear" to the contention that "an unchivalrous desire of male bartenders to . . . monopolize the calling" prompted the legislation).

In 1971, for the first time in our Nation's history, this Court ruled in favor of a woman who complained that her State had denied her the equal protection of its laws. *Reed* v. *Reed*, 404 U.S. 71, 73 (holding unconstitutional Idaho Code prescription that, among "'several persons claiming and equally entitled to administer [a decedent's estate], males must be preferred to females'"). Since *Reed*, the Court has repeatedly recognized that neither federal nor state government acts compatibly with the equal protection principle when a law or official policy denies to women, simply because they are women, full citizenship stature—equal opportunity to aspire, achieve, participate in and contribute to society based on their individual talents and capacities. See, *e.g.*, *Kirchberg* v. *Feenstra*, 450 U.S. 455, 462–463 (1981) (affirming invalidity of Louisiana law that made husband "head and master" of property jointly owned with his wife, giving him unilateral right to dispose of such property without his wife's consent); *Stanton* v. *Stanton*, 421 U.S. 7 (1975) (invalidating Utah requirement that parents support boys until age 21, girls only until age 18).

Without equating gender classifications, for all purposes, to classifications based on race or national origin,[6] the Court, in post-*Reed* decisions, has carefully inspected official action that closes a door or denies opportunity to women (or to men). See *J.E.B.*, 511 U.S., at 152 (KENNEDY, J., concurring in judgment) (case law evolving since 1971 "reveal[s] a strong presumption that gender classifications are invalid"). To summarize the Court's current directions for cases of official classification based on gender: Focusing on the differential treatment for denial of opportunity for which relief is sought, the reviewing court must determine whether the proffered justification is "exceedingly persuasive." The burden of justifica-

---

6. The Court has thus far reserved most stringent judicial scrutiny for classifications based on race or national origin, but last Term observed that strict scrutiny of such classifications is not inevitably "fatal in fact." *Adarand Constructors, Inc. v. Peña*, 515 U.S. 200, 237 (1995) (internal quotation marks omitted).

tion is demanding and it rests entirely on the State. See *Mississippi Univ. for Women,* 458 U.S., at 724. The State must show "at least that the [challenged] classification serves 'important governmental objectives and that the discriminatory means employed' are 'substantially related to the achievement of those objectives.'" *Ibid.* (quoting *Wengler* v. *Druggists Mut. Ins. Co.,* 446 U.S. 142, 150 (1980)). The justification must be genuine, not hypothesized or invented *post hoc* in response to litigation. And it must not rely on overbroad generalizations about the different talents, capacities, or preferences of males and females. See *Weinberger* v. *Wiesenfeld,* 420 U.S. 636, 643, 648 (1975); *Califano* v. *Goldfarb,* 430 U.S. 199, 223–224 (1977) (STEVENS, J., concurring in judgment).

The heightened review standard our precedent establishes does not make sex a proscribed classification. Supposed "inherent differences" are no longer accepted as a ground for race or national origin classifications. See *Loving* v. *Virginia,* 388 U.S. 1 (1967). Physical differences between men and women, however, are enduring: "[T]he two sexes are not fungible; a community made up exclusively of one [sex] is different from a community composed of both." *Ballard* v. *United States,* 329 U.S. 187, 193 (1946).

"Inherent differences" between men and women, we have come to appreciate, remain cause for celebration, but not for denigration of the members of either sex or for artificial constraints on an individual's opportunity. Sex classifications may be used to compensate women "for particular economic disabilities [they have] suffered," *Califano* v. *Webster,* 430 U.S. 313, 320 (1977) *(per curiam),* to "promot[e] equal employment opportunity," see *California Fed. Sav. & Loan Assn.* v. *Guerra,* 479 U.S. 272, 289 (1987), to advance full development of the talent and capacities of our Nation's people.[7]

---

7. Several *amici* have urged that diversity in educational opportunities is an altogether appropriate governmental pursuit and that single-sex schools can contribute importantly to such diversity. Indeed, it is the mission of some single-sex schools "to dissipate, rather than perpetuate, traditional gender classifications." See Brief for Twenty-six Private Women's Colleges as *Amici Curiae* 5. We do not question the Commonwealth's prerogative evenhandedly to support diverse educational opportunities. We address specifically and only an educational opportunity recognized by the District Court and the Court of Appeals as "unique," see 766 F. Supp., at 1413, 1432; 976 F. 2d, at 892, an opportunity available only at Virginia's premier military institute, the Commonwealth's sole single-sex public university or college. Cf. *Mississippi Univ. for Women v. Hogan,* 458 U.S. 718, 720, n. 1 (1982) ("Mississippi maintains no other single-sex public university or college. Thus, we are not faced with the question of whether States can provide 'separate but equal' undergraduate institutions for males and females.").

But such classifications may not be used, as they once were, see *Goesaert*, 335 U.S., at 467, to create or perpetuate the legal, social, and economic inferiority of women.

Measuring the record in this case against the review standard just described, we conclude that Virginia has shown no "exceedingly persuasive justification" for excluding all women from the citizen-soldier training afforded by VMI. We therefore affirm the Fourth Circuit's initial judgment, which held that Virginia had violated the Fourteenth Amendment's Equal Protection Clause. Because the remedy proffered by Virginia—the Mary Baldwin VWIL program—does not cure the constitutional violation, *i.e.*, it does not provide equal opportunity, we reverse the Fourth Circuit's final judgment in this case.

V

The Fourth Circuit initially held that Virginia had advanced no state policy by which it could justify, under equal protection principles, its determination "to afford VMI's unique type of program to men and not to women." 976 F.2d, at 892. Virginia challenges that "liability" ruling and asserts two justifications in defense of VMI's exclusion of women. First, the Commonwealth contends, "single-sex education provides important educational benefits," Brief for Cross–Petitioners 20, and the option of single-sex education contributes to "diversity in educational approaches," *id.*, at 25. Second, the Commonwealth argues, "the unique VMI method of character development and leadership training," the school's adversative approach, would have to be modified were VMI to admit women. *Id.*, at 33–36 (internal quotation marks omitted). We consider these two justifications in turn.

A

Single-sex education affords pedagogical benefits to at least some students, Virginia emphasizes, and that reality is uncontested in this litigation.[8]

---

8. On this point, the dissent sees fire where there is no flame. See *post*, 518 U.S., at 596–598, 598–600. "Both men and women can benefit from a single-sex education," the District

Similarly, it is not disputed that diversity among public educational institutions can serve the public good. But Virginia has not shown that VMI
was established, or has been maintained, with a view to diversifying, by its
categorical exclusion of women, educational opportunities within the
Commonwealth. In cases of this genre, our precedent instructs that
"benign" justifications proffered in defense of categorical exclusions
will not be accepted automatically; a tenable justification must describe
actual state purposes, not rationalizations for actions in fact differently
grounded. See *Wiesenfeld*, 420 U.S., at 648, and n. 16 ("mere recitation of
a benign [or] compensatory purpose" does not block "inquiry into the
actual purposes" of government-maintained gender-based classifications); *Goldfarb*, 430 U.S., at 212–213 (rejecting government-proffered
purposes after "inquiry into the actual purposes" (internal quotation
marks omitted)).

Mississippi Univ. for Women is immediately in point. There the State
asserted, in justification of its exclusion of men from a nursing school, that
it was engaging in "educational affirmative action" by "compensat[ing] for
discrimination against women." 458 U.S., at 727. Undertaking a "search-
ing analysis," *id.*, at 728, the Court found no close resemblance between
"the alleged objective" and "the actual purpose underlying the discriminatory classification," *id.*, at 730. Pursuing a similar inquiry here, we reach
the same conclusion.

Neither recent nor distant history bears out Virginia's alleged pursuit of
diversity through single-sex educational options. In 1839, when the
Commonwealth established VMI, a range of educational opportunities for
men and women was scarcely contemplated. Higher education at the time

---

Court recognized, although "the beneficial effects" of such education, the court added, apparently "are stronger among women than among men." 766 F. Supp., at 1414. The United States
does not challenge that recognition. Cf. C. Jencks & D. Riesman, The Academic Revolution
297–298 (1968):

"The pluralistic argument for preserving all-male colleges is uncomfortably similar
to the pluralistic argument for preserving all-white colleges. . . . The all-male college
would be relatively easy to defend if it emerged from a world in which women were
established as fully equal to men. But it does not. It is therefore likely to be a witting
or unwitting device for preserving tacit assumptions of male superiority—assumptions for which women must eventually pay."

was considered dangerous for women;[9] reflecting widely held views about women's proper place, the Nation's first universities and colleges—for example, Harvard in Massachusetts, William and Mary in Virginia—admitted only men. See E. Farello, A History of the Education of Women in the United States 163 (1970). VMI was not at all novel in this respect: In admitting no women, VMI followed the lead of the Commonwealth's flagship school, the University of Virginia, founded in 1819.

"[N]o struggle for the admission of women to a state university," a historian has recounted, "was longer drawn out, or developed more bitterness, than that at the University of Virginia." 2 T. Woody, A History of Women's Education in the United States 254 (1929) (History of Women's Education). In 1879, the State Senate resolved to look into the possibility of higher education for women, recognizing that Virginia "'has never, at any period of her history,'" provided for the higher education of her daughters, though she "'has liberally provided for the higher education of her sons.'" Ibid. (quoting 10 Educ. J. Va. 212 (1879)). Despite this recognition, no new opportunities were instantly open to women.[10]

Virginia eventually provided for several women's seminaries and colleges. Farmville Female Seminary became a public institution in 1884. See supra, 518 U.S., at 521, n. 2. Two women's schools, Mary Washington College and James Madison University, were founded in 1908; another,

---

9. Dr. Edward H. Clarke of Harvard Medical School, whose influential book, Sex in Education, went through 17 editions, was perhaps the most well-known speaker from the medical community opposing higher education for women. He maintained that the physiological effects of hard study and academic competition with boys would interfere with the development of girls' reproductive organs. See E. Clarke, Sex in Education 38–39, 62–63 (1873); id., at 127 ("identical education of the two sexes is a crime before God and humanity, that physiology protests against, and that experience weeps over"); see also H. Maudsley, Sex in Mind and in Education 17 (1874) ("It is not that girls have not ambition, nor that they fail generally to run the intellectual race [in coeducational settings], but it is asserted that they do it at a cost to their strength and health which entails life-long suffering, and even incapacitates them for the adequate performance of the natural functions of their sex."); C. Meigs, Females and Their Diseases 350 (1848) (after five or six weeks of "mental and educational discipline," a healthy woman would "lose . . . the habit of menstruation" and suffer numerous ills as a result of depriving her body for the sake of her mind).

10. Virginia's Superintendent of Public Instruction dismissed the coeducational idea as "'repugnant to the prejudices of the people'" and proposed a female college similar in quality to Girton, Smith, or Vassar. 2 History of Women's Education 254 (quoting Dept. of Interior, 1 Report of Commissioner of Education, H.R. Doc. No. 5, 58th Cong., 2d Sess., 438 (1904)).

Radford University, was founded in 1910. 766 F. Supp., at 1418–1419. By the mid-1970's, all four schools had become coeducational. *Ibid.*

Debate concerning women's admission as undergraduates at the main university continued well past the century's midpoint. Familiar arguments were rehearsed. If women were admitted, it was feared, they "would encroach on the rights of men; there would be new problems of government, perhaps scandals; the old honor system would have to be changed; standards would be lowered to those of other coeducational schools; and the glorious reputation of the university, as a school for men, would be trailed in the dust." 2 History of Women's Education 255.

Ultimately, in 1970, "the most prestigious institution of higher education in Virginia," the University of Virginia, introduced coeducation and, in 1972, began to admit women on an equal basis with men. See *Kirstein* v. *Rector and Visitors of Univ. of Virginia*, 309 F. Supp. 184, 186 (E.D.Va. 1970). A three-judge Federal District Court confirmed: "Virginia may not now deny to women, on the basis of sex, educational opportunities at the Charlottesville campus that are not afforded in other institutions operated by the [S]tate." *Id.*, at 187.

Virginia describes the current absence of public single-sex higher education for women as "an historical anomaly." Brief for Cross–Petitioners 30. But the historical record indicates action more deliberate than anomalous: First, protection of women against higher education; next, schools for women far from equal in resources and stature to schools for men; finally, conversion of the separate schools to coeducation. The state legislature, prior to the advent of this controversy, had repealed "[a]ll Virginia statutes requiring individual institutions to admit only men or women." 766 F. Supp., at 1419. And in 1990, an official commission, "legislatively established to chart the future goals of higher education in Virginia," reaffirmed the policy "'of affording broad access'" while maintaining "'autonomy and diversity.'" 976 F.2d, at 898–899 (quoting Report of the Virginia Commission on the University of the 21st Century). Significantly, the commission reported:

"'Because colleges and universities provide opportunities for students to develop values and learn from role models, it is extremely important that they deal with faculty, staff, and students without regard to sex, race, or ethnic origin.'" *Id.*, at 899 (emphasis supplied by Court of Appeals deleted).

This statement, the Court of Appeals observed, "is the only explicit one that we have found in the record in which the Commonwealth has expressed itself with respect to gender distinctions." *Ibid.*

Our 1982 decision in *Mississippi Univ. for Women* prompted VMI to reexamine its male-only admission policy. See 766 F. Supp., at 1427–1428. Virginia relies on that reexamination as a legitimate basis for maintaining VMI's single-sex character. See Reply Brief for Cross–Petitioners 6. A Mission Study Committee, appointed by the VMI Board of Visitors, studied the problem from October 1983 until May 1986, and in that month counseled against "change of VMI status as a single-sex college." See 766 F. Supp., at 1429 (internal quotation marks omitted). Whatever internal purpose the Mission Study Committee served—and however well meaning the framers of the report—we can hardly extract from that effort any Commonwealth policy evenhandedly to advance diverse educational options. As the District Court observed, the Committee's analysis "primarily focuse[d] on anticipated difficulties in attracting females to VMI," and the report, overall, supplied "very little indication of how th[e] conclusion was reached." *Ibid.*

In sum, we find no persuasive evidence in this record that VMI's male-only admission policy "is in furtherance of a state policy of 'diversity.'" See 976 F.2d, at 899. No such policy, the Fourth Circuit observed, can be discerned from the movement of all other public colleges and universities in Virginia away from single-sex education. See *ibid.* That court also questioned "how one institution with autonomy, but with no authority over any other state institution, can give effect to a state policy of diversity among institutions." *Ibid.* A purpose genuinely to advance an array of educational options, as the Court of Appeals recognized, is not served by VMI's historic and constant plan—a plan to "affor[d] a unique educational benefit only to males." *Ibid.* However "liberally" this plan serves the Commonwealth's sons, it makes no provision whatever for her daughters. That is not *equal* protection.

B

Virginia next argues that VMI's adversative method of training provides educational benefits that cannot be made available, unmodified, to women. Alterations to accommodate women would necessarily be "radical," so "drastic," Virginia asserts, as to transform, indeed "destroy," VMI's program. See Brief for Cross–Petitioners 34–36. Neither sex would be favored by the transformation, Virginia maintains: Men would be deprived of the unique opportunity currently available to them; women would not gain that opportunity because their participation would "eliminat[e] the very aspects of [the] program that distinguish [VMI] from . . . other institutions of higher education in Virginia." *Id.*, at 34.

The District Court forecast from expert witness testimony, and the Court of Appeals accepted, that coeducation would materially affect "at least these three aspects of VMI's program—physical training, the absence of privacy, and the adversative approach." 976 F.2d, at 896–897. And it is uncontested that women's admission would require accommodations, primarily in arranging housing assignments and physical training programs for female cadets. See Brief for Cross–Respondent 11, 29–30. It is also undisputed, however, that "the VMI methodology could be used to educate women." 852 F. Supp., at 481. The District Court even allowed that some women may prefer it to the methodology a women's college might pursue. See *ibid.* "[S]ome women, at least, would want to attend [VMI] if they had the opportunity," the District Court recognized, 766 F. Supp., at 1414, and "some women," the expert testimony established, "are capable of all of the individual activities required of VMI cadets," *id.*, at 1412. The parties, furthermore, agree that "*some* women can meet the physical standards [VMI] now impose[s] on men." 976 F.2d, at 896. In sum, as the Court of Appeals stated, "neither the goal of producing citizen soldiers," VMI's *raison d'être,* "nor VMI's implementing methodology is inherently unsuitable to women." *Id.*, at 899.

In support of its initial judgment for Virginia, a judgment rejecting all equal protection objections presented by the United States, the District Court made "findings" on "gender-based developmental differences." 766 F. Supp., at 1434–1435. These "findings" restate the opinions of Virginia's expert witnesses, opinions about typically male or typically female "tendencies." *Id.*, at 1434. For example, "[m]ales tend to need an atmosphere of adversativeness," while "[f]emales tend to thrive in a cooperative atmosphere." *Ibid.* "I'm not saying that some women don't do well under [the] adversative model," VMI's expert on educational institutions testified, "undoubtedly there are some [women] who do"; but educational experiences must be designed "around the rule," this expert maintained, and not "around the exception." *Ibid.* (internal quotation marks omitted).

The United States does not challenge any expert witness estimation on average capacities or preferences of men and women. Instead, the United States emphasizes that time and again since this Court's turning point decision in *Reed* v. *Reed*, 404 U.S. 71 (1971), we have cautioned reviewing courts to take a "hard look" at generalizations or "tendencies" of the kind pressed by Virginia, and relied upon by the District Court. See O'Connor, Portia's Progress, 66 N.Y.U.L.Rev. 1546, 1551 (1991). State actors controlling gates to opportunity, we have instructed, may not exclude qualified individuals based on "fixed notions concerning the roles and abilities of males and females." *Mississippi Univ. for Women,* 458 U.S., at 725; see *J.E.B.,* 511 U.S., at 139, n. 11 (equal protection principles, as applied to gender classifications, mean state actors may not rely on "overbroad" generalizations to make "judgments about people that are likely to . . . perpetuate historical patterns of discrimination").

It may be assumed, for purposes of this decision, that most women would not choose VMI's adversative method. As Fourth Circuit Judge Motz observed, however, in her dissent from the Court of Appeals' denial of rehearing en banc, it is also probable that "many men would not want to be educated in such an environment." 52 F.3d, at 93. (On that point, even our dissenting colleague might agree.) Education, to be sure, is not a "one size fits all" business. The issue, however, is not whether "women—or men—should be forced to attend VMI"; rather, the question is whether the Commonwealth can constitutionally deny to women who have the will and capacity, the training and attendant opportunities that VMI uniquely affords. *Ibid.*

The notion that admission of women would downgrade VMI's stature, destroy the adversative system and, with it, even the school,[11] is a judg-

---

11. See *post,* 518 U.S., at 566, 598–599, 603. Forecasts of the same kind were made regarding admission of women to the federal military academies. See, *e.g.,* Hearings on H.R. 9832 et al. before Subcommittee No. 2 of the House Committee on Armed Services, 93d Cong., 2d Sess., 137 (1975) (statement of Lt. Gen. A.P. Clark, Superintendent of U.S. Air Force Academy) ("It is my considered judgment that the introduction of female cadets will inevitably erode this vital atmosphere."); *id.,* at 165 (statement of Hon. H.H. Callaway, Secretary of the Army) ("Admitting women to West Point would irrevocably change the Academy. . . . The Spartan atmosphere—which is so important to producing the final product—would surely be diluted, and would in all probability disappear.").

ment hardly proved,[12] a prediction hardly different from other "self-fulfilling prophec[ies]," see *Mississippi Univ. for Women,* 458 U.S., at 730, once routinely used to deny rights or opportunities. When women first sought admission to the bar and access to legal education, concerns of the same order were expressed. For example, in 1876, the Court of Common Pleas of Hennepin County, Minnesota, explained why women were thought ineligible for the practice of law. Women train and educate the young, the court said, which

> "forbids that they shall bestow that time (early and late) and labor, so essential in attaining to the eminence to which the true lawyer should ever aspire. It cannot therefore be said that the opposition of courts to the admission of females to practice . . . is to any extent the outgrowth of . . . 'old fogyism[.]' . . . [I]t arises rather from a comprehension of the magnitude of the responsibilities connected with the successful practice of law, and a desire to *grade up* the profession." In re Application of Martha Angle Dorsett to Be Admitted to Practice as Attorney and Counselor at Law (Minn. C.P. Hennepin Cty., 1876), in The Syllabi, Oct. 21, 1876, pp. 5, 6 (emphasis added).

A like fear, according to a 1925 report, accounted for Columbia Law School's resistance to women's admission, although

> "[t]he faculty . . . never maintained that women could not master legal learning. . . . No, its argument has been . . . more practical. If women were admitted to the Columbia Law School, [the faculty] said, then the choicer, more manly and red-blooded graduates of our great universities would go to the Harvard Law School!" The Nation, Feb. 18, 1925, p. 173.

---

12. See 766 F. Supp., at 1413 (describing testimony of expert witness David Riesman: "[I]f VMI were to admit women, it would eventually find it necessary to drop the adversative system altogether, and adopt a system that provides more nurturing and support for the students."). Such judgments have attended, and impeded, women's progress toward full citizenship stature throughout our Nation's history. Speaking in 1879 in support of higher education for females, for example, Virginia State Senator C. T. Smith of Nelson recounted that legislation proposed to protect the property rights of women had encountered resistance. 10 Educ. J. Va. 213 (1879). A Senator opposing the measures objected that "there [was] no formal call for the [legislation]," and "depicted in burning eloquence the terrible consequences such laws would produce." *Ibid.* The legislation passed, and a year or so later, its sponsor, C. T. Smith, reported that "not one of [the forecast "terrible consequences"] has or ever will happen, even unto the sounding of Gabriel's trumpet." *Ibid.* See also *supra,* 518 U.S., at 537–538.

Medical faculties similarly resisted men and women as partners in the study of medicine. See R. Morantz–Sanchez, Sympathy and Science: Women Physicians in American Medicine 51–54, 250 (1985); see also M. Walsh, "Doctors Wanted: No Women Need Apply" 121–122 (1977) (quoting E. Clarke, Medical Education of Women, 4 Boston Med. & Surg. J. 345, 346 (1869) ("'God forbid that I should ever see men and women aiding each other to display with the scalpel the secrets of the reproductive system. . . .'")); cf. *supra*, 518 U.S., at 536–537, n. 9. More recently, women seeking careers in policing encountered resistance based on fears that their presence would "undermine male solidarity," see F. Heidensohn, Women in Control? 201 (1992); deprive male partners of adequate assistance, see *id.*, at 184–185; and lead to sexual misconduct, see C. Milton et al., Women in Policing 32–33 (1974). Field studies did not confirm these fears. See Heidensohn, *supra*, at 92–93; P. Bloch & D. Anderson, Policewomen on Patrol: Final Report (1974).

Women's successful entry into the federal military academies,[13] and their participation in the Nation's military forces,[14] indicate that Virginia's fears for the future of VMI may not be solidly grounded.[15] The Commonwealth's justification for excluding all women from "citizen-soldier" training for which some are qualified, in any event, cannot rank as "exceedingly persuasive," as we have explained and applied that standard.

Virginia and VMI trained their argument on "means" rather than "end," and thus misperceived our precedent. Single-sex education at VMI serves

---

13. Women cadets have graduated at the top of their class at every federal military academy. See Brief for Lieutenant Colonel Rhonda Cornum et al. as *Amici Curiae* 11, n. 25; cf. Defense Advisory Committee on Women in the Services, Report on the Integration and Performance of Women at West Point 64 (1992).

14. Brief for Lieutenant Colonel Rhonda Cornum, *supra*, at 5–9 (reporting the vital contributions and courageous performance of women in the military); see Mintz, President Nominates 1st Woman to Rank of Three–Star General, Washington Post, Mar. 27, 1996, p. A19, col. 1 (announcing President's nomination of Marine Corps Major General Carol Mutter to rank of Lieutenant General; Mutter will head corps manpower and planning); M. Tousignant, A New Era for the Old Guard, Washington Post, Mar. 23, 1996, p. C1, col. 2 (reporting admission of Sergeant Heather Johnsen to elite Infantry unit that keeps round-the-clock vigil at Tomb of the Unknowns in Arlington National Cemetery).

15. Inclusion of women in settings where, traditionally, they were not wanted inevitably entails a period of adjustment. As one West Point cadet squad leader recounted: "[T]he classes of '78 and '79 see the women as women, but the classes of '80 and '81 see them as classmates." U.S. Military Academy, A. Vitters, Report of Admission of Women (Project Athena II) 84 (1978) (internal quotation marks omitted).

an "important governmental objective," they maintained, and exclusion of women is not only "substantially related," it is essential to that objective. By this notably circular argument, the "straightforward" test *Mississippi Univ. for Women* described, see 458 U.S., at 724–725, was bent and bowed.

The Commonwealth's misunderstanding and, in turn, the District Court's, is apparent from VMI's mission: to produce "citizen-soldiers," individuals

"'imbued with love of learning, confident in the functions and attitudes of leadership, possessing a high sense of public service, advocates of the American democracy and free enterprise system, and ready . . . to defend their country in time of national peril.'" 766 F. Supp., at 1425 (quoting Mission Study Committee of the VMI Board of Visitors, Report, May 16, 1986).

Surely that goal is great enough to accommodate women, who today count as citizens in our American democracy equal in stature to men. Just as surely, the Commonwealth's great goal is not substantially advanced by women's categorical exclusion, in total disregard of their individual merit, from the Commonwealth's premier "citizen-soldier" corps.[16] Virginia, in sum, "has fallen far short of establishing the 'exceedingly persuasive justification,'" *Mississippi Univ. for Women,* 458 U.S., at 731, that must be the solid base for any gender-defined classification.

VI

In the second phase of the litigation, Virginia presented its remedial plan—maintain VMI as a male-only college and create VWIL as a separate program for women. The plan met District Court approval. The Fourth Circuit, in turn, deferentially reviewed the Commonwealth's proposal and

---

16. VMI has successfully managed another notable change. The school admitted its first African–American cadets in 1968. See The VMI Story 347–349 (students no longer sing "Dixie," salute the Confederate flag or the tomb of General Robert E. Lee at ceremonies and sports events). As the District Court noted, VMI established a program on "retention of black cadets" designed to offer academic and social-cultural support to "minority members of a dominantly white and tradition-oriented student body." 766 F. Supp., at 1436–1437. The school maintains a "special recruitment program for blacks" which, the District Court found, "has had little, if any, effect on VMI's method of accomplishing its mission." *Id.,* at 1437.

decided that the two single-sex programs directly served Virginia's reas-
serted purposes: single-gender education, and "achieving the results of an
adversative method in a military environment." See 44 F.3d, at 1236, 1239.
Inspecting the VMI and VWIL educational programs to determine whether
they "afford[ed] to both genders benefits comparable in substance, [if] not
in form and detail," *id.*, at 1240, the Court of Appeals concluded that
Virginia had arranged for men and women opportunities "sufficiently comparable" to survive equal protection evaluation, *id.*, at 1240–1241. The
United States challenges this "remedial" ruling as pervasively misguided.

A

A remedial decree, this Court has said, must closely fit the constitutional
violation; it must be shaped to place persons unconstitutionally denied an
opportunity or advantage in "the position they would have occupied in the
absence of [discrimination]." See *Milliken* v. *Bradley*, 433 U.S. 267, 280
(1977) (internal quotation marks omitted). The constitutional violation in
this suit is the categorical exclusion of women from an extraordinary educational opportunity afforded men. A proper remedy for an unconstitutional exclusion, we have explained, aims to "eliminate [so far as possible]
the discriminatory effects of the past" and to "bar like discrimination in the
future." *Louisiana* v. *United States*, 380 U.S. 145, 154 (1965).

Virginia chose not to eliminate, but to leave untouched, VMI's exclusionary policy. For women only, however, Virginia proposed a separate
program, different in kind from VMI and unequal in tangible and intangible facilities.[17] Having violated the Constitution's equal protection requirement, Virginia was obliged to show that its remedial proposal "directly

---

17. As earlier observed, see *supra*, 518 U.S., at 529, Judge Phillips, in dissent, measured
Virginia's plan against a paradigm arrangement, one that "could survive equal protection
scrutiny": single-sex schools with "substantially comparable curricular and extra-curricular
programs, funding, physical plant, administration and support services, . . . faculty[,] and
library resources." 44 F.3d 1229, 1250 (C.A.4 1995). Cf. *Bray v. Lee*, 337 F. Supp. 934 (Mass.
1972) (holding inconsistent with the Equal Protection Clause admission of males to Boston's
Boys Latin School with a test score of 120 or higher (up to a top score of 200) while requiring
a score, on the same test, of at least 133 for admission of females to Girls Latin School, but
not ordering coeducation). Measuring VMI/VWIL against the paradigm, Judge Phillips
said, "reveals how far short the [Virginia] plan falls from providing substantially equal tangible and intangible educational benefits to men and women." 44 F.3d, at 1250.

address[ed] and relate[d] to" the violation, see *Milliken,* 433 U.S., at 282, *i.e.,* the equal protection denied to women ready, willing, and able to benefit from educational opportunities of the kind VMI offers. Virginia described VWIL as a "parallel program," and asserted that VWIL shares VMI's mission of producing "citizen-soldiers" and VMI's goals of providing "education, military training, mental and physical discipline, character . . . and leadership development." Brief for Respondents 24 (internal quotation marks omitted). If the VWIL program could not "eliminate the discriminatory effects of the past," could it at least "bar like discrimination in the future"? See *Louisiana,* 380 U.S., at 154. A comparison of the programs said to be "parallel" informs our answer. In exposing the character of, and differences in, the VMI and VWIL programs, we recapitulate facts earlier presented. See *supra,* 518 U.S., at 520–523, 526–527.

VWIL affords women no opportunity to experience the rigorous military training for which VMI is famed. See 766 F. Supp., at 1413–1414 ("No other school in Virginia or in the United States, public or private, offers the same kind of rigorous military training as is available at VMI."); *id.,* at 1421 (VMI "is known to be the most challenging military school in the United States"). Instead, the VWIL program "deemphasize[s]" military education, 44 F.3d, at 1234, and uses a "cooperative method" of education "which reinforces self-esteem," 852 F. Supp., at 476.

VWIL students participate in ROTC and a "largely ceremonial" Virginia Corps of Cadets, see 44 F.3d, at 1234, but Virginia deliberately did not make VWIL a military institute. The VWIL House is not a military-style residence and VWIL students need not live together throughout the 4–year program, eat meals together, or wear uniforms during the schoolday. See 852 F. Supp., at 477, 495. VWIL students thus do not experience the "barracks" life "crucial to the VMI experience," the spartan living arrangements designed to foster an "egalitarian ethic." See 766 F. Supp., at 1423–1424. "[T]he most important aspects of the VMI educational experience occur in the barracks," the District Court found, *id.,* at 1423, yet Virginia deemed that core experience nonessential, indeed inappropriate, for training its female citizen-soldiers.

VWIL students receive their "leadership training" in seminars, externships, and speaker series, see 852 F. Supp., at 477, episodes and encounters lacking the "[p]hysical rigor, mental stress, . . . minute regulation of behavior, and indoctrination in desirable values" made hallmarks of VMI's citizen-soldier training, see 766 F. Supp., at 1421.[18] Kept away from the pressures, hazards, and psychological bonding characteristic of VMI's adversative training, see *id.*, at 1422, VWIL students will not know the "feeling of tremendous accomplishment" commonly experienced by VMI's successful cadets, *id.*, at 1426.

Virginia maintains that these methodological differences are "justified pedagogically," based on "important differences between men and women in learning and developmental needs," "psychological and sociological differences" Virginia describes as "real" and "not stereotypes." Brief for Respondents 28 (internal quotation marks omitted). The Task Force charged with developing the leadership program for women, drawn from the staff and faculty at Mary Baldwin College, "determined that a military model and, especially VMI's adversative method, would be wholly inappropriate for educating and training *most women.*" 852 F. Supp., at 476 (emphasis added). See also 44 F.3d, at 1233–1234 (noting Task Force conclusion that, while "some women would be suited to and interested in [a VMI-style experience]," VMI's adversative method "would not be effective for *women as a group*" (emphasis added)). The Commonwealth embraced the Task Force view, as did expert witnesses who testified for Virginia. See 852 F. Supp., at 480–481.

As earlier stated, see *supra*, 518 U.S., at 541–542, generalizations about "the way women are," estimates of what is appropriate for *most women,* no longer justify denying opportunity to women whose talent and capacity place them outside the average description. Notably, Virginia never asserted that VMI's method of education suits *most men.* It is also revealing that Virginia accounted for its failure to make the VWIL experience "the entirely militaristic experience of VMI" on the ground that VWIL "is planned for women who do not necessarily expect to pursue military careers." 852 F. Supp., at 478. By that reasoning, VMI's "entirely militaristic" program would be inappropriate for men in general or *as a group,* for "[o]nly about 15% of VMI cadets enter career military service." See 766 F. Supp., at 1432.

---

18. Both programs include an honor system. Students at VMI are expelled forthwith for honor code violations, see 766 F. Supp., at 1423; the system for VWIL students, see 852 F. Supp., at 496–497, is less severe, see Tr. 414–415 (testimony of Mary Baldwin College President Cynthia Tyson).

In contrast to the generalizations about women on which Virginia rests, we note again these dispositive realities: VMI's "implementing methodology" is not "inherently unsuitable to women," 976 F.2d, at 899; "some women . . . do well under [the] adversative model," 766 F. Supp., at 1434 (internal quotation marks omitted); "some women, at least, would want to attend [VMI] if they had the opportunity," *id.*, at 1414; "some women are capable of all of the individual activities required of VMI cadets," *id.*, at 1412, and "can meet the physical standards [VMI] now impose[s] on men," 976 F.2d, at 896. It is on behalf of these women that the United States has instituted this suit, and it is for them that a remedy must be crafted,[19] a remedy that will end their exclusion from a state-supplied educational opportunity for which they are fit, a decree that will "bar like discrimination in the future." *Louisiana,* 380 U.S., at 154.

B

In myriad respects other than military training, VWIL does not qualify as VMI's equal. VWIL's student body, faculty, course offerings, and facilities hardly match VMI's. Nor can the VWIL graduate anticipate the benefits associated with VMI's 157–year history, the school's prestige, and its influential alumni network.

Mary Baldwin College, whose degree VWIL students will gain, enrolls first-year women with an average combined SAT score about 100 points lower than the average score for VMI freshmen. 852 F. Supp., at 501. The Mary Baldwin faculty holds "significantly fewer Ph.D.'s," *id.*, at 502, and receives substantially lower salaries, see Tr. 158 (testimony of James Lott, Dean of Mary Baldwin College), than the faculty at VMI.

---

19. Admitting women to VMI would undoubtedly require alterations necessary to afford members of each sex privacy from the other sex in living arrangements, and to adjust aspects of the physical training programs. See Brief for Petitioner 27–29; cf. note following 10 U.S.C. § 4342 (academic and other standards for women admitted to the Military, Naval, and Air Force Academies "shall be the same as those required for male individuals, except for those minimum essential adjustments in such standards required because of physiological differences between male and female individuals"). Experience shows such adjustments are manageable. See U.S. Military Academy, A. Vitters, N. Kinzer, & J. Adams, Report of Admission of Women (Project Athena I–IV) (1977–1980) (4–year longitudinal study of the admission of women to West Point); Defense Advisory Committee on Women in the Services, Report on the Integration and Performance of Women at West Point 17–18 (1992).

Mary Baldwin does not offer a VWIL student the range of curricular choices available to a VMI cadet. VMI awards baccalaureate degrees in liberal arts, biology, chemistry, civil engineering, electrical and computer engineering, and mechanical engineering. See 852 F. Supp., at 503; Virginia Military Institute: More than an Education 11 (Govt. exh. 75, lodged with Clerk of this Court). VWIL students attend a school that "does not have a math and science focus," 852 F. Supp., at 503; they cannot take at Mary Baldwin any courses in engineering or the advanced math and physics courses VMI offers, see *id.*, at 477.

For physical training, Mary Baldwin has "two multi-purpose fields" and "[o]ne gymnasium." *Id.*, at 503. VMI has "an NCAA competition level indoor track and field facility; a number of multi-purpose fields; baseball, soccer and lacrosse fields; an obstacle course; large boxing, wrestling and martial arts facilities; an 11–laps–to–the–mile indoor running course; an indoor pool; indoor and outdoor rifle ranges; and a football stadium that also contains a practice field and outdoor track." *Ibid.*

Although Virginia has represented that it will provide equal financial support for in-state VWIL students and VMI cadets, *id.*, at 483, and the VMI Foundation has agreed to endow VWIL with $5.4625 million, *id.*, at 499, the difference between the two schools' financial reserves is pronounced. Mary Baldwin's endowment, currently about $19 million, will gain an additional $35 million based on future commitments; VMI's current endowment, $131 million—the largest public college per-student endowment in the Nation—will gain $220 million. *Id.*, at 503.

The VWIL student does not graduate with the advantage of a VMI degree. Her diploma does not unite her with the legions of VMI "graduates [who] have distinguished themselves" in military and civilian life. See 976 F.2d, at 892–893. "[VMI] alumni are exceptionally close to the school," and that closeness accounts, in part, for VMI's success in attracting applicants. See 766 F. Supp., at 1421. A VWIL graduate cannot assume that the "network of business owners, corporations, VMI graduates and nongraduate employers . . . interested in hiring VMI graduates," 852 F. Supp., at 499, will be equally responsive to her search for employment, see 44 F.3d, at 1250 (Phillips, J., dissenting) ("the powerful political and economic ties of the VMI alumni network cannot be expected to open" for graduates of the fledgling VWIL program).

Virginia, in sum, while maintaining VMI for men only, has failed to provide any "comparable single-gender women's institution." *Id.*, at 1241. Instead, the Commonwealth has created a VWIL program fairly appraised as a "pale shadow" of VMI in terms of the range of curricular choices and faculty stature, funding, prestige, alumni support and influence. See *id.*, at 1250 (Phillips, J., dissenting).

Virginia's VWIL solution is reminiscent of the remedy Texas proposed 50 years ago, in response to a state trial court's 1946 ruling that, given the equal protection guarantee, African–Americans could not be denied a legal education at a state facility. See *Sweatt* v. *Painter*, 339 U.S. 629 (1950). Reluctant to admit African–Americans to its flagship University of Texas Law School, the State set up a separate school for Heman Sweatt and other black law students. *Id.*, at 632. As originally opened, the new school had no independent faculty or library, and it lacked accreditation. *Id.*, at 633. Nevertheless, the state trial and appellate courts were satisfied that the new school offered Sweatt opportunities for the study of law "substantially equivalent to those offered by the State to white students at the University of Texas." *Id.*, at 632 (internal quotation marks omitted).

Before this Court considered the case, the new school had gained "a faculty of five full-time professors; a student body of 23; a library of some 16,500 volumes serviced by a full-time staff; a practice court and legal aid association; and one alumnus who ha[d] become a member of the Texas Bar." *Id.*, at 633. This Court contrasted resources at the new school with those at the school from which Sweatt had been excluded. The University of Texas Law School had a full-time faculty of 16, a student body of 850, a library containing over 65,000 volumes, scholarship funds, a law review, and moot court facilities. *Id.*, at 632–633.

More important than the tangible features, the Court emphasized, are "those qualities which are incapable of objective measurement but which make for greatness" in a school, including "reputation of the faculty, experience of the administration, position and influence of the alumni, standing in the community, traditions and prestige." *Id.*, at 634. Facing the marked differences reported in the *Sweatt* opinion, the Court unanimously ruled that Texas had not shown "substantial equality in the [separate] educational opportunities" the State offered. *Id.*, at 633. Accordingly, the Court held, the Equal Protection Clause required Texas to admit

African–Americans to the University of Texas Law School. *Id.*, at 636. In line with *Sweatt,* we rule here that Virginia has not shown substantial equality in the separate educational opportunities the Commonwealth supports at VWIL and VMI.

C

When Virginia tendered its VWIL plan, the Fourth Circuit did not inquire whether the proposed remedy, approved by the District Court, placed women denied the VMI advantage in "the position they would have occupied in the absence of [discrimination]." *Milliken,* 433 U.S., at 280 (internal quotation marks omitted). Instead, the Court of Appeals considered whether the Commonwealth could provide, with fidelity to the equal protection principle, separate and unequal educational programs for men and women.

The Fourth Circuit acknowledged that "the VWIL degree from Mary Baldwin College lacks the historical benefit and prestige of a degree from VMI." 44 F.3d, at 1241. The Court of Appeals further observed that VMI is "an ongoing and successful institution with a long history," and there remains no "comparable single-gender women's institution." *Ibid.* Nevertheless, the appeals court declared the substantially different and significantly unequal VWIL program satisfactory. The court reached that result by revising the applicable standard of review. The Fourth Circuit displaced the standard developed in our precedent, see *supra,* 518 U.S., at 532–534, and substituted a standard of its own invention.

We have earlier described the deferential review in which the Court of Appeals engaged, see *supra,* 518 U.S., at 528–529, a brand of review inconsistent with the more exacting standard our precedent requires, see *supra,* 518 U.S., at 532–534. Quoting in part from *Mississippi Univ. for Women,* the Court of Appeals candidly described its own analysis as one capable of checking a legislative purpose ranked as "pernicious," but generally according "deference to [the] legislative will." 44 F.3d, at 1235, 1236. Recognizing that it had extracted from our decisions a test yielding "little or no scrutiny of the effect of a classification directed at [single-gender education]," the Court of Appeals devised another test, a "substantive comparability" inquiry, *id.,* at 1237, and proceeded to find that new test satisfied, *id.,* at 1241.

The Fourth Circuit plainly erred in exposing Virginia's VWIL plan to a deferential analysis, for "all gender-based classifications today" warrant "heightened scrutiny." See *J.E.B.*, 511 U.S., at 136. Valuable as VWIL may prove for students who seek the program offered, Virginia's remedy affords no cure at all for the opportunities and advantages withheld from women who want a VMI education and can make the grade. See *supra*, 518 U.S., at 549–554.[20] In sum, Virginia's remedy does not match the constitutional violation; the Commonwealth has shown no "exceedingly persuasive justification" for withholding from women qualified for the experience premier training of the kind VMI affords.

VII

A generation ago, "the authorities controlling Virginia higher education," despite long established tradition, agreed "to innovate and favorably entertain[ed] the [then] relatively new idea that there must be no discrimination by sex in offering educational opportunity." *Kirstein*, 309

---

20. Virginia's prime concern, it appears, is that "plac[ing] men and women into the adversative relationship inherent in the VMI program . . . would destroy, at least for that period of the adversative training, any sense of decency that still permeates the relationship between the sexes." 44 F.3d, at 1239; see *supra*, 518 U.S., at 540–546. It is an ancient and familiar fear. Compare *In re Lavinia Goodell*, 39 Wis. 232, 246 (1875) (denying female applicant's motion for admission to the bar of its court, Wisconsin Supreme Court explained: "Discussions are habitually necessary in courts of justice, which are unfit for female ears. The habitual presence of women at these would tend to relax the public sense of decency and propriety."), with Levine, Closing Comments, 6 Law & Inequality 41 (1988) (presentation at Eighth Circuit Judicial Conference, Colorado Springs, Colo., July 17, 1987) (footnotes omitted):

> "Plato questioned whether women should be afforded equal opportunity to become guardians, those elite Rulers of Platonic society. Ironically, in that most undemocratic system of government, the Republic, women's native ability to serve as guardians was not seriously questioned. The concern was over the wrestling and exercise class in which all candidates for guardianship had to participate, for rigorous physical and mental training were prerequisites to attain the exalted status of guardian. And in accord with Greek custom, those exercise classes were conducted in the nude. Plato concluded that their virtue would clothe the women's nakedness and that Platonic society would not thereby be deprived of the talent of qualified citizens for reasons of mere gender."

For Plato's full text on the equality of women, see 2 The Dialogues of Plato 302–312 (B. Jowett transl., 4th ed. 1953). Virginia, not bound to ancient Greek custom in its "rigorous physical and mental training" programs, could more readily make the accommodations necessary to draw on "the talent of [all] qualified citizens." Cf. *supra*, 518 U.S., at 550–551, n. 19.

F. Supp., at 186. Commencing in 1970, Virginia opened to women "educational opportunities at the Charlottesville campus that [were] not afforded in other [state-operated] institutions." *Id.*, at 187; see *supra*, 518 U.S., at 538. A federal court approved the Commonwealth's innovation, emphasizing that the University of Virginia "offer[ed] courses of instruction . . . not available elsewhere." 309 F. Supp., at 187. The court further noted: "[T]here exists at Charlottesville a 'prestige' factor [not paralleled in] other Virginia educational institutions." *Ibid.*

VMI, too, offers an educational opportunity no other Virginia institution provides, and the school's "prestige"—associated with its success in developing "citizen-soldiers"—is unequaled. Virginia has closed this facility to its daughters and, instead, has devised for them a "parallel program," with a faculty less impressively credentialed and less well paid, more limited course offerings, fewer opportunities for military training and for scientific specialization. Cf. *Sweatt*, 339 U.S., at 633. VMI, beyond question, "possesses to a far greater degree" than the VWIL program "those qualities which are incapable of objective measurement but which make for greatness in a . . . school," including "position and influence of the alumni, standing in the community, traditions and prestige." *Id.*, at 634. Women seeking and fit for a VMI-quality education cannot be offered anything less, under the Commonwealth's obligation to afford them genuinely equal protection.

A prime part of the history of our Constitution, historian Richard Morris recounted, is the story of the extension of constitutional rights and protections to people once ignored or excluded.[21] VMI's story continued as our comprehension of "We the People" expanded. See *supra*, 518 U.S. at 546, n. 16. There is no reason to believe that the admission of women

---

21. R. Morris, The Forging of the Union, 1781–1789, p. 193 (1987); see *id.*, at 191, setting out letter to a friend from Massachusetts patriot (later second President) John Adams, on the subject of qualifications for voting in his home State:

"[I]t is dangerous to open so fruitful a source of controversy and altercation as would be opened by attempting to alter the qualifications of voters; there will be no end of it. New claims will arise; women will demand a vote; lads from twelve to twenty-one will think their rights not enough attended to; and every man who has not a farthing, will demand an equal voice with any other, in all acts of state. It tends to confound and destroy all distinctions, and prostrate all ranks to one common level." Letter from John Adams to James Sullivan (May 26, 1776), in 9 Works of John Adams 378 (C. Adams ed. 1854).

capable of all the activities required of VMI cadets would destroy the Institute rather than enhance its capacity to serve the "more perfect Union."

*   *   *

For the reasons stated, the initial judgment of the Court of Appeals, 976 F.2d 890 (C.A.4 1992), is affirmed, the final judgment of the Court of Appeals, 44 F.3d 1229 (C.A.4 1995), is reversed, and the case is remanded for further proceedings consistent with this opinion.

It is so ordered.

Justice THOMAS took no part in the consideration or decision of these cases.

[The opinion of Chief Justice REHNQUIST concurring in the judgment and the dissenting opinion of Justice SCALIA are omitted.]

LEDBETTER V. GOODYEAR TIRE & RUBBER CO. (2007)

In *Ledbetter* v. *Goodyear Tire & Rubber Co.*, the Supreme Court had to decide what time limitations exist on an employee's ability to file a pay discrimination claim under Title VII of the Civil Rights Act of 1964. The plaintiff in the case, Lilly Ledbetter, sued Goodyear, her employer, contending that she had been paid less than her male counterparts in violation of Title VII for much of her almost twenty years with the company. In an opinion for a five-justice majority, Justice Samuel A. Alito, Jr., held that a party must file any complaint under the Title VII framework within 180 days of a challenged "discrete unlawful practice." It followed, on the majority's view, that Ledbetter could not challenge any pay discrimination that may have pre-dated such period. Bolstering this conclusion, the majority rejected Ledbetter's argument that Title VII treated any current pay disparity as the product of longstanding and cumulative discrimination.

Writing on behalf of four dissenting justices, Justice Ginsburg believed, as she phrases it in her bench announcement that follows, that "the Court does not comprehend, or is indifferent to, the insidious way in which women can be victims of pay discrimination." As she viewed matters, "Title VII was meant to govern real-world employment practices, and that world is what the Court today ignores. Pay disparities often occur, as they did in Ledbetter's case, in small increments; only over time is there strong cause to suspect that discrimination is at work." For this reason, she argues in her dissent that follows that the majority's "cramped interpretation of Title VII" is entirely "at odds with the robust protection against workplace discrimination Congress intended Title VII to secure." Ever hopeful, Justice Ginsburg concludes her opinion by pointing out that Congress had the power to "correct this Court's parsimonious reading of Title VII."

It took Congress little time to take up Justice Ginsburg's invitation and enact the Lilly Ledbetter Fair Pay Act of 2009, codified at 42 U.S.C. § 2000e-5(e)(3)(A), which became one of the first bills President Obama signed into law after taking office in January 2009.

Justice Ginsburg's statement read from the bench on the day the Court announced its decision, along with her dissenting opinion, follow.

LEDBETTER V. GOODYEAR TIRE & RUBBER CO., NO. 05-1074

BENCH ANNOUNCEMENT

Supreme Court of the United States (May 29, 2007)

Four members of this Court, Justices Stevens, Souter, Breyer and I, dissent from today's decision. In our view, the Court does not comprehend, or is indifferent to, the insidious way in which women can be victims of pay discrimination. Today's decision counsels: Sue early on, when it is uncertain whether discrimination accounts for the pay disparity you are beginning to experience. Indeed, initially you may not know that men are receiving more for substantially similar work. (Of course, you are likely to lose such a less-than-fully baked case.) If you sue only when the pay disparity becomes steady and large enough to enable you to mount a winnable case, you will be cut off at the court's threshold for suing too late. That situation cannot be what Congress intended when, in Title VII, it outlawed discrimination based on race, color, religion, sex, or national origin in our Nation's workplaces.

Lilly Ledbetter, the plaintiff in this case, was engaged as an area manager at a Goodyear Tire and Rubber plant in Alabama in 1979. Her starting salary was in line with the salaries of men performing similar work. But over time, her pay slipped in comparison to the pay of male employees with equal or less seniority. By the end of 1997, Ledbetter was the only woman left working as an area manager and the pay discrepancy between

Ledbetter and her 15 male counterparts was stark: Ledbetter's pay was *15 to 40 percent less* than every other area manager.

Ledbetter complained to the Equal Employment Opportunity Commission in March 1998. She charged that, in violation of Title VII, Goodyear paid her a discriminatorily low salary because of her sex. The charge was eventually brought to court and tried to a jury. The jury found it "more likely than not that [Goodyear] paid [Ledbetter] a[n] unequal salary because of her sex." The Court today nullifies that verdict, holding that Ledbetter's claim is time barred.

Title VII provides that a charge of discrimination "shall be filed within [180] days after the alleged unlawful employment practice occurred." Ledbetter charged, and proved at trial, that the paychecks she received within the 180-day filing period were substantially lower than the paychecks received by men doing the same work. Further, she introduced substantial evidence showing that discrimination accounted for the pay differential, indeed, that discrimination against women as supervisors was pervasive at Goodyear's plant. That evidence was unavailing, the Court holds, because it was incumbent on Ledbetter to file charges of discrimination year-by-year, each time Goodyear failed to increase her salary commensurate with the salaries of her male peers. Any annual pay decision not contested promptly (within 180 days), the Court affirms, becomes grandfathered, beyond the province of Title VII ever to repair.

Title VII was meant to govern real-world employment practices, and that world is what the Court today ignores. Pay disparities often occur, as they did in Ledbetter's case, in small increments; only over time is there strong cause to suspect that discrimination is at work. Comparative pay information is not routinely communicated to employees. Instead, it is often hidden from the employee's view. Small initial discrepancies, even if the employee knows they exist, may not be seen as grounds for a federal case. An employee like Ledbetter, trying to succeed in a male-dominated workplace, in a job filled only by men before she was hired, understandably may be anxious to avoid making waves.

Pay discrimination that recurs and swells in impact, is significantly different from discrete adverse actions promptly communicated and "easy to identify" as discriminatory. Events in that category include firing, denial of a promotion, or refusal to hire. In contrast to those unambiguous actions, until a pay disparity becomes apparent and sizable, an employee is unlikely to comprehend her plight and, therefore, to complain about it. Ledbetter's initial readiness to give her employer the benefit of the doubt should not preclude her from later seeking redress for the continuing payment to her of a salary depressed because of her sex.

Yet, as the Court reads Title VII, each and every pay decision Ledbetter did not promptly challenge wiped the slate clean. Nevermind the cumulative effect of a series of decisions that, together, set her pay well below that of every male area manager. Knowingly carrying past pay discrimination forward must be treated as lawful. Ledbetter may not be compensated under Title VII for the lower pay she was in fact receiving when she complained to the EEOC. Notably, the same denial of relief would occur had Ledbetter encountered pay discrimination based on race, religion, age, national origin, or disability.

This is not the first time the Court has ordered a cramped interpretation of Title VII, incompatible with the statute's broad remedial purpose. In 1991, Congress passed a Civil Rights Act that effectively overruled several of this Court's similarly restrictive decisions, including one, *Lorance*, upon which the Court relies today. Today, the ball again lies in Congress' court. As in 1991, the Legislature has cause to note and correct this Court's parsimonious reading of Title VII.

LEDBETTER V. GOODYEAR TIRE & RUBBER CO., 550 U.S. 618

DISSENTING OPINION

Supreme Court of the United States

Lilly M. LEDBETTER, Petitioner,

v.

The GOODYEAR TIRE & RUBBER CO., INC.

No. 05-1074.

Argued Nov. 27, 2006.

Decided May 29, 2007.

[The majority opinion of Justice ALITO is omitted.]

Justice GINSBURG, with whom Justice STEVENS, Justice SOUTER, and Justice BREYER join, dissenting.

Lilly Ledbetter was a supervisor at Goodyear Tire & Rubber's plant in Gadsden, Alabama, from 1979 until her retirement in 1998. For most of those years, she worked as an area manager, a position largely occupied by men. Initially, Ledbetter's salary was in line with the salaries of men performing substantially similar work. Over time, however, her pay slipped in comparison to the pay of male area managers with equal or less seniority. By the end of 1997, Ledbetter was the only woman working as an area manager and the pay discrepancy between Ledbetter and her 15 male counterparts was stark: Ledbetter was paid $3,727 per month; the lowest paid male area manager received $4,286 per month, the highest paid, $5,236. See 421 F.3d 1169, 1174 (C.A.11 2005); Brief for Petitioner 4.

Ledbetter launched charges of discrimination before the Equal Employment Opportunity Commission (EEOC) in March 1998. Her formal administrative complaint specified that, in violation of Title VII, Goodyear paid her a discriminatorily low salary because of her sex. See 42 U.S.C. § 2000e–2(a)(1) (rendering it unlawful for an employer "to discriminate against any individual with respect to [her] compensation . . . because of such individual's . . . sex"). That charge was eventually tried to a jury, which found it "more likely than not that [Goodyear] paid [Ledbetter] a[n] unequal salary because of her sex." App. 102. In accord with the jury's liability determination, the District Court entered judgment for Ledbetter for backpay and damages, plus counsel fees and costs.

The Court of Appeals for the Eleventh Circuit reversed. Relying on Goodyear's system of annual merit-based raises, the court held that Ledbetter's claim, in relevant part, was time barred. 421 F.3d, at 1171, 1182–1183. Title VII provides that a charge of discrimination "shall be filed within [180] days after the alleged unlawful employment practice occurred." 42 U.S.C. § 2000e–5(e)(1).[1] Ledbetter charged, and proved at trial, that within the 180-day period, her pay was substantially less than the pay of men doing the same work. Further, she introduced evidence sufficient to establish that discrimination against female managers at the Gadsden plant, not performance inadequacies on her part, accounted for

---

1. If the complainant has first instituted proceedings with a state or local agency, the filing period is extended to 300 days or 30 days after the denial of relief by the agency. 42 U.S.C. § 2000e–5(e)(1). Because the 180-day period applies to Ledbetter's case, that figure will be used throughout. See *ante*, 550 U.S., at 622, 624.

the pay differential. See, *e.g.*, App. 36–47, 51–68, 82–87, 90–98, 112–113. That evidence was unavailing, the Eleventh Circuit held, and the Court today agrees, because it was incumbent on Ledbetter to file charges year by year, each time Goodyear failed to increase her salary commensurate with the salaries of male peers. Any annual pay decision not contested immediately (within 180 days), the Court affirms, becomes grandfathered, a *fait accompli* beyond the province of Title VII ever to repair.

The Court's insistence on immediate contest overlooks common characteristics of pay discrimination. Pay disparities often occur, as they did in Ledbetter's case, in small increments; cause to suspect that discrimination is at work develops only over time. Comparative pay information, moreover, is often hidden from the employee's view. Employers may keep under wraps the pay differentials maintained among supervisors, no less the reasons for those differentials. Small initial discrepancies may not be seen as meet for a federal case, particularly when the employee, trying to succeed in a nontraditional environment, is averse to making waves.

Pay disparities are thus significantly different from adverse actions "such as termination, failure to promote, . . . or refusal to hire," all involving fully communicated discrete acts, "easy to identify" as discriminatory. See *National Railroad Passenger Corporation v. Morgan*, 536 U.S. 101, 114 (2002). It is only when the disparity becomes apparent and sizable, *e.g.*, through future raises calculated as a percentage of current salaries, that an employee in Ledbetter's situation is likely to comprehend her plight and, therefore, to complain. Her initial readiness to give her employer the benefit of the doubt should not preclude her from later challenging the then current and continuing payment of a wage depressed on account of her sex.

On questions of time under Title VII, we have identified as the critical inquiries: "What constitutes an 'unlawful employment practice' and when has that practice 'occurred'?" *Id.*, at 110. Our precedent suggests, and lower courts have overwhelmingly held, that the unlawful practice is the current payment of salaries infected by gender-based (or race-based) discrimination—a practice that occurs whenever a paycheck delivers less to a woman than to a similarly situated man. See *Bazemore v. Friday*, 478 U.S. 385, 395 (1986) (Brennan, J., joined by all other Members of the Court, concurring in part).

I

Title VII proscribes as an "unlawful employment practice" discrimination "against any individual with respect to his compensation . . . because of such individual's race, color, religion, sex, or national origin." 42 U.S.C. § 2000e–2(a)(1). An individual seeking to challenge an employment practice under this proscription must file a charge with the EEOC within 180 days "after the alleged unlawful employment practice occurred." § 2000e–5(e)(1). See *ante*, 550 U.S., at 624; *supra*, 550 U.S., at 644, n. 1.

Ledbetter's petition presents a question important to the sound application of Title VII: What activity qualifies as an unlawful employment practice in cases of discrimination with respect to compensation. One answer identifies the pay-setting decision, and that decision alone, as the unlawful practice. Under this view, each particular salary-setting decision is discrete from prior and subsequent decisions, and must be challenged within 180 days on pain of forfeiture. Another response counts both the pay-setting decision and the actual payment of a discriminatory wage as unlawful practices. Under this approach, each payment of a wage or salary infected by sex-based discrimination constitutes an unlawful employment practice; prior decisions, outside the 180-day charge-filing period, are not themselves actionable, but they are relevant in determining the lawfulness of conduct within the period. The Court adopts the first view, see *ante*, 550 U.S., at 621, 624, 628–629, but the second is more faithful to precedent, more in tune with the realities of the workplace, and more respectful of Title VII's remedial purpose.

A

In *Bazemore*, we unanimously held that an employer, the North Carolina Agricultural Extension Service, committed an unlawful employment practice each time it paid black employees less than similarly situated white employees. 478 U.S., at 395 (opinion of Brennan, J.). Before 1965, the Extension Service was divided into two branches: a white branch and a "Negro branch." *Id.*, at 390. Employees in the "Negro branch" were paid less than their white counterparts. In response to the Civil Rights Act of 1964, which included Title VII, the State merged the two branches into a single organization, made adjustments to reduce the salary disparity, and began giving annual raises based on nondiscriminatory factors. *Id.*, at 390–391, 394–395. Nonetheless, "some pre-existing salary disparities continued to linger on." *Id.*, at 394 (internal quotation marks omitted). We rejected the Court of Appeals' conclusion that the plaintiffs could not prevail because the lingering disparities were simply a continuing effect of a decision lawfully made prior to the effective date of Title VII. See *id.*, at 395–396. Rather, we reasoned, "[e]ach week's paycheck that delivers less to a black than to a similarly situated white is a wrong actionable under Title VII." *Id.*, at 395. Paychecks perpetuating past discrimination, we thus recognized, are actionable not simply because they are "related" to a decision made outside the charge-filing period, cf. *ante*, 550 U.S., at 636, but because they discriminate anew each time they issue, see *Bazemore*, 478 U.S., at 395–396, and n. 6; *Morgan*, 536 U.S., at 111–112.

Subsequently, in *Morgan*, we set apart, for purposes of Title VII's timely filing requirement, unlawful employment actions of two kinds: "discrete acts" that are "easy to identify" as discriminatory, and acts that recur and are cumulative in impact. See *id.*, at 110, 113–115. "[A] [d]iscrete ac[t] such as termination, failure to promote, denial of transfer, or refusal to hire," *id.*, at 114, we explained, "'occur[s]' on the day that it 'happen[s].' A party, therefore, must file a charge within . . . 180 . . . days of the date of the act or lose the ability to recover for it." *Id.*, at 110; see *id.*, at 113 ("[D]iscrete discriminatory acts are not actionable if time barred, even when they are related to acts alleged in timely filed charges. Each discrete discriminatory act starts a new clock for filing charges alleging that act.").

"[D]ifferent in kind from discrete acts," we made clear, are "claims . . . based on the cumulative effect of individual acts." *Id.*, at 115. The *Morgan* decision placed hostile work environment claims in that category. "Their very nature involves repeated conduct." *Ibid.* "The unlawful employment practice" in hostile work environment claims "cannot be said to occur on any particular day. It occurs over a series of days or perhaps years and, in direct contrast to discrete acts, a single act of harassment may not be actionable on its own." *Ibid.* (internal quotation marks omitted). The persistence of the discriminatory conduct both indicates that management should have known of its existence and produces a cognizable harm. *Ibid.* Because the very nature of the hostile work environment claim involves repeated conduct, "[i]t does not matter, for purposes of the statute, that some of the component acts of the hostile work environment fall outside the statutory time period. Provided that an act contributing to the claim occurs within the filing period, the entire time period of the hostile environment may be considered by a court for the purposes of determining liability." *Id.*, at 117.

Consequently, although the unlawful conduct began in the past, "a charge may be filed at a later date and still encompass the whole." *Ibid.*

Pay disparities, of the kind Ledbetter experienced, have a closer kinship to hostile work environment claims than to charges of a single episode of discrimination. Ledbetter's claim, resembling Morgan's, rested not on one particular paycheck, but on "the cumulative effect of individual acts." See *id.*, at 115. See also Brief for Petitioner 13, 15–17, and n. 9 (analogizing Ledbetter's claim to the recurring and cumulative harm at issue in *Morgan*); Reply Brief for Petitioner 13 (distinguishing pay discrimination from "easy to identify" discrete acts (internal quotation marks omitted)). She charged insidious discrimination building up slowly but steadily. See Brief for Petitioner 5–8. Initially in line with the salaries of men performing substantially the same work, Ledbetter's salary fell 15 to 40 percent behind her male counterparts only after successive evaluations and percentage-based pay adjustments. See *supra*, 550 U.S., at 643–644. Over time, she alleged and proved, the repetition of pay decisions undervaluing her work gave rise to the current discrimination of which she complained. Though component acts fell outside the charge-filing period, with each new paycheck, Goodyear contributed incrementally to the accumulating harm. See *Morgan*, 536 U.S., at 117; *Bazemore*, 478 U.S., at 395–396; cf. *Hanover Shoe, Inc.* v. *United Shoe Machinery Corp.*, 392 U.S. 481, 502, n. 15 (1968).[2]

---

2. *National Railroad Passenger Corporation v. Morgan*, 536 U.S. 101, 117 (2002), the Court emphasizes, required that "an act contributing to the claim occu[r] within the [charge-]filing period." *Ante*, 550 U.S., at 638, and n. 7 (emphasis deleted; internal quotation marks omitted). Here, each paycheck within the filing period compounded the discrimination Ledbetter encountered, and thus contributed to the "actionable wrong," *i.e.*, the succession of acts composing the pattern of discriminatory pay, of which she complained.

B

The realities of the workplace reveal why the discrimination with respect to compensation that Ledbetter suffered does not fit within the category of singular discrete acts "easy to identify." A worker knows immediately if she is denied a promotion or transfer, if she is fired or refused employment. And promotions, transfers, hirings, and firings are generally public events, known to co-workers. When an employer makes a decision of such open and definitive character, an employee can immediately seek out an explanation and evaluate it for pretext. Compensation disparities, in contrast, are often hidden from sight. It is not unusual, decisions in point illustrate, for management to decline to publish employee pay levels, or for employees to keep private their own salaries. See, *e.g., Goodwin* v. *General Motors Corp.*, 275 F.3d 1005, 1008–1009 (C.A.10 2002) (plaintiff did not know what her colleagues earned until a printout listing of salaries appeared on her desk, seven years after her starting salary was set lower than her co-workers' salaries); *McMillan* v. *Massachusetts Soc. for Prevention of Cruelty to Animals*, 140 F.3d 288, 296 (C.A.1 1998) (plaintiff worked for employer for years before learning of salary disparity published in a newspaper).[3] Tellingly, as the record in this case bears out, Goodyear kept salaries confidential; employees had only limited access to information regarding their colleagues' earnings. App. 56–57, 89.

The problem of concealed pay discrimination is particularly acute where the disparity arises not because the female employee is flatly denied a raise but because male counterparts are given larger raises. Having received a pay increase, the female employee is unlikely to discern at once that she has experienced an adverse employment decision. She may have little reason even to suspect discrimination until a pattern develops incrementally and she ultimately becomes aware of the disparity. Even if an employee suspects that the reason for a comparatively low raise is not performance but sex (or another protected ground), the amount involved

---

3. See also Bierman & Gely, "Love, Sex and Politics? Sure. Salary? No Way": Workplace Social Norms and the Law, 25 Berkeley J. Emp. & Lab. L. 167, 168, 171 (2004) (one-third of private sector employers have adopted specific rules prohibiting employees from discussing their wages with co-workers; only one in ten employers has adopted a pay openness policy).

may seem too small, or the employer's intent too ambiguous, to make the issue immediately actionable—or winnable.

Further separating pay claims from the discrete employment actions identified in *Morgan*, an employer gains from sex-based pay disparities in a way it does not from a discriminatory denial of promotion, hiring, or transfer. When a male employee is selected over a female for a higher level position, someone still gets the promotion and is paid a higher salary; the employer is not enriched. But when a woman is paid less than a similarly situated man, the employer reduces its costs each time the pay differential is implemented. Furthermore, decisions on promotions, like decisions installing seniority systems, often implicate the interests of third-party employees in a way that pay differentials do not. Cf. *Teamsters* v. *United States*, 431 U.S. 324, 352–353 (1977) (recognizing that seniority systems involve "vested . . . rights of employees" and concluding that Title VII was not intended to "destroy or water down" those rights). Disparate pay, by contrast, can be remedied at any time solely at the expense of the employer who acts in a discriminatory fashion.

C

In light of the significant differences between pay disparities and discrete employment decisions of the type identified in *Morgan*, the cases on which the Court relies hold no sway. See *ante*, 550 U.S., at 625–629 (discussing *United Air Lines, Inc.* v. *Evans*, 431 U.S. 553 (1977), *Delaware State College* v. *Ricks*, 449 U.S. 250 (1980), and *Lorance* v. *AT&T Technologies, Inc.*, 490 U.S. 900 (1989)). *Evans* and *Ricks* both involved a single, immediately identifiable act of discrimination: in *Evans*, a constructive discharge, 431 U.S., at 554; in *Ricks*, a denial of tenure, 449 U.S., at 252. In each case, the employee filed charges well after the discrete discriminatory act occurred: When United Airlines forced Evans to resign because of its policy barring married female flight attendants, she filed no charge; only four years later, when Evans was rehired, did she allege that the airline's former no-marriage rule was unlawful and therefore should not operate to deny her seniority credit for her prior service. See *Evans*, 431 U.S., at 554–557. Similarly, when Delaware State College denied Ricks tenure, he did not object until his terminal contract came to an end, one year later. *Ricks*, 449 U.S., at 253–254, 257–258. No repetitive, cumulative discriminatory employment practice was at issue in either case. See *Evans*, 431 U.S., at 557–558; *Ricks*, 449 U.S., at 258.[4]

Lorance is also inapposite, for, in this Court's view, it too involved a one-time discrete act: the adoption of a new seniority system that "had its genesis in sex discrimination." See 490 U.S., at 902, 905 (internal quotation marks omitted). The Court's extensive reliance on *Lorance, ante,* 550 U.S., at 626–629, 633, 636–637, moreover, is perplexing for that decision is no longer effective: In the 1991 Civil Rights Act, Congress superseded *Lorance*'s holding. § 112, 105 Stat. 1079 (codified as amended at 42 U.S.C. § 2000e–5(e)(2)). Repudiating our judgment that a facially neutral seniority system adopted with discriminatory intent must be challenged immediately, Congress provided:

> "For purposes of this section, an unlawful employment practice occurs . . . when the seniority system is adopted, when an individual becomes subject to the seniority system, or when a person aggrieved is injured by the application of the seniority system or provision of the system." *Ibid.*

Congress thus agreed with the dissenters in *Lorance* that "the harsh reality of [that] decision" was "glaringly at odds with the purposes of Title VII." 490 U.S., at 914 (opinion of Marshall, J.). See also § 3, 105 Stat. 1071 (1991 Civil Rights Act was designed "to respond to recent decisions of the Supreme Court by expanding the scope of relevant civil rights statutes in order to provide adequate protection to victims of discrimination").

True, § 112 of the 1991 Civil Rights Act directly addressed only seniority systems. See *ante,* 550 U.S., at 627, and n. 2. But Congress made clear (1) its view that this Court had unduly contracted the scope of protection afforded by Title VII and other civil rights statutes, and (2) its aim to gen-

---

4. The Court also relies on *Machinists v. NLRB,* 362 U.S. 411 (1960), which like *Evans* and *Ricks,* concerned a discrete act: the execution of a collective-bargaining agreement containing a union security clause. 362 U.S., at 412, 417. In *Machinists,* it was undisputed that under the National Labor Relations Act (NLRA), a union and an employer may not agree to a union security clause "if at the time of original execution the union does not represent a majority of the employees in the [bargaining] unit." *Id.,* at 412–414, 417. The complainants, however, failed to file a charge within the NLRA's six-month charge-filing period; instead, they filed charges 10 and 12 months after the execution of the agreement, objecting to its subsequent enforcement. See *id.,* at 412, 414. Thus, as in *Evans* and *Ricks,* but in contrast to Ledbetter's case, the employment decision at issue was easily identifiable and occurred on a single day.

eralize the ruling in *Bazemore*. As the Senate Report accompanying the proposed Civil Rights Act of 1990, the precursor to the 1991 Act, explained:

> "Where, as was alleged in *Lorance*, an employer adopts a rule or decision with an unlawful discriminatory motive, each application of that rule or decision is a new violation of the law. In *Bazemore* . . . , for example, . . . the Supreme Court properly held that each application of th[e] racially motivated salary structure, *i.e.*, each new paycheck, constituted a distinct violation of Title VII. Section 7(a)(2) generalizes the result correctly reached in *Bazemore*." Civil Rights Act of 1990, S.Rep. No. 101–315, p. 54 (1990).[5]

See also 137 Cong. Rec. 29046, 29047 (1991) (Sponsors' Interpretative Memorandum) ("This legislation should be interpreted as disapproving the extension of [*Lorance*] to contexts outside of seniority systems."). But cf. *ante*, 550 U.S., at 637 (relying on *Lorance* to conclude that "when an employer issues paychecks pursuant to a system that is facially nondiscriminatory and neutrally applied" a new Title VII violation does not occur (internal quotation marks omitted)).

Until today, in the more than 15 years since Congress amended Title VII, the Court had not once relied upon *Lorance*. It is mistaken to do so now. Just as Congress' "goals in enacting Title VII . . . never included conferring absolute immunity on discriminatorily adopted seniority systems that survive their first [180] days," 490 U.S., at 914 (Marshall, J., dissenting), Congress never intended to immunize forever discriminatory pay differentials unchallenged within 180 days of their adoption. This assessment gains weight when one comprehends that even a relatively minor pay disparity will expand exponentially over an employee's working life if raises are set as a percentage of prior pay.

A clue to congressional intent can be found in Title VII's backpay provision. The statute expressly provides that backpay may be awarded for a period of up to two years before the discrimination charge is filed. 42 U.S.C. § 2000e–5(g)(1) ("Back pay liability shall not accrue from a date more than two years prior to the filing of a charge with the Commission."). This prescription indicates that Congress contemplated challenges to pay discrimination commencing before, but continuing into, the 180-day fil-

---

5. No Senate Report was submitted with the Civil Rights Act of 1991, which was in all material respects identical to the proposed 1990 Act.

ing period. See *Morgan*, 536 U.S., at 119 ("If Congress intended to limit liability to conduct occurring in the period within which the party must file the charge, it seems unlikely that Congress would have allowed recovery for two years of backpay."). As we recognized in *Morgan*, "the fact that Congress expressly limited the amount of recoverable damages elsewhere to a particular time period [*i.e.*, two years] indicates that the [180–day] timely filing provision was not meant to serve as a specific limitation ... [on] the conduct that may be considered." *Ibid.*

D

In tune with the realities of wage discrimination, the Courts of Appeals have overwhelmingly judged as a present violation the payment of wages infected by discrimination: Each paycheck less than the amount payable had the employer adhered to a nondiscriminatory compensation regime, courts have held, constitutes a cognizable harm. See, *e.g.*, *Forsyth* v. *Federation Employment and Guidance Serv.*, 409 F.3d 565, 573 (C.A.2 2005) ("Any paycheck given within the [charge-filing] period ... would be actionable, even if based on a discriminatory pay scale set up outside of the statutory period."); *Shea* v. *Rice*, 409 F.3d 448, 452–453 (C.A.D.C. 2005) ("[An] employer commit[s] a separate unlawful employment practice each time he pa[ys] one employee less than another for a discriminatory reason" (citing *Bazemore*, 478 U.S., at 396)); *Goodwin*, 275 F.3d, at 1009–1010 ("[*Bazemore*] has taught a crucial distinction with respect to discriminatory disparities in pay, establishing that a discriminatory salary is not merely a lingering effect of past discrimination—instead it is itself a continually recurring violation. . . . [E]ach race-based discriminatory salary payment constitutes a fresh violation of Title VII." (footnote omitted)); *Anderson* v. *Zubieta*, 180 F.3d 329, 335 (C.A.D.C. 1999) ("The Courts of Appeals have repeatedly reached the ... conclusion" that pay discrimination is "actionable upon receipt of each paycheck."); accord *Hildebrandt* v. *Illinois Dept. of Natural Resources*, 347 F.3d 1014, 1025–1029 (C.A.7 2003); *Cardenas* v. *Massey*, 269 F.3d 251, 257 (C.A.3 2001); *Ashley* v. *Boyle's Famous Corned Beef Co.*, 66 F.3d 164, 167–168 (C.A.8 1995) (en banc); *Brinkley–Obu* v. *Hughes Training, Inc.*, 36 F.3d 336, 347–349 (C.A.4 1994); *Gibbs* v. *Pierce Cty. Law Enforcement Support Agcy.*, 785 F.2d 1396, 1399–1400 (C.A.9 1986).

Similarly in line with the real-world characteristics of pay discrimination, the EEOC—the federal agency responsible for enforcing Title VII, see, *e.g.*, 42 U.S.C. §§ 2000e–5(f), 2000e–12(a)—has interpreted the Act to permit employees to challenge disparate pay each time it is received. The EEOC's Compliance Manual provides that "[r]epeated occurrences of the same discriminatory employment action, such as discriminatory paychecks, can be challenged as long as one discriminatory act occurred within the charge filing period." 2 EEOC Compliance Manual § 2–IV–C(1)(a), p. 605:0024, and n. 183 (2006); cf. *id.*, § 10–III, p. 633:0002 (Title VII requires an employer to eliminate pay disparities attributable to a discriminatory system, even if that system has been discontinued).

The EEOC has given effect to its interpretation in a series of administrative decisions. See *Albritton* v. *Potter*, No. 01A44063, 2004 WL 2983682, *2 (EEOC Office of Fed. Operations, Dec. 17, 2004) (although disparity arose and employee became aware of the disparity outside the charge-filing period, claim was not time barred because "[e]ach paycheck that complainant receives which is less than that of similarly situated employees outside of her protected classes could support a claim under Title VII if discrimination is found to be the reason for the pay discrepancy." (citing *Bazemore*, 478 U.S., at 396)). See also *Bynum–Doles* v. *Winter*, No. 01A53973, 2006 WL 2096290 (EEOC Office of Fed. Operations, July 18, 2006); *Ward* v. *Potter*, No. 01A60047, 2006 WL 721992 (EEOC Office of Fed. Operations, Mar. 10, 2006). And in this very case, the EEOC urged the Eleventh Circuit to recognize that Ledbetter's failure to challenge any particular pay-setting decision when that decision was made "does not deprive her of the right to seek relief for discriminatory paychecks she received in 1997 and 1998." Brief of EEOC in Support of Petition for Rehearing and Suggestion for Rehearing En Banc, in No. 03–15264–GG (CA11), p. 14 (hereinafter EEOC Brief) (citing *Morgan*, 536 U.S., at 113).[6]

---

6. The Court dismisses the EEOC's considerable "experience and informed judgment," *Firefighters* v. *Cleveland*, 478 U.S. 501, 518 (1986) (internal quotation marks omitted), as unworthy of any deference in this case, see *ante*, 550 U.S., at 642–643, n. 11. But the EEOC's interpretations mirror workplace realities and merit at least respectful attention. In any event, the level of deference due the EEOC here is an academic question, for the agency's conclusion that Ledbetter's claim is not time barred is the best reading of the statute even if the Court "were interpreting [Title VII] from scratch." See *Edelman* v. *Lynchburg College*, 535 U.S. 106, 114 (2002); see *supra*, 550 U.S., at 646–655 and this page.

II

The Court asserts that treating pay discrimination as a discrete act, limited to each particular pay-setting decision, is necessary to "protec[t] employers from the burden of defending claims arising from employment decisions that are long past." *Ante*, 550 U.S., at 630 (quoting *Ricks*, 449 U.S., at 256–257). But the discrimination of which Ledbetter complained is not long past. As she alleged, and as the jury found, Goodyear continued to treat Ledbetter differently because of sex each pay period, with mounting harm. Allowing employees to challenge discrimination "that extend[s] over long periods of time," into the charge-filing period, we have previously explained, "does not leave employers defenseless" against unreasonable or prejudicial delay. *Morgan*, 536 U.S., at 121. Employers disadvantaged by such delay may raise various defenses. *Id.*, at 122. Doctrines such as "waiver, estoppel, and equitable tolling" "allow us to honor Title VII's remedial purpose without negating the particular purpose of the filing requirement, to give prompt notice to the employer." *Id.*, at 121 (quoting *Zipes* v. *Trans World Airlines, Inc.*, 455 U.S. 385, 398 (1982)); see 536 U.S., at 121 (defense of laches may be invoked to block an employee's suit "if he unreasonably delays in filing [charges] and as a result harms the defendant"); EEOC Brief 15 ("[I]f Ledbetter unreasonably delayed challenging an earlier decision, and that delay significantly impaired Goodyear's ability to defend itself . . . Goodyear can raise a defense of laches. . . .").[7]

In a last-ditch argument, the Court asserts that this dissent would allow a plaintiff to sue on a single decision made 20 years ago "even if the employee had full knowledge of all the circumstances relating to the . . . decision at the time it was made." *Ante*, 550 U.S., at 639. It suffices to point out that the defenses just noted would make such a suit foolhardy. No sensible judge would tolerate such inexcusable neglect. See *Morgan*, 536 U.S., at 121 ("In such cases, the federal courts have the discretionary power

---

7. Further, as the EEOC appropriately recognized in its brief to the Eleventh Circuit, Ledbetter's failure to challenge particular pay raises within the charge-filing period "significantly limit[s] the relief she can seek. By waiting to file a charge, Ledbetter lost her opportunity to seek relief for any discriminatory paychecks she received between 1979 and late 1997." EEOC Brief 14. See also *supra*, 550 U.S., at 654–656.

. . . to locate a just result in light of the circumstances peculiar to the case."
(internal quotation marks omitted)).

Ledbetter, the Court observes, *ante*, 550 U.S., at 640–641, n. 9, dropped
an alternative remedy she could have pursued: Had she persisted in press-
ing her claim under the Equal Pay Act of 1963 (EPA), 77 Stat. 56, 29 U.S.C.
§ 206(d), she would not have encountered a time bar.[8] See *ante*, 550 U.S.,
at 640 ("If Ledbetter had pursued her EPA claim, she would not face the
Title VII obstacles that she now confronts."); cf. *Corning Glass Works* v.
Brennan, 417 U.S. 188, 208–210 (1974). Notably, the EPA provides no
relief when the pay discrimination charged is based on race, religion,
national origin, age, or disability. Thus, in truncating the Title VII rule this
Court announced in *Bazemore*, the Court does not disarm female workers
from achieving redress for unequal pay, but it does impede racial and
other minorities from gaining similar relief.[9]

Furthermore, the difference between the EPA's prohibition against paying unequal wages and Title VII's ban on discrimination with regard to
compensation is not as large as the Court's opinion might suggest. See
ante, 550 U.S., at 640. The key distinction is that Title VII requires a
showing of intent. In practical effect, "if the trier of fact is in equipoise
about whether the wage differential is motivated by gender discrimination," Title VII compels a verdict for the employer, while the EPA compels
a verdict for the plaintiff. 2 C. Sullivan, M. Zimmer, & R. White,
Employment Discrimination: Law and Practice § 7.08[F][3], p. 532 (3d
ed. 2002). In this case, Ledbetter carried the burden of persuading the
jury that the pay disparity she suffered was attributable to intentional sex

---

8. Under the EPA, 29 U.S.C. § 206(d), which is subject to the Fair Labor Standards Act's
time prescriptions, a claim charging denial of equal pay accrues anew with each paycheck.
1 B. Lindemann & P. Grossman, Employment Discrimination Law 529 (3d ed. 1996); cf. 29
U.S.C. § 255(a) (prescribing a two-year statute of limitations for violations generally, but a
three-year limitation period for willful violations).

9. For example, under today's decision, if a black supervisor initially received the same salary
as his white colleagues, but annually received smaller raises, there would be no right to sue
under Title VII outside the 180-day window following each annual salary change, however
strong the cumulative evidence of discrimination might be. The Court would thus force
plaintiffs, in many cases, to sue too soon to prevail, while cutting them off as time barred
once the pay differential is large enough to enable them to mount a winnable case.

discrimination. See *supra*, 550 U.S., at 643–644; *infra*, this page and 550 U.S., at 660.

III

To show how far the Court has strayed from interpretation of Title VII with fidelity to the Act's core purpose, I return to the evidence Ledbetter presented at trial. Ledbetter proved to the jury the following: She was a member of a protected class; she performed work substantially equal to work of the dominant class (men); she was compensated less for that work; and the disparity was attributable to gender-based discrimination. See *supra*, 550 U.S., at 643–644.

Specifically, Ledbetter's evidence demonstrated that her current pay was discriminatorily low due to a long series of decisions reflecting Goodyear's pervasive discrimination against women managers in general and Ledbetter in particular. Ledbetter's former supervisor, for example, admitted to the jury that Ledbetter's pay, during a particular one-year period, fell below Goodyear's minimum threshold for her position. App. 93–97. Although Goodyear claimed the pay disparity was due to poor performance, the supervisor acknowledged that Ledbetter received a "Top Performance Award" in 1996. *Id.*, at 90–93. The jury also heard testimony that another supervisor—who evaluated Ledbetter in 1997 and whose evaluation led to her most recent raise denial—was openly biased against women. *Id.*, at 46, 77–82. And two women who had previously worked as managers at the plant told the jury they had been subject to pervasive discrimination and were paid less than their male counterparts. One was paid less than the men she supervised. *Id.*, at 51–68. Ledbetter herself testified about the discriminatory animus conveyed to her by plant officials. Toward the end of her career, for instance, the plant manager told Ledbetter that the "plant did not need women, that [women] didn't help it, [and] caused problems." *Id.*, at 36.[10] After weighing all the evidence,

---

10. Given this abundant evidence, the Court cannot tenably maintain that Ledbetter's case "turned principally on the misconduct of a single Goodyear supervisor." See *ante*, 550 U.S., at 632, n. 4.

the jury found for Ledbetter, concluding that the pay disparity was due to intentional discrimination.

Yet, under the Court's decision, the discrimination Ledbetter proved is not redressable under Title VII. Each and every pay decision she did not immediately challenge wiped the slate clean. Consideration may not be given to the cumulative effect of a series of decisions that, together, set her pay well below that of every male area manager. Knowingly carrying past pay discrimination forward must be treated as lawful conduct. Ledbetter may not be compensated for the lower pay she was in fact receiving when she complained to the EEOC. Nor, were she still employed by Goodyear, could she gain, on the proof she presented at trial, injunctive relief requiring, prospectively, her receipt of the same compensation men receive for substantially similar work. The Court's approbation of these consequences is totally at odds with the robust protection against workplace discrimination Congress intended Title VII to secure. See, e.g., *Teamsters* v. *United States*, 431 U.S., at 348 ("The primary purpose of Title VII was to assure equality of employment opportunities and to eliminate . . . discriminatory practices and devices. . . ." (internal quotation marks omitted)); *Albemarle Paper Co.* v. *Moody*, 422 U.S. 405, 418 (1975) ("It is . . . the purpose of Title VII to make persons whole for injuries suffered on account of unlawful employment discrimination.").

This is not the first time the Court has ordered a cramped interpretation of Title VII, incompatible with the statute's broad remedial purpose. See *supra*, 550 U.S., at 652–654. See also *Wards Cove Packing Co.* v. *Atonio*, 490 U.S. 642 (1989) (superseded in part by the Civil Rights Act of 1991); *Price Waterhouse* v. *Hopkins*, 490 U.S. 228 (1989) (plurality opinion) (same); 1 B. Lindemann & P. Grossman, Employment Discrimination Law 2 (3d ed. 1996) ("A spate of Court decisions in the late 1980s drew congressional fire and resulted in demands for legislative change[,]" culminating in the 1991 Civil Rights Act (footnote omitted)). Once again, the ball is in Congress' court. As in 1991, the Legislature may act to correct this Court's parsimonious reading of Title VII.

*   *   *

For the reasons stated, I would hold that Ledbetter's claim is not time barred and would reverse the Eleventh Circuit's judgment.

SHELBY COUNTY V. HOLDER
(2013)

Shelby County v. *Holder* involved the constitutionality of two provisions of the Voting Rights Act of 1965, which Congress enacted in response to decades of discriminatory voting policies that governed in many parts of the United States. As Justice Ginsburg notes in her dissenting opinion that follows, the Voting Rights Act stands as "one of the most consequential, efficacious, and amply justified exercises of federal legislative power in our Nation's history." Section 2 of the original Act closely followed the language of the Fifteenth Amendment to the United States Constitution and applied a nationwide prohibition of the denial or abridgement of the right to vote on account of race. The Act also contained special enforcement provisions targeted at specific areas of the country where Congress believed the potential for ongoing discrimination in voting policies was the greatest. Section 5 of the Voting Rights Act prohibits certain voting districts from changing their election laws and procedures without obtaining "preclearance"—that is, prior approval—from the federal government. Section 4 of the Act in turn defines those districts that must comply with the Section 5 preclearance procedures. Together, Sections 4 and 5 mandate that covered jurisdictions seeking to change their election laws or procedures must demonstrate that a proposed change will not have "the purpose [or] . . . the effect of denying or abridging the right to vote on account of race or color."

In passing the Voting Rights Act, Congress relied upon its authority under the Fifteenth Amendment to the United States Constitution, which provides that "[t]he right of citizens of the United States to vote shall not be denied or abridged by the United States or by any State on account of race, color, or previous condition of servitude" and vests Congress with the "power to enforce this article by appropriate legislation."

In 2013, Shelby County, Alabama, a jurisdiction covered by Section 4 of the Voting Rights Act, sued the United States Attorney General seeking to enjoin the continued enforcement of Sections 4 and 5 of the Act on the basis that the provisions were unconstitutional. In an opinion written by Chief Justice John G. Roberts, Jr., on behalf of five justices, the Supreme Court held that Congress exceeded its authority in enacting Section 4 because its coverage formula, when combined with Section 5's preclearance requirements, imposed burdens on covered jurisdictions that are no longer responsive to current circumstances. Any departure from equal treatment of the states and the power to regulate elections that the Constitution reserves to the states, the Court held, may only be justified by "exceptional conditions still exist[ing]" in the relevant jurisdictions. In so holding, the Chief Justice opined that Congress had not sufficiently confronted the fact that voting conditions had "changed dramatically" since the 1960s. He did not, however, rule out that Congress "may draft another formula based on current conditions," nor did the Court's holding determine whether the separate requirements set forth in Section 5 of the Voting Rights Act might be independently problematic.

Writing on behalf of four dissenting justices, Justice Ginsburg argues in the opinion that follows that the majority misunderstood both the constitutional questions in the case and the reality on the ground. In her view, "Congress' judgment regarding exercise of its power to enforce the Fourteenth and Fifteenth Amendments warrants substantial deference." Continuing, she maintains that when employed to confront "the combination of race discrimination and the right to vote . . . , Congress' power to act is at its height." Citing the legislative record supporting Congress's most recent reauthorization of the Voting Rights Act, Justice Ginsburg asserts that considerable work remains to be done to rid "all vestiges of discrimination against the exercise of the franchise by minority citizens" and that Congress was well within its powers to leave the Voting Rights Act preclearance framework in place to "guard against backsliding." On the day the Court handed down its decision in *Shelby County*, Justice Ginsburg read a summary of her dissent. In it, she criticizes the majority's disregard for Congress's findings on this score and asks, "What has become of the Court's usual restraint?" The importance of the case, she also observes, is hard to overstate—at issue is nothing less than "the equal citizenship stature of all in our polity, a voice to every voter in our democracy undiluted by race."

Justice Ginsburg's bench statement in *Shelby County* and her dissenting opinion follow.

SHELBY COUNTY V. HOLDER, NO. 12-96

BENCH ANNOUNCEMENT

Supreme Court of the United States (June 25, 2013)

The majority and the dissenters agree on two points. First, race-based voting discrimination still exists; no one doubts that. Second, the Voting Rights Act addresses an extraordinary problem—a near century of disregard for the dictates of the Fifteenth Amendment—and Congress has taken extraordinary measures to meet the problem. Beyond those two points, the Court divides sharply.

Congress' failure to redo the coverage formula, the Court holds, renders inoperative the preclearance remedy of § 5, the provision far more effective than any other in securing minority voting rights and stopping backsliding. Justices Breyer, Sotomayor, Kagan, and I are of the view that Congress' decision to renew the Act and keep the coverage formula was an altogether rational means to serve the end of achieving what was once the subject of a dream: the equal citizenship stature of all in our polity, a voice to every voter in our democracy undiluted by race.

Most fundamentally, we see the issue as a "who decides" question. In this regard, we note that the very First Amendment to our Constitution exhibits a certain suspicion of Congress. It instructs: Congress shall make no law abridging the freedom of speech or of the press. The Civil War Amendments are of a distinctly different thrust. Thus the Fifteenth

Amendment instructs that the right to vote shall not be denied or abridged on account of race, and it vests in Congress, as do the Thirteenth and Fourteenth Amendments, power to enforce the guaranteed right by appropriate legislation. As the standard-setting decision, *South Carolina* v. *Katzenbach*, put it: "As against the reserved powers of the States, Congress may use any rational means to effectuate the constitutional prohibition of race discrimination in voting."

Congress sought to do just that in 1965, when it initially passed the Voting Rights Act, and in each reauthorization, including the most recent one. Indeed, the 2006 reauthorization was the product of the most earnest consideration. Over a span of more than 20 months, the House and Senate Judiciary Committees held 21 hearings, heard from scores of witnesses, received numerous investigative reports and other documentation showing that "serious and widespread intentional discrimination persists in covered jurisdictions."

In all, the legislative record filled more than 15,000 pages. Representative Sensenbrenner, then Chair of the House Judiciary Committee, described the record supporting reauthorization as "one of the most extensive considerations of any piece of legislation that the United States Congress has dealt with in the 27½ years" he had served in the House. The reauthorization passed the House by a vote of 390 to 33. The vote in the Senate was 98 to 0. President Bush signed the reauthorization a week after he received it, noting the need for "further work . . . in the fight against injustice" and calling the extension "an example of our continued commitment to a united America where every person is treated with dignity and respect."

Why was Congress intent on renewing § 5 particularly? As the Chief Justice explained, § 5 requires covered jurisdictions to obtain preclearance before making changes in voting laws that might introduce new methods of voting discrimination. Congress found, first of all, that § 5 had been enormously successful in increasing minority registration and access to the ballot. But it also learned how essential § 5 was to prevent a return to old ways. In 1995, for example, the State of Mississippi was stopped by § 5 from bringing back its Jim Crow-era dual voter registration system, and in 2006, Texas was stopped from curtailing early voting in a predominantly Latino district, in defiance of this Court's order to reinstate the district after Texas tried to eliminate it. Congress confronted similar examples of discrimination in covered jurisdictions by the score.

Of signal importance, Congress found that as registration and voting by minority citizens impressively increased, other barriers sprang up to replace the tests and devices that once impeded access to the ballot. These second generation barriers included racial gerrymandering, switches from district-by-district voting to at-large voting, discriminatory annexations—methods more subtle than the visible methods used in 1965, but serving effectively to diminish a minority community's ability to exercise clout in the electoral process.

Congress retained § 5 to put down the second generation barriers before they got off the ground.

But the coverage formula is no good, the Court insists, for it is based on "decades-old data and eradicated practices," so Congress must start from scratch. Suppose the record shows, however, as engaging with it would reveal, that the formula continues to identify the jurisdictions of greatest concern, jurisdictions with the worst current records of voting discrimination. If Congress could determine from the reams of evidence it gathered that these jurisdictions still belonged under the preclearance regime, why did it need to alter the formula?

Bear in mind that Shelby County has mounted a facial challenge to the reauthorization. By what right does the Court address the County's claim? On other days, this Court has explained that facial challenges are the most difficult to mount successfully. The challenger will not be heard to complain on the ground that the statute in question might be applied unconstitutionally to others in situations not before the Court. Congress continued preclearance over Alabama, including Shelby County, only after considering barriers there to minority voting clout. There were many, they were shocking, and they were recent. They are spelled out in the dissenting opinion. What has become of the Court's usual restraint, its readiness to turn away facial attacks unless there is "no set of circumstances . . . under which [an] Act would be valid"?

The Court points to the success of § 5 in eliminating the tests and devices extant in 1965 and in increasing minority citizens' registration and ballot access. Does that provide cause to believe § 5's potent remedy is no longer needed? The notion that it does is hardly new. The same assumption, that the problem can be solved when particular methods of voting discrimination are identified and eliminated, was indulged and proved wrong repeatedly prior to enactment of the Voting Rights Act. That is why the 2006 renewal targeted no particular practices, but instead aimed to reach, in all their variety and persistence, measures that effectively impaired minority voting rights. And it is why Congress found in the second generation barriers demonstrative evidence that a remedy as strong as preclearance remains vital and should not be removed from the federal arsenal.

It was the judgment of Congress that "40 years has not been a sufficient amount of time to eliminate the vestiges of discrimination following nearly 100 years of disregard for the dictates of the 15th Amendment." That judgment of the body empowered to enforce the Civil War Amendments "by appropriate legislation" should garner this Court's unstinting approbation. The great man who led the march from Selma to Montgomery and there called for the passage of the Voting Rights Act foresaw progress, even in Alabama. "The arc of the moral universe is long," he said, but "it bends toward justice," if there is a steadfast commitment to see the task through to completion. That commitment has been disserved by today's decision.

SHELBY COUNTY V. HOLDER, 570 U.S. 529

DISSENTING OPINION

Supreme Court of the United States

SHELBY COUNTY, ALABAMA, Petitioner

v.

Eric H. HOLDER, Jr., Attorney General, et al.

No. 12-96.

Argued Feb. 27, 2013.

Decided June 25, 2013.

[The majority opinion of Chief Justice ROBERTS and the concurring opinion of Justice THOMAS are omitted.]

Justice GINSBURG, with whom Justice BREYER, Justice SOTOMAYOR, and Justice KAGAN join, dissenting.

In the Court's view, the very success of § 5 of the Voting Rights Act demands its dormancy. Congress was of another mind. Recognizing that large progress has been made, Congress determined, based on a voluminous record, that the scourge of discrimination was not yet extirpated. The question this case presents is who decides whether, as currently operative, § 5 remains justifiable,[1] this Court, or a Congress charged with the obligation to enforce the post-Civil War Amendments "by appropriate legislation." With overwhelming support in both Houses, Congress concluded that, for two prime reasons, § 5 should continue in force, unabated. First, continuance would facilitate completion of the impressive gains thus far made; and second, continuance would guard against backsliding. Those assessments were well within Congress' province to make and should elicit this Court's unstinting approbation.

I

"[V]oting discrimination still exists; no one doubts that." *Ante,* 570 U.S., at 536. But the Court today terminates the remedy that proved to be best suited to block that discrimination. The Voting Rights Act of 1965 (VRA or Act) has worked to combat voting discrimination where other remedies had been tried and failed. Particularly effective is the VRA's requirement of federal preclearance for all changes to voting laws in the regions of the country with the most aggravated records of rank discrimination against minority voting rights.

A century after the Fourteenth and Fifteenth Amendments guaranteed citizens the right to vote free of discrimination on the basis of race, the "blight of racial discrimination in voting" continued to "infec[t] the electoral process in parts of our country." *South Carolina* v. *Katzenbach,* 383 U.S. 301, 308 (1966). Early attempts to cope with this vile infection resembled battling the Hydra. Whenever one form of voting discrimination was identified and prohibited, others sprang up in its place. This Court repeatedly encountered the remarkable "variety and persistence" of laws disen-

---

1. The Court purports to declare unconstitutional only the coverage formula set out in § 4(b). See *ante,* 570 U.S., at 557. But without that formula, § 5 is immobilized.

franchising minority citizens. *Id.*, at 311. To take just one example, the Court, in 1927, held unconstitutional a Texas law barring black voters from participating in primary elections, *Nixon* v. *Herndon*, 273 U.S. 536, 541; in 1944, the Court struck down a "reenacted" and slightly altered version of the same law, *Smith* v. *Allwright*, 321 U.S. 649, 658; and in 1953, the Court once again confronted an attempt by Texas to "circumven[t]" the Fifteenth Amendment by adopting yet another variant of the all-white primary, *Terry* v. *Adams*, 345 U.S. 461, 469.

During this era, the Court recognized that discrimination against minority voters was a quintessentially political problem requiring a political solution. As Justice Holmes explained: If "the great mass of the white population intends to keep the blacks from voting," "relief from [that] great political wrong, if done, as alleged, by the people of a State and the State itself, must be given by them or by the legislative and political department of the government of the United States." *Giles* v. *Harris*, 189 U.S. 475, 488 (1903).

Congress learned from experience that laws targeting particular electoral practices or enabling case-by-case litigation were inadequate to the task. In the Civil Rights Acts of 1957, 1960, and 1964, Congress authorized and then expanded the power of "the Attorney General to seek injunctions against public and private interference with the right to vote on racial grounds." *Katzenbach*, 383 U.S., at 313. But circumstances reduced the ameliorative potential of these legislative Acts:

> "Voting suits are unusually onerous to prepare, sometimes requiring as many as 6,000 man-hours spent combing through registration records in preparation for trial. Litigation has been exceedingly slow, in part because of the ample opportunities for delay afforded voting officials and others involved in the proceedings. Even when favorable decisions have finally been obtained, some of the States affected have merely switched to discriminatory devices not covered by the federal decrees or have enacted difficult new tests designed to prolong the existing disparity between white and Negro registration. Alternatively, certain local officials have defied and evaded court orders or have simply closed their registration offices to freeze the voting rolls." *Id.*, at 314 (footnote omitted).

Patently, a new approach was needed.

Answering that need, the Voting Rights Act became one of the most consequential, efficacious, and amply justified exercises of federal legislative power in our Nation's history. Requiring federal preclearance of changes in voting laws in the covered jurisdictions—those States and localities where opposition to the Constitution's commands were most virulent—the VRA provided a fit solution for minority voters as well as for States. Under the preclearance regime established by § 5 of the VRA, covered jurisdictions must submit proposed changes in voting laws or procedures to the Department of Justice (DOJ), which has 60 days to respond to the changes. 79 Stat. 439, codified at 42 U.S.C. § 1973c(a). A change will be approved unless DOJ finds it has "the purpose [or] . . . the effect of denying or abridging the right to vote on account of race or color." *Ibid.* In the alternative, the covered jurisdiction may seek approval by a three-judge District Court in the District of Columbia.

After a century's failure to fulfill the promise of the Fourteenth and Fifteenth Amendments, passage of the VRA finally led to signal improvement on this front. "The Justice Department estimated that in the five years after [the VRA's] passage, almost as many blacks registered [to vote] in Alabama, Mississippi, Georgia, Louisiana, North Carolina, and South Carolina as in the entire century before 1965." Davidson, The Voting Rights Act: A Brief History, in Controversies in Minority Voting 7, 21 (B. Grofman & C. Davidson eds. 1992). And in assessing the overall effects of the VRA in 2006, Congress found that "[s]ignificant progress has been made in eliminating first generation barriers experienced by minority voters, including increased numbers of registered minority voters, minority voter turnout, and minority representation in Congress, State legislatures, and local elected offices. This progress is the direct result of the Voting Rights Act of 1965." Fannie Lou Hamer, Rosa Parks, and Coretta Scott King Voting Rights Act Reauthorization and Amendments Act of 2006 (hereinafter 2006 Reauthorization), § 2(b)(1), 120 Stat. 577. On that matter of cause and effects there can be no genuine doubt.

Although the VRA wrought dramatic changes in the realization of minority voting rights, the Act, to date, surely has not eliminated all vestiges of discrimination against the exercise of the franchise by minority citizens. Jurisdictions covered by the preclearance requirement continued to submit, in large numbers, proposed changes to voting laws that the Attorney General declined to approve, auguring that barriers to minority voting would quickly resurface were the preclearance remedy eliminated.

City of Rome v. *United States*, 446 U.S. 156, 181 (1980). Congress also found that as "registration and voting of minority citizens increas[ed], other measures may be resorted to which would dilute increasing minority voting strength." *Ibid.* (quoting H.R.Rep. No. 94–196, p. 10 (1975)). See also *Shaw* v. *Reno*, 509 U.S. 630, 640 (1993) ("[I]t soon became apparent that guaranteeing equal access to the polls would not suffice to root out other racially discriminatory voting practices" such as voting dilution). Efforts to reduce the impact of minority votes, in contrast to direct attempts to block access to the ballot, are aptly described as "second-generation barriers" to minority voting.

Second-generation barriers come in various forms. One of the blockages is racial gerrymandering, the redrawing of legislative districts in an "effort to segregate the races for purposes of voting." *Id.*, at 642. Another is adoption of a system of at-large voting in lieu of district-by-district voting in a city with a sizable black minority. By switching to at-large voting, the overall majority could control the election of each city council member, effectively eliminating the potency of the minority's votes. Grofman & Davidson, The Effect of Municipal Election Structure on Black Representation in Eight Southern States, in Quiet Revolution in the South 301, 319 (C. Davidson & B. Grofman eds. 1994) (hereinafter Quiet Revolution). A similar effect could be achieved if the city engaged in discriminatory annexation by incorporating majority-white areas into city limits, thereby decreasing the effect of VRA-occasioned increases in black voting. Whatever the device employed, this Court has long recognized that vote dilution, when adopted with a discriminatory purpose, cuts down the right to vote as certainly as denial of access to the ballot. *Shaw*, 509 U.S., at 640–641; *Allen* v. *State Bd. of Elections*, 393 U.S. 544, 569 (1969); *Reynolds* v. *Sims*, 377 U.S. 533, 555 (1964). See also H.R.Rep. No. 109–478, p. 6 (2006) (although "[d]iscrimination today is more subtle than the visible methods used in 1965," "the effect and results are the same, namely a diminishing of the minority community's ability to fully participate in the electoral process and to elect their preferred candidates").

In response to evidence of these substituted barriers, Congress reauthorized the VRA for five years in 1970, for seven years in 1975, and for 25 years in 1982. *Ante*, 570 U.S., at 538–539. Each time, this Court upheld the reauthorization as a valid exercise of congressional power. *Ante*, 570 U.S., at 539. As the 1982 reauthorization approached its 2007 expiration date, Congress again considered whether the VRA's preclearance mechanism remained an appropriate response to the problem of voting discrimination in covered jurisdictions.

Congress did not take this task lightly. Quite the opposite. The 109th Congress that took responsibility for the renewal started early and conscientiously. In October 2005, the House began extensive hearings, which continued into November and resumed in March 2006. S.Rep. No. 109–295, p. 2 (2006). In April 2006, the Senate followed suit, with hearings of its own. *Ibid.* In May 2006, the bills that became the VRA's reauthorization were introduced in both Houses. *Ibid.* The House held further hearings of considerable length, as did the Senate, which continued to hold hearings into June and July. H.R.Rep. No. 109–478, at 5; S.Rep. No. 109–295, at 3–4. In mid-July, the House considered and rejected four amendments, then passed the reauthorization by a vote of 390 yeas to 33 nays. 152 Cong. Rec. 14303–14304 (2006); Persily, The Promise and Pitfalls of the New Voting Rights Act, 117 Yale L.J. 174, 182–183 (2007) (hereinafter Persily). The bill was read and debated in the Senate, where it passed by a vote of 98 to 0. 152 Cong. Rec. 15325 (2006). President Bush signed it a week later, on July 27, 2006, recognizing the need for "further work . . . in the fight against injustice," and calling the reauthorization "an example of our continued commitment to a united America where every person is valued and treated with dignity and respect." 152 Cong. Rec. 16946–16947 (2006).

In the long course of the legislative process, Congress "amassed a sizable record." *Northwest Austin Municipal Util. Dist. No. One* v. *Holder,* 557 U.S. 193, 205 (2009). See also 679 F.3d 848, 865–873 (C.A.D.C. 2012) (describing the "extensive record" supporting Congress' determination that "serious and widespread intentional discrimination persisted in covered jurisdictions"). The House and Senate Judiciary Committees held 21 hearings, heard from scores of witnesses, and received a number of investigative reports and other written documentation of continuing discrimination in covered jurisdictions. In all, the legislative record Congress compiled filled more than 15,000 pages. H.R.Rep. No. 109–478, at 5, 11–12; S.Rep. No. 109–295, at 2–4, 15. The compilation presents countless "examples of flagrant racial discrimination" since the last reauthorization; Congress also brought to light systematic evidence that "intentional racial discrimination in voting remains so serious and widespread in covered jurisdictions that section 5 preclearance is still needed." 679 F.3d, at 866.

After considering the full legislative record, Congress made the following findings: The VRA has directly caused significant progress in eliminating first-generation barriers to ballot access, leading to a marked increase in minority voter registration and turnout and the number of minority elected officials. 2006 Reauthorization § 2(b)(1). But despite this progress, "second generation barriers constructed to prevent minority voters from fully participating in the electoral process" continued to exist, as well as racially polarized voting in the covered jurisdictions, which increased the political vulnerability of racial and language minorities in those jurisdictions. §§ 2(b)(2)–(3), 120 Stat. 577. Extensive "[e]vidence of continued discrimination," Congress concluded, "clearly show[ed] the continued need for Federal oversight" in covered jurisdictions. §§ 2(b)(4)–(5), *id.*, at 577–578. The overall record demonstrated to the federal lawmakers that, "without the continuation of the Voting Rights Act of 1965 protections, racial and language minority citizens will be deprived of the opportunity to exercise their right to vote, or will have their votes diluted, undermining the significant gains made by minorities in the last 40 years." § 2(b)(9), *id.*, at 578.

Based on these findings, Congress reauthorized preclearance for another 25 years, while also undertaking to reconsider the extension after 15 years to ensure that the provision was still necessary and effective. 42 U.S.C. §§ 1973b(a)(7), (8) (2006 ed., Supp. V). The question before the Court is whether Congress had the authority under the Constitution to act as it did.

II

In answering this question, the Court does not write on a clean slate. It is well established that Congress' judgment regarding exercise of its power to enforce the Fourteenth and Fifteenth Amendments warrants substantial deference. The VRA addresses the combination of race discrimination and the right to vote, which is "preservative of all rights." *Yick Wo* v. *Hopkins*, 118 U.S. 356, 370 (1886). When confronting the most constitutionally invidious form of discrimination, and the most fundamental right in our democratic system, Congress' power to act is at its height.

The basis for this deference is firmly rooted in both constitutional text and precedent. The Fifteenth Amendment, which targets precisely and only racial discrimination in voting rights, states that, in this domain, "Congress shall have power to enforce this article by appropriate legislation."[2] In choosing this language, the Amendment's framers invoked Chief Justice Marshall's formulation of the scope of Congress' powers under the Necessary and Proper Clause:

> "Let the end be legitimate, let it be within the scope of the constitution, and *all means which are appropriate, which are plainly adapted to that end,* which are not prohibited, but consist with the letter and spirit of the constitution, are constitutional." *McCulloch* v. *Maryland,* 17 U.S. (4 Wheat.) 316, 421 (1819) (emphasis added).

It cannot tenably be maintained that the VRA, an Act of Congress adopted to shield the right to vote from racial discrimination, is inconsistent with the letter or spirit of the Fifteenth Amendment, or any provision of the Constitution read in light of the Civil War Amendments. Nowhere in today's opinion, or in *Northwest Austin,*[3] is there clear recognition of the transformative effect the Fifteenth Amendment aimed to achieve. Notably, "the Founders' first successful amendment told Congress that it could 'make no law' over a certain domain"; in contrast, the Civil War Amendments used "language [that] authorized transformative new federal statutes to uproot all vestiges of unfreedom and inequality" and pro-

---

2. The Constitution uses the words "right to vote" in five separate places: the Fourteenth, Fifteenth, Nineteenth, Twenty-Fourth, and Twenty-Sixth Amendments. Each of these Amendments contains the same broad empowerment of Congress to enact "appropriate legislation" to enforce the protected right. The implication is unmistakable: Under our constitutional structure, Congress holds the lead rein in making the right to vote equally real for all U.S. citizens. These Amendments are in line with the special role assigned to Congress in protecting the integrity of the democratic process in federal elections. U.S. Const., Art. I, § 4 ("[T]he Congress may at any time by Law make or alter" regulations concerning the "Times, Places and Manner of holding Elections for Senators and Representatives."); *Arizona* v. *Inter Tribal Council of Ariz., Inc.,* 570 U.S. 1, 8 (2013).

3. Acknowledging the existence of "serious constitutional questions," see *ante,* 570 U.S., at 555 (internal quotation marks omitted), does not suggest how those questions should be answered.

vided "sweeping enforcement powers ... to enact 'appropriate' legislation targeting state abuses." A. Amar, America's Constitution: A Biography 361, 363, 399 (2005). See also McConnell, Institutions and Interpretation: A Critique of *City of Boerne* v. *Flores*, 111 Harv. L.Rev. 153, 182 (1997) (quoting Civil War-era framer: "[T]he remedy for the violation of the fourteenth and fifteenth amendments was expressly not left to the courts. The remedy was legislative.").

The stated purpose of the Civil War Amendments was to arm Congress with the power and authority to protect all persons within the Nation from violations of their rights by the States. In exercising that power, then, Congress may use "all means which are appropriate, which are plainly adapted" to the constitutional ends declared by these Amendments. *McCulloch*, 17 U.S. (4 Wheat.), at 421. So when Congress acts to enforce the right to vote free from racial discrimination, we ask not whether Congress has chosen the means most wise, but whether Congress has rationally selected means appropriate to a legitimate end. "It is not for us to review the congressional resolution of [the need for its chosen remedy]. It is enough that we be able to perceive a basis upon which the Congress might resolve the conflict as it did." *Katzenbach* v. *Morgan*, 384 U.S. 641, 653 (1966).

Until today, in considering the constitutionality of the VRA, the Court has accorded Congress the full measure of respect its judgments in this domain should garner. *South Carolina* v. *Katzenbach* supplies the standard of review: "As against the reserved powers of the States, Congress may use any rational means to effectuate the constitutional prohibition of racial discrimination in voting." 383 U.S., at 324. Faced with subsequent reauthorizations of the VRA, the Court has reaffirmed this standard. *E.g.*, *City of Rome*, 446 U.S., at 178. Today's Court does not purport to alter settled precedent establishing that the dispositive question is whether Congress has employed "rational means."

For three reasons, legislation reauthorizing an existing statute is especially likely to satisfy the minimal requirements of the rational-basis test. First, when reauthorization is at issue, Congress has already assembled a legislative record justifying the initial legislation. Congress is entitled to consider that pre-existing record as well as the record before it at the time of the vote on reauthorization. This is especially true where, as here, the Court has repeatedly affirmed the statute's constitutionality and Congress has adhered to the very model the Court has upheld. See *id.*, at 174 ("The appellants are asking us to do nothing less than overrule our decision in *South Carolina* v. *Katzenbach* . . . , in which we upheld the constitutionality of the Act."); *Lopez* v. *Monterey County*, 525 U.S. 266, 283 (1999) (similar).

Second, the very fact that reauthorization is necessary arises because Congress has built a temporal limitation into the Act. It has pledged to review, after a span of years (first 15, then 25) and in light of contemporary evidence, the continued need for the VRA. Cf. *Grutter* v. *Bollinger*, 539 U.S. 306, 343 (2003) (anticipating, but not guaranteeing, that, in 25 years, "the use of racial preferences [in higher education] will no longer be necessary").

Third, a reviewing court should expect the record supporting reauthorization to be less stark than the record originally made. Demand for a record of violations equivalent to the one earlier made would expose Congress to a catch-22. If the statute was working, there would be less evidence of discrimination, so opponents might argue that Congress should not be allowed to renew the statute. In contrast, if the statute was not working, there would be plenty of evidence of discrimination, but scant reason to renew a failed regulatory regime. See Persily 193–194.

This is not to suggest that congressional power in this area is limitless. It is this Court's responsibility to ensure that Congress has used appropriate means. The question meet for judicial review is whether the chosen means are "adapted to carry out the objects the amendments have in view." *Ex parte Virginia*, 100 U.S. 339, 346 (1880). The Court's role, then, is not to substitute its judgment for that of Congress, but to determine whether the legislative record sufficed to show that "Congress could rationally have determined that [its chosen] provisions were appropriate methods." *City of Rome*, 446 U.S., at 176–177.

In summary, the Constitution vests broad power in Congress to protect the right to vote, and in particular to combat racial discrimination in voting. This Court has repeatedly reaffirmed Congress' prerogative to use any rational means in exercise of its power in this area. And both precedent and logic dictate that the rational-means test should be easier to satisfy, and the burden on the statute's challenger should be higher, when what is at issue is the reauthorization of a remedy that the Court has previously affirmed, and that Congress found, from contemporary evidence, to be working to advance the legislature's legitimate objective.

III

The 2006 reauthorization of the Voting Rights Act fully satisfies the standard stated in *McCulloch*, 17 U.S. (4 Wheat.), at 421: Congress may choose any means "appropriate" and "plainly adapted to" a legitimate constitutional end. As we shall see, it is implausible to suggest otherwise.

A

I begin with the evidence on which Congress based its decision to continue the preclearance remedy. The surest way to evaluate whether that remedy remains in order is to see if preclearance is still effectively preventing discriminatory changes to voting laws. See *City of Rome*, 446 U.S., at 181 (identifying "information on the number and types of submissions made by covered jurisdictions and the number and nature of objections interposed by the Attorney General" as a primary basis for upholding the 1975 reauthorization). On that score, the record before Congress was huge. In fact, Congress found there were *more* DOJ objections between 1982 and 2004 (626) than there were between 1965 and the 1982 reauthorization (490). 1 Voting Rights Act: Evidence of Continued Need, Hearing before the Subcommittee on the Constitution of the House Committee on the Judiciary, 109th Cong., 2d Sess., 172 (2006) (hereinafter Evidence of Continued Need).

All told, between 1982 and 2006, DOJ objections blocked over 700 voting changes based on a determination that the changes were discriminatory. H.R.Rep. No. 109–478, at 21. Congress found that the majority of DOJ objections included findings of discriminatory intent, see 679 F.3d, at 867, and that the changes blocked by preclearance were "calculated decisions to keep minority voters from fully participating in the political process," H.R.Rep. No. 109–478, at 21. On top of that, over the same time period DOJ and private plaintiffs succeeded in more than 100 actions to enforce the § 5 preclearance requirements. 1 Evidence of Continued Need 186, 250.

In addition to blocking proposed voting changes through preclearance, DOJ may request more information from a jurisdiction proposing a change. In turn, the jurisdiction may modify or withdraw the proposed change. The number of such modifications or withdrawals provides an indication of how many discriminatory proposals are deterred without need for formal objection. Congress received evidence that more than 800 proposed changes were altered or withdrawn since the last reauthorization in 1982. H.R.Rep. No. 109-478, at 40-41.[4] Congress also received empirical studies finding that DOJ's requests for more information had a significant effect on the degree to which covered jurisdictions "compl[ied] with their obligatio[n]" to protect minority voting rights. 2 Evidence of Continued Need 2555.

Congress also received evidence that litigation under § 2 of the VRA was an inadequate substitute for preclearance in the covered jurisdictions. Litigation occurs only after the fact, when the illegal voting scheme has already been put in place and individuals have been elected pursuant to it, thereby gaining the advantages of incumbency. 1 id., at 97. An illegal scheme might be in place for several election cycles before a § 2 plaintiff can gather sufficient evidence to challenge it. 1 Voting Rights Act: Section 5 of the Act— History, Scope, and Purpose: Hearing before the Subcommittee on the Constitution of the House Committee on the Judiciary, 109th Cong., 1st Sess., 92 (2005) (hereinafter Section 5 Hearing). And litigation places a heavy financial burden on minority voters. See id., at 84. Congress also received evidence that preclearance lessened the litigation burden on covered jurisdictions themselves, because the preclearance process is far less costly than defending against a § 2 claim, and clearance by DOJ substantially reduces the likelihood that a § 2 claim will be mounted. Reauthorizing the Voting Rights Act's Temporary Provisions: Policy Perspectives and Views

---

4. This number includes only changes actually proposed. Congress also received evidence that many covered jurisdictions engaged in an "informal consultation process" with DOJ before formally submitting a proposal, so that the deterrent effect of preclearance was far broader than the formal submissions alone suggest. The Continuing Need for Section 5 Pre-Clearance: Hearing before the Senate Committee on the Judiciary, 109th Cong., 2d Sess., 53-54 (2006). All agree that an unsupported assertion about "deterrence" would not be sufficient to justify keeping a remedy in place in perpetuity. See ante, 570 U.S., at 550. But it was certainly reasonable for Congress to consider the testimony of witnesses who had worked with officials in covered jurisdictions and observed a real-world deterrent effect.

From the Field: Hearing before the Subcommittee on the Constitution, Civil Rights and Property Rights of the Senate Committee on the Judiciary, 109th Cong., 2d Sess., 13, 120–121 (2006). See also Brief for State of New York as *Amici Curiae* 8–9 (Section 5 "reduc[es] the likelihood that a jurisdiction will face costly and protracted Section 2 litigation.").

The number of discriminatory changes blocked or deterred by the preclearance requirement suggests that the state of voting rights in the covered jurisdictions would have been significantly different absent this remedy. Surveying the type of changes stopped by the preclearance procedure conveys a sense of the extent to which § 5 continues to protect minority voting rights. Set out below are characteristic examples of changes blocked in the years leading up to the 2006 reauthorization:

- In 1995, Mississippi sought to reenact a dual voter registration system, "which was initially enacted in 1892 to disenfranchise Black voters," and for that reason, was struck down by a federal court in 1987. H.R.Rep. No. 109–478, at 39.

- Following the 2000 census, the city of Albany, Georgia, proposed a redistricting plan that DOJ found to be "designed with the purpose to limit and retrogress the increased black voting strength . . . in the city as a whole." *Id.*, at 37 (internal quotation marks omitted).

- In 2001, the mayor and all-white five-member Board of Aldermen of Kilmichael, Mississippi, abruptly canceled the town's election after "an unprecedented number" of African-American candidates announced they were running for office. DOJ required an election, and the town elected its first black mayor and three black aldermen. *Id.*, at 36–37.

- In 2006, this Court found that Texas' attempt to redraw a congressional district to reduce the strength of Latino voters bore "the mark of intentional discrimination that could give rise to an equal protection violation," and ordered the district redrawn in compliance with the VRA. *League of United Latin American Citizens* v. *Perry*, 548 U.S. 399, 440 (2006). In response, Texas sought to undermine this Court's order by curtailing early voting in the district, but was blocked by an action to enforce the § 5 preclearance requirement. See Order in *League of United Latin American Citizens* v. *Texas*, No. 06–cv–1046 (W.D.Tex., Dec. 5, 2006), Doc. 8.

- In 2003, after African-Americans won a majority of the seats on the school board for the first time in history, Charleston County, South Carolina, proposed an at-large voting mechanism for the board. The proposal, made without consulting any of the African-American members of the school board, was found to be an "'exact replica'" of an earlier voting scheme that, a federal court had determined, violated the VRA. 811 F. Supp.2d 424, 483 (D.D.C. 2011). See also S.Rep. No. 109–295, at 309. DOJ invoked § 5 to block the proposal.

- In 1993, the city of Millen, Georgia, proposed to delay the election in a majority-black district by two years, leaving that district without representation on the city council while the neighboring majority-white district would have three representatives. 1 Section 5 Hearing 744. DOJ blocked the proposal. The county then sought to move a polling place from a predominantly black neighborhood in the city to an inaccessible location in a predominantly white neighborhood outside city limits. *Id.*, at 816.

- In 2004, Waller County, Texas, threatened to prosecute two black students after they announced their intention to run for office. The county then attempted to reduce the availability of early voting in that election at polling places near a historically black university. 679 F.3d, at 865–866.

- In 1990, Dallas County, Alabama, whose county seat is the city of Selma, sought to purge its voter rolls of many black voters. DOJ rejected the purge as discriminatory, noting that it would have disqualified many citizens from voting "simply because they failed to pick up or return a voter update form, when there was no valid requirement that they do so." 1 Section 5 Hearing 356.

These examples, and scores more like them, fill the pages of the legislative record. The evidence was indeed sufficient to support Congress' conclusion that "racial discrimination in voting in covered jurisdictions [remained] serious and pervasive." 679 F.3d, at 865.[5]

---

5. For an illustration postdating the 2006 reauthorization, see *South Carolina* v. *United States*, 898 F. Supp.2d 30 (D.D.C. 2012), which involved a South Carolina voter-identification law enacted in 2011. Concerned that the law would burden minority voters, DOJ brought a § 5 enforcement action to block the law's implementation. In the course of the litigation, South Carolina officials agreed to binding interpretations that made it "far easier than some might have expected or feared" for South Carolina citizens to vote. *Id.*, at 37. A three-judge panel precleared the law after adopting both interpretations as an express "condition of pre-clearance." *Id.*, at 37–38. Two of the judges commented that the case demonstrated "the continuing utility of Section 5 of the Voting Rights Act in deterring problematic, and hence encouraging non-discriminatory, changes in state and local voting laws." *Id.*, at 54 (Bates, J., concurring).

Congress further received evidence indicating that formal requests of the kind set out above represented only the tip of the iceberg. There was what one commentator described as an "avalanche of case studies of voting rights violations in the covered jurisdictions," ranging from "outright intimidation and violence against minority voters" to "more subtle forms of voting rights deprivations." Persily 202. This evidence gave Congress ever more reason to conclude that the time had not yet come for relaxed vigilance against the scourge of race discrimination in voting.

True, conditions in the South have impressively improved since passage of the Voting Rights Act. Congress noted this improvement and found that the VRA was the driving force behind it. 2006 Reauthorization § 2(b) (1). But Congress also found that voting discrimination had evolved into subtler second-generation barriers, and that eliminating preclearance would risk loss of the gains that had been made. §§ 2(b)(2), (9). Concerns of this order, the Court previously found, gave Congress adequate cause to reauthorize the VRA. *City of Rome*, 446 U.S., at 180–182 (congressional reauthorization of the preclearance requirement was justified based on "the number and nature of objections interposed by the Attorney General" since the prior reauthorization; extension was "necessary to preserve the limited and fragile achievements of the Act and to promote further amelioration of voting discrimination") (internal quotation marks omitted). Facing such evidence then, the Court expressly rejected the argument that disparities in voter turnout and number of elected officials were the only metrics capable of justifying reauthorization of the VRA. *Ibid.*

B

I turn next to the evidence on which Congress based its decision to reauthorize the coverage formula in § 4(b). Because Congress did not alter the coverage formula, the same jurisdictions previously subject to preclearance continue to be covered by this remedy. The evidence just described, of preclearance's continuing efficacy in blocking constitutional violations in the covered jurisdictions, itself grounded Congress' conclusion that the remedy should be retained for those jurisdictions.

There is no question, moreover, that the covered jurisdictions have a unique history of problems with racial discrimination in voting. *Ante*, 570 U.S., at 545–546. Consideration of this long history, still in living memory, was altogether appropriate. The Court criticizes Congress for failing to recognize that "history did not end in 1965." *Ante*, 570 U.S., at 552. But the Court ignores that "what's past is prologue." W. Shakespeare, The Tempest, act 2, sc. 1. And "[t]hose who cannot remember the past are condemned to repeat it." 1 G. Santayana, The Life of Reason 284 (1905). Congress was especially mindful of the need to reinforce the gains already made and to prevent backsliding. 2006 Reauthorization § 2(b)(9).

Of particular importance, even after 40 years and thousands of discriminatory changes blocked by preclearance, conditions in the covered jurisdictions demonstrated that the formula was still justified by "current needs." *Northwest Austin*, 557 U.S., at 203.

Congress learned of these conditions through a report, known as the Katz study, that looked at § 2 suits between 1982 and 2004. To Examine the Impact and Effectiveness of the Voting Rights Act: Hearing before the Subcommittee on the Constitution of the House Committee on the Judiciary, 109th Cong., 1st Sess., 964–1124 (2005) (hereinafter Impact and Effectiveness). Because the private right of action authorized by § 2 of the VRA applies nationwide, a comparison of § 2 lawsuits in covered and noncovered jurisdictions provides an appropriate yardstick for measuring differences between covered and noncovered jurisdictions. If differences in the risk of voting discrimination between covered and noncovered jurisdictions had disappeared, one would expect that the rate of successful § 2 lawsuits would be roughly the same in both areas.[6] The study's findings, however, indicated that racial discrimination in voting remains "concentrated in the jurisdictions singled out for preclearance." *Northwest Austin*, 557 U.S., at 203.

Although covered jurisdictions account for less than 25 percent of the country's population, the Katz study revealed that they accounted for 56 percent of successful § 2 litigation since 1982. Impact and Effectiveness 974. Controlling for population, there were nearly *four* times as many successful § 2 cases in covered jurisdictions as there were in noncovered jurisdictions. 679 F.3d, at 874. The Katz study further found that § 2 lawsuits are more

---

6. Because preclearance occurs only in covered jurisdictions and can be expected to stop the most obviously objectionable measures, one would expect a *lower* rate of successful § 2 lawsuits in those jurisdictions if the risk of voting discrimination there were the same as elsewhere in the country.

likely to succeed when they are filed in covered jurisdictions than in non-covered jurisdictions. Impact and Effectiveness 974. From these findings—ignored by the Court—Congress reasonably concluded that the coverage formula continues to identify the jurisdictions of greatest concern.

The evidence before Congress, furthermore, indicated that voting in the covered jurisdictions was more racially polarized than elsewhere in the country. H.R.Rep. No. 109–478, at 34–35. While racially polarized voting alone does not signal a constitutional violation, it is a factor that increases the vulnerability of racial minorities to discriminatory changes in voting law. The reason is twofold. First, racial polarization means that racial minorities are at risk of being systematically outvoted and having their interests underrepresented in legislatures. Second, "when political preferences fall along racial lines, the natural inclinations of incumbents and ruling parties to entrench themselves have predictable racial effects. Under circumstances of severe racial polarization, efforts to gain political advantage translate into race-specific disadvantages." Ansolabehere, Persily, & Stewart, Regional Differences in Racial Polarization in the 2012 Presidential Election: Implications for the Constitutionality of Section 5 of the Voting Rights Act, 126 Harv. L.Rev. Forum 205, 209 (2013).

In other words, a governing political coalition has an incentive to prevent changes in the existing balance of voting power. When voting is racially polarized, efforts by the ruling party to pursue that incentive "will inevitably discriminate against a racial group." *Ibid.* Just as buildings in California have a greater need to be earthquake-proofed, places where there is greater racial polarization in voting have a greater need for prophylactic measures to prevent purposeful race discrimination. This point was understood by Congress and is well recognized in the academic literature. See 2006 Reauthorization § 2(b)(3), 120 Stat. 577 ("The continued evidence of racially polarized voting in each of the jurisdictions covered by the [preclearance requirement] demonstrates that racial and language minorities remain politically vulnerable"); H.R.Rep. No. 109–478, at 35; Davidson, The Recent Evolution of Voting Rights Law Affecting Racial and Language Minorities, in Quiet Revolution 21, 22.

The case for retaining a coverage formula that met needs on the ground was therefore solid. Congress might have been charged with rigidity had it afforded covered jurisdictions no way out or ignored jurisdictions that needed superintendence. Congress, however, responded to this concern. Critical components of the congressional design are the statutory provisions allowing jurisdictions to "bail out" of preclearance, and for court-ordered "bail ins." See *Northwest Austin*, 557 U.S., at 199. The VRA permits a jurisdiction to bail out by showing that it has complied with the Act for ten years, and has engaged in efforts to eliminate intimidation and harassment of voters. 42 U.S.C. § 1973b(a) (2006 ed. and Supp. V). It also authorizes a court to subject a noncovered jurisdiction to federal preclearance upon finding that violations of the Fourteenth and Fifteenth Amendments have occurred there. § 1973a(c) (2006 ed.).

Congress was satisfied that the VRA's bailout mechanism provided an effective means of adjusting the VRA's coverage over time. H.R.Rep. No. 109–478, at 25 (the success of bailout "illustrates that: (1) covered status is neither permanent nor over-broad; and (2) covered status has been and continues to be within the control of the jurisdiction such that those jurisdictions that have a genuinely clean record and want to terminate coverage have the ability to do so"). Nearly 200 jurisdictions have successfully bailed out of the preclearance requirement, and DOJ has consented to every bailout application filed by an eligible jurisdiction since the current bailout procedure became effective in 1984. Brief for Federal Respondent 54. The bail-in mechanism has also worked. Several jurisdictions have been subject to federal preclearance by court orders, including the States of New Mexico and Arkansas. App. to Brief for Federal Respondent 1a–3a.

This experience exposes the inaccuracy of the Court's portrayal of the Act as static, unchanged since 1965. Congress designed the VRA to be a dynamic statute, capable of adjusting to changing conditions. True, many covered jurisdictions have not been able to bail out due to recent acts of noncompliance with the VRA, but that truth reinforces the congressional judgment that these jurisdictions were rightfully subject to preclearance, and ought to remain under that regime.

IV

Congress approached the 2006 reauthorization of the VRA with great care and seriousness. The same cannot be said of the Court's opinion today. The Court makes no genuine attempt to engage with the massive legislative record that Congress assembled. Instead, it relies on increases in voter registration and turnout as if that were the whole story. See *supra*, 570 U.S., at 551. Without even identifying a standard of review, the Court dismissively brushes off arguments based on "data from the record," and declines to enter the "debat[e about] what [the] record shows." *Ante*, 570 U.S., at 553. One would expect more from an opinion striking at the heart of the Nation's signal piece of civil-rights legislation.

I note the most disturbing lapses. First, by what right, given its usual restraint, does the Court even address Shelby County's facial challenge to the VRA? Second, the Court veers away from controlling precedent regarding the "equal sovereignty" doctrine without even acknowledging that it is doing so. Third, hardly showing the respect ordinarily paid when Congress acts to implement the Civil War Amendments, and as just stressed, the Court does not even deign to grapple with the legislative record.

A

Shelby County launched a purely facial challenge to the VRA's 2006 reauthorization. "A facial challenge to a legislative Act," the Court has other times said, "is, of course, the most difficult challenge to mount successfully, since the challenger must establish that no set of circumstances exists under which the Act would be valid." *United States* v. *Salerno*, 481 U.S. 739, 745 (1987).

"[U]nder our constitutional system[,] courts are not roving commissions assigned to pass judgment on the validity of the Nation's laws." *Broadrick* v. *Oklahoma*, 413 U.S. 601, 610–611 (1973). Instead, the "judicial Power" is limited to deciding particular "Cases" and "Controversies." U.S. Const., Art. III, § 2. "Embedded in the traditional rules governing constitutional adjudication is the principle that a person to whom a statute may constitutionally be applied will not be heard to challenge that statute on the ground that it may conceivably be applied unconstitutionally to others, in other situations not before the Court." *Broadrick*, 413 U.S., at 610. Yet the Court's opinion in this case contains not a word explaining why Congress lacks the power to subject to preclearance the particular plaintiff that initiated this lawsuit—Shelby County, Alabama. The reason for the

Court's silence is apparent, for as applied to Shelby County, the VRA's pre-clearance requirement is hardly contestable.

Alabama is home to Selma, site of the "Bloody Sunday" beatings of civil-rights demonstrators that served as the catalyst for the VRA's enactment. Following those events, Martin Luther King, Jr., led a march from Selma to Montgomery, Alabama's capital, where he called for passage of the VRA. If the Act passed, he foresaw, progress could be made even in Alabama, but there had to be a steadfast national commitment to see the task through to completion. In King's words, "the arc of the moral universe is long, but it bends toward justice." G. May, Bending Toward Justice: The Voting Rights Act and the Transformation of American Democracy 144 (2013).

History has proved King right. Although circumstances in Alabama have changed, serious concerns remain. Between 1982 and 2005, Alabama had one of the highest rates of successful § 2 suits, second only to its VRA-covered neighbor Mississippi. 679 F.3d, at 897 (Williams, J., dissenting). In other words, even while subject to the restraining effect of § 5, Alabama was found to have "deni[ed] or abridge[d]" voting rights "on account of race or color" more frequently than nearly all other States in the Union. 42 U.S.C. § 1973(a). This fact prompted the dissenting judge below to concede that "a more narrowly tailored coverage formula" capturing Alabama and a handful of other jurisdictions with an established track record of racial discrimination in voting "might be defensible." 679 F.3d, at 897 (opinion of Williams, J.). That is an understatement. Alabama's sorry history of § 2 violations alone provides sufficient justification for Congress' determination in 2006 that the State should remain subject to § 5's preclearance requirement.[7]

A few examples suffice to demonstrate that, at least in Alabama, the "current burdens" imposed by § 5's preclearance requirement are "justified by current needs." *Northwest Austin*, 557 U.S., at 203. In the interim

---

7. This lawsuit was filed by Shelby County, a political subdivision of Alabama, rather than by the State itself. Nevertheless, it is appropriate to judge Shelby County's constitutional challenge in light of instances of discrimination statewide because Shelby County is subject to § 5's preclearance requirement by virtue of *Alabama's* designation as a covered jurisdiction under § 4(b) of the VRA. See *ante*, 570 U.S., at 540. In any event, Shelby County's recent record of employing an at-large electoral system tainted by intentional racial discrimination is by itself sufficient to justify subjecting the county to § 5's preclearance mandate. See *infra*, 570 U.S., at 583–584.

between the VRA's 1982 and 2006 reauthorizations, this Court twice confronted purposeful racial discrimination in Alabama. In *Pleasant Grove* v. *United States*, 479 U.S. 462 (1987), the Court held that Pleasant Grove—a city in Jefferson County, Shelby County's neighbor—engaged in purposeful discrimination by annexing all-white areas while rejecting the annexation request of an adjacent black neighborhood. The city had "shown unambiguous opposition to racial integration, both before and after the passage of the federal civil rights laws," and its strategic annexations appeared to be an attempt "to provide for the growth of a monolithic white voting block" for "the impermissible purpose of minimizing future black voting strength." *Id.*, at 465, 471–472.

Two years before *Pleasant Grove*, the Court in *Hunter* v. *Underwood*, 471 U.S. 222 (1985), struck down a provision of the Alabama Constitution that prohibited individuals convicted of misdemeanor offenses "involving moral turpitude" from voting. *Id.*, at 223 (internal quotation marks omitted). The provision violated the Fourteenth Amendment's Equal Protection Clause, the Court unanimously concluded, because "its original enactment was motivated by a desire to discriminate against blacks on account of race[,] and the [provision] continues to this day to have that effect." *Id.*, at 233.

Pleasant Grove and *Hunter* were not anomalies. In 1986, a Federal District Judge concluded that the at-large election systems in several Alabama counties violated § 2. *Dillard* v. *Crenshaw Cty.*, 640 F. Supp. 1347, 1354–1363 (M.D.Ala. 1986). Summarizing its findings, the court stated that "[f]rom the late 1800's through the present, [Alabama] has consistently erected barriers to keep black persons from full and equal participation in the social, economic, and political life of the state." *Id.*, at 1360.

The *Dillard* litigation ultimately expanded to include 183 cities, counties, and school boards employing discriminatory at-large election systems. *Dillard* v. *Baldwin Cty. Bd. of Ed.*, 686 F. Supp. 1459, 1461 (M.D.Ala. 1988). One of those defendants was Shelby County, which eventually signed a consent decree to resolve the claims against it. See *Dillard* v. *Crenshaw Cty.*, 748 F. Supp. 819 (M.D.Ala. 1990).

Although the *Dillard* litigation resulted in overhauls of numerous electoral systems tainted by racial discrimination, concerns about backsliding persist. In 2008, for example, the city of Calera, located in Shelby County, requested preclearance of a redistricting plan that "would have eliminated the city's sole majority-black district, which had been created pursuant to the consent decree in *Dillard*." 811 F. Supp.2d, at 443. Although DOJ objected to the plan, Calera forged ahead with elections based on the unprecleared voting changes, resulting in the defeat of the incumbent African-American councilman who represented the former majority-black district. *Ibid.* The city's defiance required DOJ to bring a § 5 enforcement action that ultimately yielded appropriate redress, including restoration of the majority-black district. *Ibid.*; Brief for Respondent-Intervenors Earl Cunningham et al. 20.

A recent Federal Bureau of Investigation (FBI) investigation provides a further window into the persistence of racial discrimination in state politics. See *United States* v. *McGregor*, 824 F. Supp.2d 1339, 1344–1348 (M.D.Ala. 2011). Recording devices worn by state legislators cooperating with the FBI's investigation captured conversations between members of the state legislature and their political allies. The recorded conversations are shocking. Members of the state Senate derisively refer to African-Americans as "Aborigines" and talk openly of their aim to quash a particular gambling-related referendum because the referendum, if placed on the ballot, might increase African-American voter turnout. *Id.*, at 1345–1346 (internal quotation marks omitted). See also *id.*, at 1345 (legislators and their allies expressed concern that if the referendum were placed on the ballot, "'[e]very black, every illiterate' would be 'bused [to the polls] on HUD financed buses'"). These conversations occurred not in the 1870's, or even in the 1960's, they took place in 2010. *Id.*, at 1344–1345. The District Judge presiding over the criminal trial at which the recorded conversations were introduced commented that the "recordings represent compelling evidence that political exclusion through racism remains a real and enduring problem" in Alabama. *Id.*, at 1347. Racist sentiments, the judge observed, "remain regrettably entrenched in the high echelons of state government." *Ibid.*

These recent episodes forcefully demonstrate that § 5's preclearance requirement is constitutional as applied to Alabama and its political subdivisions.[8] And under our case law, that conclusion should suffice to resolve

---

8. Congress continued preclearance over Alabama, including Shelby County, *after* considering evidence of current barriers there to minority voting clout. Shelby County, thus, is no "redhead" caught up in an arbitrary scheme. See *ante*, 570 U.S., at 554.

this case. See *United States* v. *Raines*, 362 U.S. 17, 24–25 (1960) ("[I]f the complaint here called for an application of the statute clearly constitutional under the Fifteenth Amendment, that should have been an end to the question of constitutionality."). See also *Nev. Dep't of Human Res.* v. *Hibbs*, 538 U.S. 721, 743 (2003) (Scalia, J., dissenting) (where, as here, a state or local government raises a facial challenge to a federal statute on the ground that it exceeds Congress' enforcement powers under the Civil War Amendments, the challenge fails if the opposing party is able to show that the statute "could constitutionally be applied to *some* jurisdictions").

This Court has consistently rejected constitutional challenges to legislation enacted pursuant to Congress' enforcement powers under the Civil War Amendments upon finding that the legislation was constitutional as applied to the particular set of circumstances before the Court. See *United States* v. *Georgia*, 546 U.S. 151, 159 (2006) (Title II of the Americans with Disabilities Act of 1990 (ADA) validly abrogates state sovereign immunity "insofar as [it] creates a private cause of action . . . for conduct that *actually* violates the Fourteenth Amendment"); *Tennessee* v. *Lane*, 541 U.S. 509, 530–534 (2004) (Title II of the ADA is constitutional "as it applies to the class of cases implicating the fundamental right of access to the courts"); *Raines*, 362 U.S., at 24–26 (federal statute proscribing deprivations of the right to vote based on race was constitutional as applied to the state officials before the Court, even if it could not constitutionally be applied to other parties). A similar approach is warranted here.[9]

The VRA's exceptionally broad severability provision makes it particularly inappropriate for the Court to allow Shelby County to mount a facial challenge to §§ 4(b) and 5 of the VRA, even though application of those provisions to the county falls well within the bounds of Congress' legislative authority. The severability provision states:

---

9. The Court does not contest that Alabama's history of racial discrimination provides a sufficient basis for Congress to require Alabama and its political subdivisions to preclear electoral changes. Nevertheless, the Court asserts that Shelby County may prevail on its facial challenge to § 4's coverage formula because it is subject to § 5's preclearance requirement by virtue of that formula. See *ante*, 570 U.S., at 554–555 ("The county was selected [for preclearance] based on th[e coverage] formula."). This misses the reality that Congress decided to subject Alabama to preclearance based on evidence of continuing constitutional violations in that State. See *supra*, 570 U.S., at 585, n. 8.

"If any provision of [this Act] or the application thereof to any person or circumstances is held invalid, the remainder of [the Act] and the application of the provision to other persons not similarly situated or to other circumstances shall not be affected thereby." 42 U.S.C. § 1973p.

In other words, even if the VRA could not constitutionally be applied to certain States—*e.g.*, Arizona and Alaska, see *ante*, 570 U.S., at 542—§ 1973p calls for those unconstitutional applications to be severed, leaving the Act in place for jurisdictions as to which its application does not transgress constitutional limits.

Nevertheless, the Court suggests that limiting the jurisdictional scope of the VRA in an appropriate case would be to "try our hand at updating the statute." *Ante*, 570 U.S., at 554. Just last Term, however, the Court rejected this very argument when addressing a materially identical severability provision, explaining that such a provision is "Congress' explicit textual instruction to leave unaffected the remainder of [the Act]" if any particular "application is unconstitutional." *National Federation of Independent Business* v. *Sebelius*, 567 U.S. 519, 586 (2012) (plurality opinion) (internal quotation marks omitted); *id.*, at 645–646 (Ginsburg, J., concurring in part, concurring in judgment in part, and dissenting in part) (agreeing with the plurality's severability analysis). See also *Raines*, 362 U.S., at 23 (a statute capable of some constitutional applications may nonetheless be susceptible to a facial challenge only in "that rarest of cases where this Court can justifiably think itself able confidently to discern that Congress would not have desired its legislation to stand at all unless it could validly stand in its every application"). Leaping to resolve Shelby County's facial challenge without considering whether application of the VRA to Shelby County is constitutional, or even addressing the VRA's severability provision, the Court's opinion can hardly be described as an exemplar of restrained and moderate decisionmaking. Quite the opposite. Hubris is a fit word for today's demolition of the VRA.

B

The Court stops any application of § 5 by holding that § 4(b)'s coverage formula is unconstitutional. It pins this result, in large measure, to "the fundamental principle of equal sovereignty." *Ante*, 570 U.S., at 542,

544–545, 556. In *Katzenbach*, however, the Court held, in no uncertain terms, that the principle *"applies only to the terms upon which States are admitted to the Union*, and not to the remedies for local evils which have subsequently appeared." 383 U.S., at 328–329 (emphasis added).

Katzenbach, the Court acknowledges, "rejected the notion that the [equal sovereignty] principle operate[s] as a bar on differential treatment outside ⌊the⌋ context ⌊of the admission of new States]." *Ante*, 570 U.S., at 544 (citing 383 U.S., at 328–329) (emphasis deleted). But the Court clouds that once clear understanding by citing dictum from *Northwest Austin* to convey that the principle of equal sovereignty "remains highly pertinent in assessing subsequent disparate treatment of States." *Ante*, 570 U.S., at 544 (citing 557 U.S., at 203). See also *ante*, 570 U.S., at 556 (relying on *Northwest Austin*'s "emphasis on [the] significance" of the equal-sovereignty principle). If the Court is suggesting that dictum in *Northwest Austin* silently overruled *Katzenbach*'s limitation of the equal sovereignty doctrine to "the admission of new States," the suggestion is untenable. *Northwest Austin* cited *Katzenbach*'s holding in the course of *declining to decide* whether the VRA was constitutional or even what standard of review applied to the question. 557 U.S., at 203–204. In today's decision, the Court ratchets up what was pure dictum in *Northwest Austin*, attributing breadth to the equal sovereignty principle in flat contradiction of *Katzenbach*. The Court does so with nary an explanation of why it finds *Katzenbach* wrong, let alone any discussion of whether *stare decisis* nonetheless counsels adherence to *Katzenbach*'s ruling on the limited "significance" of the equal sovereignty principle.

Today's unprecedented extension of the equal sovereignty principle outside its proper domain—the admission of new States—is capable of much mischief. Federal statutes that treat States disparately are hardly novelties. See, *e.g.*, 28 U.S.C. § 3704(a)(1) (no State may operate or permit a sports-related gambling scheme, unless that State conducted such a scheme "at any time during the period beginning January 1, 1976, and ending August 31, 1990"); 26 U.S.C. § 142(l) (Environmental Protection Agency required to locate green building project in a State meeting specified population criteria); 42 U.S.C. § 3796bb(b) (at least 50 percent of rural drug enforcement assistance funding must be allocated to States with "a population density of fifty-two or fewer persons per square mile or a State in which the largest county has fewer than one hundred and fifty thousand people, based on the decennial census of 1990 through fiscal year 1997"); §§ 13925, 13971 (similar population criteria for funding to combat rural domestic violence); § 10136(c)(6) (specifying rules applicable to Nevada's Yucca Mountain nuclear waste site, and providing that "[n]o State, other than the State of Nevada, may receive financial assistance under this subsection after December 22, 1987"). Do such provisions remain safe given the Court's expansion of equal sovereignty's sway?

Of gravest concern, Congress relied on our pathmarking *Katzenbach* decision in each reauthorization of the VRA. It had every reason to believe that the Act's limited geographical scope would weigh in favor of, not against, the Act's constitutionality. See, *e.g.*, *United States* v. *Morrison*, 529 U.S. 598, 626–627 (2000) (confining preclearance regime to States with a record of discrimination bolstered the VRA's constitutionality). Congress could hardly have foreseen that the VRA's limited geographic reach would render the Act constitutionally suspect. See Persily 195 ("[S]upporters of the Act sought to develop an evidentiary record for the principal purpose of explaining why the covered jurisdictions should remain covered, rather than justifying the coverage of certain jurisdictions but not others.").

In the Court's conception, it appears, defenders of the VRA could not prevail upon showing what the record overwhelmingly bears out, *i.e.*, that there is a need for continuing the preclearance regime in covered States. In addition, the defenders would have to disprove the existence of a comparable need elsewhere. See Tr. of Oral Arg. 61–62 (suggesting that proof of egregious episodes of racial discrimination in covered jurisdictions would not suffice to carry the day for the VRA, unless such episodes are shown to be absent elsewhere). I am aware of no precedent for imposing such a double burden on defenders of legislation.

C

The Court has time and again declined to upset legislation of this genre unless there was no or almost no evidence of unconstitutional action by States. See, *e.g.*, *City of Boerne* v. *Flores*, 521 U.S. 507, 530 (1997) (legislative record "mention[ed] no episodes [of the kind the legislation aimed to check] occurring in the past 40 years"). No such claim can be made about the congressional record for the 2006 VRA reauthorization. Given a record replete with examples of denial or abridgment of a paramount federal right, the Court should have left the matter where it belongs: in Congress' bailiwick.

Instead, the Court strikes § 4(b)'s coverage provision because, in its view, the provision is not based on "current conditions." *Ante*, 570 U.S., at 550. It discounts, however, that one such condition was the preclearance remedy in place in the covered jurisdictions, a remedy Congress designed both to catch discrimination before it causes harm, and to guard against return to old ways. 2006 Reauthorization §§ 2(b)(3), (9). Volumes of evidence supported Congress' determination that the prospect of retrogression was real. Throwing out preclearance when it has worked and is continuing to work to stop discriminatory changes is like throwing away your umbrella in a rainstorm because you are not getting wet.

But, the Court insists, the coverage formula is no good; it is based on "decades-old data and eradicated practices." *Ante*, 570 U.S., at 551. Even if the legislative record shows, as engaging with it would reveal, that the formula accurately identifies the jurisdictions with the worst conditions of voting discrimination, that is of no moment, as the Court sees it. Congress, the Court decrees, must "star[t] from scratch." *Ante*, 570 U.S., at 556. I do not see why that should be so.

Congress' chore was different in 1965 than it was in 2006. In 1965, there were a "small number of States . . . which in most instances were familiar to Congress by name," on which Congress fixed its attention. *Katzenbach*, 383 U.S., at 328. In drafting the coverage formula, "Congress began work with reliable evidence of actual voting discrimination in a great majority of the States" it sought to target. *Id.*, at 329. "The formula [Congress] eventually evolved to describe these areas" also captured a few States that had not been the subject of congressional factfinding. *Ibid.* Nevertheless, the Court upheld the formula in its entirety, finding it fair "to infer a significant danger of the evil" in all places the formula covered. *Ibid.*

The situation Congress faced in 2006, when it took up reauthorization of the coverage formula, was not the same. By then, the formula had been in effect for many years, and all of the jurisdictions covered by it were "familiar to Congress by name." *Id.*, at 328. The question before Congress: Was there still a sufficient basis to support continued application of the preclearance remedy in each of those already-identified places? There was at that point no chance that the formula might inadvertently sweep in new areas that were not the subject of congressional findings. And Congress could determine from the record whether the jurisdictions captured by the coverage formula still belonged under the preclearance regime. If they did, there was no need to alter the formula. That is why the Court, in addressing prior reauthorizations of the VRA, did not question the continuing "relevance" of the formula.

Consider once again the components of the record before Congress in 2006. The coverage provision identified a known list of places with an undisputed history of serious problems with racial discrimination in voting. Recent evidence relating to Alabama and its counties was there for all to see. Multiple Supreme Court decisions had upheld the coverage provision, most recently in 1999. There was extensive evidence that, due to the preclearance mechanism, conditions in the covered jurisdictions had notably improved. And there was evidence that preclearance was still having a substantial real-world effect, having stopped hundreds of discriminatory voting changes in the covered jurisdictions since the last reauthorization. In addition, there was evidence that racial polarization in voting was higher in covered jurisdictions than elsewhere, increasing the vulnerability of minority citizens in those jurisdictions. And countless witnesses, reports, and case studies documented continuing problems with voting discrimination in those jurisdictions. In light of this record, Congress had more than a reasonable basis to conclude that the existing coverage formula was not out of sync with conditions on the ground in covered areas. And certainly Shelby County was no candidate for release through the mechanism Congress provided. See *supra*, 570 U.S., at 581, 583–584.

The Court holds § 4(b) invalid on the ground that it is "irrational to base coverage on the use of voting tests 40 years ago, when such tests have been illegal since that time." *Ante*, 570 U.S., at 556. But the Court disregards what Congress set about to do in enacting the VRA. That extraordinary legislation scarcely stopped at the particular tests and devices that happened to exist in 1965. The grand aim of the Act is to secure to all in our polity equal citizenship stature, a voice in our democracy undiluted by race. As the record for the 2006 reauthorization makes abundantly clear, second-generation barriers to minority voting rights have emerged in the covered jurisdictions as attempted *substitutes* for the first-generation barriers that originally triggered preclearance in those jurisdictions. See *supra*, 570 U.S., at 563–564, 566, 573–575.

The sad irony of today's decision lies in its utter failure to grasp why the VRA has proved effective. The Court appears to believe that the VRA's success in eliminating the specific devices extant in 1965 means that preclearance is no longer needed. *Ante*, 570 U.S., at 552–553, 554, 556. With that belief, and the argument derived from it, history repeats itself. The same assumption—that the problem could be solved when particular methods of voting discrimination are identified and eliminated—was indulged and proved wrong repeatedly prior to the VRA's enactment. Unlike prior statutes, which singled out particular tests or devices, the VRA is grounded in Congress' recognition of the "variety and persistence" of measures designed to impair minority voting rights. *Katzenbach*, 383 U.S., at 311; *supra*, 570 U.S., at 560. In truth, the evolution of voting discrimination into more subtle second-generation barriers is powerful evidence that a remedy as effective as preclearance remains vital to protect minority voting rights and prevent backsliding.

Beyond question, the VRA is no ordinary legislation. It is extraordinary because Congress embarked on a mission long delayed and of extraordinary importance: to realize the purpose and promise of the Fifteenth Amendment. For a half century, a concerted effort has been made to end racial discrimination in voting. Thanks to the VRA, progress once the subject of a dream has been achieved and continues to be made.

The record supporting the 2006 reauthorization of the VRA is also extraordinary. It was described by the Chairman of the House Judiciary Committee as "one of the most extensive considerations of any piece of legislation that the United States Congress has dealt with in the 27½ years" he had served in the House. 152 Cong. Rec. 14230 (2006) (statement of Rep. Sensenbrenner). After exhaustive evidence gathering and deliberative process, Congress reauthorized the VRA, including the coverage provision, with overwhelming bipartisan support. It was the judgment of Congress that "40 years has not been a sufficient amount of time to eliminate the vestiges of discrimination following nearly 100 years of disregard for the dictates of the 15th amendment and to ensure that the right of all citizens to vote is protected as guaranteed by the Constitution." 2006 Reauthorization § 2(b)(7), 120 Stat. 578. That determination of the body empowered to enforce the Civil War Amendments "by appropriate legislation" merits this Court's utmost respect. In my judgment, the Court errs egregiously by overriding Congress' decision.

*   *   *

For the reasons stated, I would affirm the judgment of the Court of Appeals.

BURWELL V. HOBBY LOBBY STORES, INC. (2014)

Burwell v. *Hobby Lobby Stores, Inc.*, concerned the contraceptive mandate in the Patient Protection and Affordable Care Act (ACA). The ACA permits religious employers and nonprofit religious institutions to opt out of its contraceptive mandate for religious reasons. It does not expressly provide an exemption for privately held, for-profit corporations to do the same. Plaintiff Hobby Lobby Stores and other closely held for-profit corporations sued the United States Secretary of Health and Human Services, contending that the obligation to comply with the contraceptive mandate violated the religious views of their owners and therefore the Free Exercise Clause of the First Amendment to the United States Constitution and the Religious Freedom Restoration Act of 1993 (RFRA).

Writing for a five-justice majority, Justice Samuel A. Alito, Jr., did not reach the plaintiffs' First Amendment claims and instead decided the case solely on the basis of RFRA. The Court began by holding that RFRA extends its protections to for-profit corporations. Next, the Court concluded that the contraceptive mandate substantially burdens the exercise of religion because the mandate required, under threat of significant financial penalties, the plaintiff corporations to participate in conduct at odds with their owners' sincerely held religious beliefs. Justice Alito's opinion for the Court assumed the government had a compelling interest in guaranteeing cost-free access to the specific contraceptive methods challenged in the case, but nonetheless concluded that the government had failed to show that the contraceptive mandate was the least restrictive means of furthering that interest, as required by RFRA.

Justice Ginsburg's dissent, joined in substantial measure by three of her colleagues, follows here. Criticizing the majority's "decision of startling breadth," she initially dismisses the plaintiffs' First Amendment claims as wanting. Continuing, her dissent emphasizes that the Court had never before "recognized a for-profit corporation's qualification for a religious exemption from a generally applicable law, whether under the Free Exercise Clause or RFRA." "The absence of such precedent is just what one would expect," she writes, "for the exercise of religion is characteristic of natural persons, not artificial legal entities."

More generally, in her bench announcement summarizing her dissent in this case, Justice Ginsburg asserts that with respect to free exercise claims no less than free speech claims, "Your right to swing your arms ends just where the other [person's] nose begins." In her view, moreover, Congress did not intend to upend this understanding in RFRA.

Justice Ginsburg also explains in her dissent that requiring plaintiffs to comply with the contraceptive mandate could not be said to impose a "substantial" burden on their religious beliefs for many reasons, including the fact that "the decisions whether to claim benefits under the plans are made not by [the plaintiff corporations], but by the covered employees and dependents. . . . " With respect to those employees and dependents, Justice Ginsburg notes the significant expenses that contraception would impose upon them without the promise of coverage under the ACA. She also emphasizes the "compelling interests in public health and women's well being" advanced by the law's mandate. Finally, Justice Ginsburg rejects the majority's assertion that the government could advance those interests meaningfully by less restrictive alternatives. The result of the majority's holding, she fears, will be to "deny legions of women who do not hold their employers' beliefs access to contraceptive coverage." Concerned by the potential breadth of the majority's holding, she closes by asking, "where is the stopping point[?]"

Justice Ginsburg's statement read from the bench on the day the Court announced its decision, along with her dissenting opinion, follow.

BURWELL V. HOBBY LOBBY STORES, INC., NO. 13-354

CONESTOGA WOOD SPECIALTIES CORP. V. BURWELL, NO. 13-356

BENCH ANNOUNCEMENT

Supreme Court of the United States (June 30, 2014)

Under the Affordable Care Act, employers with health plans must provide women with access to contraceptives at no cost to the insured employee. The Court holds today that commercial enterprises, employing workers of diverse faiths, can opt out of contraceptive coverage if contraceptive use is incompatible with the employers' religious beliefs. When an employer's religious practice detrimentally affects others, however, the First Amendment's Free Exercise Clause does not require accommodation to that practice. Because precedent to that effect is well established, the Court rests its decision not on the Free Exercise Clause of the Constitution, but solely on the Religious Freedom Restoration Act (RFRA).

Justices Breyer, Sotomayor, Kagan, and I find in that Act no design to permit the opt-outs in question. RFRA targeted this Court's decision in a particular case, one holding that Native Americans could be denied unemployment benefits because they had ingested peyote at, and as an essential part of, a religious ceremony. Congress sought to override that decision and to restore by statute the respect for religious exercise as it existed before the sacramental peyote decision was rendered. Nothing more.

Reading the Act expansively, as the Court does, raises a host of "Me, too" questions. Can an employer in business for profit opt out of coverage for blood transfusions, vaccinations, antidepressants, or medications derived from pigs, based on the employer's sincerely held religious beliefs opposing those medical practices? What of the employer whose religious faith teaches that it is sinful to employ a single woman without her father's consent, or a married woman, without her husband's consent? Can those employers opt out of Title VII's ban on gender discrimination in employment? These examples, by the way, are not hypothetical.

A wise legal scholar famously said of the First Amendment's Free Speech guarantee: "Your right to swing your arms ends just where the other [person's] nose begins." The dissenters believe the same is true of the Free Exercise Clause, and that Congress meant RFRA to be interpreted in line with that principle.

The genesis of the contraceptive coverage regulations should have enlightened the Court's decision. "The ability of women to participate equally in the economic and social life of the Nation," the Court appreciated over two decades ago, "has been facilitated by their ability to control their reproductive lives." Congress acted on that understanding when it called for coverage of preventive care responsive to women's needs as part of the Affordable Care Act, a nationwide insurance program intended to be comprehensive.

Carrying out Congress' direction, the Department of Health and Human Services (HHS) promulgated regulations requiring group health plans to cover, without cost-sharing, all contraceptives approved by the Food and Drug Administration (FDA). The scientific studies informing the HHS regulations demonstrate compellingly the benefits to public health and to women's well being attending improved contraceptive access.

Notably, the Court assumes that contraceptive coverage under the Affordable Care Act furthers compelling interests. The Court's reasoning, however, subordinates those interests. Nor is the subordination limited to the four contraceptives Hobby Lobby and Conestoga object to. At oral argument, counsel for Hobby Lobby forthrightly acknowledged that his argument "would apply just as well" if an employer's religion ruled out use of every one of the 20 contraceptives the FDA has approved.

A threshold issue the parties dispute: Does RFRA, which speaks of "a person's" exercise of religion, even apply to for-profit corporations, for they are not flesh-and-blood "person[s]," they are artificial entities created by law. True enough, the First Amendment's free exercise protections, and RFRA's safeguards, shelter not only natural persons, they shield as well churches and other nonprofit religion-based organizations. Yes, the Court's decisions have accorded "special solicitude" to religious institutions. But until today, no similar solicitude has been extended to for-profit commercial entities.

The reason why is not obscure. Religious organizations exist to foster the interests of persons subscribing to the same religious faith. Not so of for-profit corporations. Workers who sustain the operations of for-profit corporations commonly are not drawn from one religious community. Indeed, by law, no religion-based criterion can restrict the workforce of for-profit corporations. The difference between a community of believers in the same religion and a business embracing persons of diverse beliefs is slighted in today's decision.

Justice Sotomayor and I would hold that for-profit corporations should not be equated to nonprofits existing to serve a religious community, and would place them outside RFRA's domain. Justices Breyer and Kagan would not decide the threshold question whether for-profit corporations or their owners can bring RFRA claims, and therefore do not join this part of the dissenting opinion. All four of us, however, agree in unison that RFRA gives Hobby Lobby and Conestoga no right to opt out of contraceptive coverage.

The Court rejects the contraceptive coverage requirement on the ground that it fails to meet RFRA's least restrictive means test. But the Government has shown that there is no less restrictive, equally effective means that would both satisfy the challengers' religious objections and ensure that women employees receive, at no cost to them, the preventive care needed to safeguard their health and well being.

Well, let the government pay for the contraceptives (rather than the employees who do not share their employer's faith), the Court suggests. The Care Act, however, requires coverage of preventive services through the existing employer-based system of health insurance, not through substitution of the government (in effect, the general public) as payor.

And where is the stopping point to the "let the government pay" solution? Suppose it offends an employer's religious belief to pay the minimum wage, or to accord women equal pay for substantially similar work. Such claims, in fact, have been made and accepted as sincere. Does it rank as a less restrictive alternative to require the government to provide the pay to which the employer has a religion-based objection?

Perhaps because these questions are not so easy to answer, the Court rests on a different solution: Extend to commercial enterprises the accommodation already afforded to nonprofit religion-based organizations. This extension solution was barely addressed in the parties' briefs. Asked about it at oral argument, Hobby Lobby's counsel responded: "We haven't been offered that accommodation, so we haven't had to decide what kind of objection, if any, we would make to that."

Ultimately, the Court hedges. It declines to decide whether the extension solution "complies with RFRA for purposes of all religious claims." The fatal flaw, in any event, bears reiteration. The extension cure would equate two dissimilar categories: on the one hand, commercial businesses like Hobby Lobby and Conestoga, whose workforces, by law, are open to persons of all faiths, and on the other, nonprofit organizations designed to further the mission of a particular community of believers.

A pathmarking 1982 decision RFRA preserved is highly instructive in this regard: *United States* v. *Lee. Lee* rejected the exemption claim of an Amish entrepreneur whose religious tenets were offended by the payment of Social Security taxes. Tax cases are in a discrete category, today's Court responds. But *Lee* made two key points that cannot be confined to tax cases. First, "[w]hen followers of a particular sect enter into commercial activity as a matter of choice," the *Lee* Court observed, "the limits they accept on their own conduct as a matter of conscience and faith are not to be superimposed on statutory schemes ... binding on others in that activity." Second, the *Lee* Court said, allowing a religion-based exemption to a commercial employer would "operat[e] to impose the employer's religious faith on the employees." Working for Hobby Lobby or Conestoga, in other words, should not deprive employees holding different beliefs of the employer-insured preventive care available to workers at the shop next door.

Hobby Lobby and Conestoga, as shown by the real cases I described, hardly stand alone as commercial enterprises seeking religion-based exemptions from generally applicable laws, among them, laws prohibiting discrimination in the workplace. How is the Court to divine when a religious belief is feigned "to escape legal sanction," or which genuine beliefs are worthy of accommodation and which are not? Those questions are all the more perplexing given the majority opinion's repeated insistence that "courts may not presume to determine ... the plausibility of a religious claim."

In sum, today's potentially sweeping decision minimizes the government's compelling interest in uniform compliance with laws governing workplaces, in particular, the Affordable Care Act. And it discounts the disadvantages religion-based opt-outs impose on others, in particular, employees who do not share their employer's religious beliefs.

Our cosmopolitan nation is made up of people of almost every conceivable religious preference. In passing RFRA, Congress did not alter a tradition in which one person's right to free exercise of her religion must be kept in harmony with the rights of her fellow citizens, and with the common good.

For the reasons I summarized, all of them and others developed in the dissenting opinion, I would reverse the judgment of the Tenth Circuit and affirm the judgment of the Third Circuit.

BURWELL V. HOBBY LOBBY STORES, INC., 573 U.S. 682

DISSENTING OPINION

Supreme Court of the United States

Sylvia BURWELL, Secretary of Health and Human Services, et al., Petitioners

v.

HOBBY LOBBY STORES, INC., et al.

Conestoga Wood Specialties Corporation et al., Petitioners

v.

Sylvia Burwell, Secretary of Health and Human Services, et al.

Nos. 13-354, 13-356.

Argued March 25, 2014.

Decided June 30, 2014.

[The majority opinion of Justice ALITO, the concurring opinion of Justice KENNEDY, and the dissenting opinion of Justices BREYER and KAGAN are omitted.]

Justice GINSBURG, with whom Justice SOTOMAYOR joins, and with whom Justice BREYER and Justice KAGAN join as to all but Part III-C-1, dissenting.

In a decision of startling breadth, the Court holds that commercial enterprises, including corporations, along with partnerships and sole proprietorships, can opt out of any law (saving only tax laws) they judge incompatible with their sincerely held religious beliefs. See *ante*, 573 U.S., at 705–736. Compelling governmental interests in uniform compliance with the law, and disadvantages that religion-based opt-outs impose on others, hold no sway, the Court decides, at least when there is a "less restrictive alternative." And such an alternative, the Court suggests, there always will be whenever, in lieu of tolling an enterprise claiming a religion-based exemption, the government, *i.e.*, the general public, can pick up the tab. See *ante*, 573 U.S., at 728–731.[1]

The Court does not pretend that the First Amendment's Free Exercise Clause demands religion-based accommodations so extreme, for our decisions leave no doubt on that score. See *infra*, 573 U.S., at 744–746. Instead, the Court holds that Congress, in the Religious Freedom Restoration Act of 1993 (RFRA), 42 U.S.C. § 2000bb *et seq.*, dictated the extraordinary religion-based exemptions today's decision endorses. In the Court's view, RFRA demands accommodation of a for-profit corporation's religious beliefs no matter the impact that accommodation may have on third parties who do not share the corporation owners' religious faith—in these cases, thousands of women employed by Hobby Lobby and Conestoga or dependents of persons those corporations employ. Persuaded that Congress enacted RFRA to serve a far less radical purpose, and mindful of the havoc the Court's judgment can introduce, I dissent.

---

1. The Court insists it has held none of these things, for another less restrictive alternative is at hand: extending an existing accommodation, currently limited to religious nonprofit organizations, to encompass commercial enterprises. See *ante*, 573 U.S., at 692–693. With that accommodation extended, the Court asserts, "women would still be entitled to all [Food and Drug Administration]-approved contraceptives without cost sharing." *Ante*, 573 U.S., at 693. In the end, however, the Court is not so sure. In stark contrast to the Court's initial emphasis on this accommodation, it ultimately declines to decide whether the highlighted accommodation is even lawful. See *ante*, 573 U.S., at 731 ("We do not decide today whether an approach of this type complies with RFRA. . . .").

I

"The ability of women to participate equally in the economic and social life of the Nation has been facilitated by their ability to control their reproductive lives." *Planned Parenthood of Southeastern Pa.* v. *Casey*, 505 U.S. 833, 856 (1992). Congress acted on that understanding when, as part of a nationwide insurance program intended to be comprehensive, it called for coverage of preventive care responsive to women's needs. Carrying out Congress' direction, the Department of Health and Human Services (HHS), in consultation with public health experts, promulgated regulations requiring group health plans to cover all forms of contraception approved by the Food and Drug Administration (FDA). The genesis of this coverage should enlighten the Court's resolution of these cases.

A

The Affordable Care Act (ACA), in its initial form, specified three categories of preventive care that health plans must cover at no added cost to the plan participant or beneficiary.[2] Particular services were to be recommended by the U.S. Preventive Services Task Force, an independent panel of experts. The scheme had a large gap, however; it left out preventive services that "many women's health advocates and medical professionals believe are critically important." 155 Cong. Rec. 28841 (2009) (statement of Sen. Boxer). To correct this oversight, Senator Barbara Mikulski introduced the Women's Health Amendment, which added to the ACA's minimum coverage requirements a new category of preventive services specific to women's health.

Women paid significantly more than men for preventive care, the amendment's proponents noted; in fact, cost barriers operated to block many women from obtaining needed care at all. See, *e.g., id.*, at 29070 (statement of Sen. Feinstein) ("Women of childbearing age spend

---

2. See 42 U.S.C. § 300gg-13(a)(1)–(3) (group health plans must provide coverage, without cost sharing, for (1) certain "evidence-based items or services" recommended by the U.S. Preventive Services Task Force; (2) immunizations recommended by an advisory committee of the Centers for Disease Control and Prevention; and (3) "with respect to infants, children, and adolescents, evidence-informed preventive care and screenings provided for in the comprehensive guidelines supported by the Health Resources and Services Administration").

68 percent more in out-of-pocket health care costs than men.”); *id.*, at 29302 (statement of Sen. Mikulski) (“copayments are [often] so high that [women] avoid getting [preventive and screening services] in the first place”). And increased access to contraceptive services, the sponsors comprehended, would yield important public health gains. See, *e.g.*, *id.*, at 29768 (statement of Sen. Durbin) (“This bill will expand health insurance coverage to the vast majority of [the 17 million women of reproductive age in the United States who are uninsured]. . . . This expanded access will reduce unintended pregnancies.”).

As altered by the Women’s Health Amendment’s passage, the ACA requires new insurance plans to include coverage without cost sharing of “such additional preventive care and screenings . . . as provided for in comprehensive guidelines supported by the Health Resources and Services Administration [(HRSA)],” a unit of HHS. 42 U.S.C. § 300gg-13(a)(4). Thus charged, the HRSA developed recommendations in consultation with the Institute of Medicine (IOM). See 77 Fed.Reg. 8725–8726 (2012).[3] The IOM convened a group of independent experts, including “specialists in disease prevention [and] women’s health”; those experts prepared a report evaluating the efficacy of a number of preventive services. IOM, Clinical Preventive Services for Women: Closing the Gaps 2 (2011) (hereinafter IOM Report). Consistent with the findings of “[n]umerous health professional associations” and other organizations, the IOM experts determined that preventive coverage should include the “full range” of FDA-approved contraceptive methods. *Id.*, at 10. See also *id.*, at 102–110.

In making that recommendation, the IOM’s report expressed concerns similar to those voiced by congressional proponents of the Women’s Health Amendment. The report noted the disproportionate burden women carried for comprehensive health services and the adverse health consequences of excluding contraception from preventive care available to employees without cost sharing. See, *e.g.*, *id.*, at 19 (“[W]omen are consistently more likely than men to report a wide range of cost-related barriers to receiving . . . medical tests and treatments and to filling prescriptions

---

3. The IOM is an arm of the National Academy of Sciences, an organization Congress established “for the explicit purpose of furnishing advice to the Government.” *Public Citizen* v. *Department of Justice*, 491 U.S. 440, 460, n. 11 (1989) (internal quotation marks omitted).

for themselves and their families."); *id.*, at 103–104, 107 (pregnancy may be contraindicated for women with certain medical conditions, for example, some congenital heart diseases, pulmonary hypertension, and Marfan syndrome, and contraceptives may be used to reduce risk of endometrial cancer, among other serious medical conditions); *id.*, at 103 (women with unintended pregnancies are more likely to experience depression and anxiety, and their children face "increased odds of preterm birth and low birth weight").

In line with the IOM's suggestions, the HRSA adopted guidelines recommending coverage of "[a]ll [FDA-] approved contraceptive methods, sterilization procedures, and patient education and counseling for all women with reproductive capacity."[4] Thereafter, HHS, the Department of Labor, and the Department of Treasury promulgated regulations requiring group health plans to include coverage of the contraceptive services recommended in the HRSA guidelines, subject to certain exceptions, described *infra*, 573 U.S., at 763–764.[5] This opinion refers to these regulations as the contraceptive coverage requirement.

B

While the Women's Health Amendment succeeded, a countermove proved unavailing. The Senate voted down the so-called "conscience amendment," which would have enabled any employer or insurance provider to deny coverage based on its asserted "religious beliefs or moral convictions." 158 Cong. Rec. S539 (Feb. 9, 2012); see *id.*, at S1162–S1173 (Mar. 1, 2012) (debate and vote).[6] That amendment, Senator Mikulski observed, would have "pu[t] the personal opinion of employers and insurers over the practice of medicine." *Id.*, at S1127 (Feb. 29, 2012). Rejecting the "conscience amendment," Congress left health care

---

4. HRSA, HHS, Women's Preventive Services Guidelines, available at http://www.hrsa.gov/womensguidelines/ (all Internet materials as visited June 27, 2014, and available in Clerk of Court's case file), reprinted in App. to Brief for Petitioners in No. 13–354, pp. 43–44a. See also 77 Fed.Reg. 8725–8726 (2012).

5. 45 CFR § 147.130(a)(1)(iv) (2013) (HHS); 29 CFR § 2590.715–2713(a)(1)(iv) (2013) (Labor); 26 CFR § 54.9815–2713(a)(1)(iv) (2013) (Treasury).

6. Separating moral convictions from religious beliefs would be of questionable legitimacy. See *Welsh* v. *United States*, 398 U.S. 333, 357–358 (1970) (Harlan, J., concurring in result).

decisions—including the choice among contraceptive methods—in the hands of women, with the aid of their health care providers.

II

Any First Amendment Free Exercise Clause claim Hobby Lobby or Conestoga[7] might assert is foreclosed by this Court's decision in *Employment Div., Dept. of Human Resources of Ore. v. Smith*, 494 U.S. 872 (1990). In *Smith*, two members of the Native American Church were dismissed from their jobs and denied unemployment benefits because they ingested peyote at, and as an essential element of, a religious ceremony. Oregon law forbade the consumption of peyote, and this Court, relying on that prohibition, rejected the employees' claim that the denial of unemployment benefits violated their free exercise rights. The First Amendment is not offended, *Smith* held, when "prohibiting the exercise of religion . . . is not the object of [governmental regulation] but merely the incidental effect of a generally applicable and otherwise valid provision." *Id.*, at 878; see *id.*, at 878–879 ("an individual's religious beliefs [do not] excuse him from compliance with an otherwise valid law prohibiting conduct that the State is free to regulate"). The ACA's contraceptive coverage requirement applies generally, it is "otherwise valid," it trains on women's well being, not on the exercise of religion, and any effect it has on such exercise is incidental.

Even if *Smith* did not control, the Free Exercise Clause would not require the exemption Hobby Lobby and Conestoga seek. Accommodations to religious beliefs or observances, the Court has clarified, must not significantly impinge on the interests of third parties.[8]

---

7. As the Court explains, see *ante*, 573 U.S., at 700–705, these cases arise from two separate lawsuits, one filed by Hobby Lobby, its affiliated business (Mardel), and the family that operates these businesses (the Greens); the other filed by Conestoga and the family that owns and controls that business (the Hahns). Unless otherwise specified, this opinion refers to the respective groups of plaintiffs as Hobby Lobby and Conestoga.

8. See *Wisconsin v. Yoder*, 406 U.S. 205, 230 (1972) ("This case, of course, is not one in which any harm to the physical or mental health of the child or to the public safety, peace, order, or welfare has been demonstrated or may be properly inferred."); *Estate of Thornton v. Caldor, Inc.*, 472 U.S. 703 (1985) (invalidating state statute requiring employers to accom-

The exemption sought by Hobby Lobby and Conestoga would override significant interests of the corporations' employees and covered dependents. It would deny legions of women who do not hold their employers' beliefs access to contraceptive coverage that the ACA would otherwise secure. See *Catholic Charities of Sacramento, Inc.* v. *Superior Court*, 32 Cal.4th 527, 565 (2004) ("We are unaware of any decision in which ... [the U.S. Supreme Court] has exempted a religious objector from the operation of a neutral, generally applicable law despite the recognition that the requested exemption would detrimentally affect the rights of third parties."). In sum, with respect to free exercise claims no less than free speech claims, "'[y]our right to swing your arms ends just where the other man's nose begins.'" Chafee, Freedom of Speech in War Time, 32 Harv. L.Rev. 932, 957 (1919).

III

A

Lacking a tenable claim under the Free Exercise Clause, Hobby Lobby and Conestoga rely on RFRA, a statute instructing that "[g]overnment shall not substantially burden a person's exercise of religion even if the burden results from a rule of general applicability" unless the government shows that application of the burden is "the least restrictive means" to further a "compelling governmental interest." 42 U.S.C. § 2000bb–1(a), (b) (2). In RFRA, Congress "adopt[ed] a statutory rule comparable to the constitutional rule rejected in *Smith*." *Gonzales* v. *Ó Centro Espírita Beneficente União do Vegetal*, 546 U.S. 418, 424 (2006).

RFRA's purpose is specific and written into the statute itself. The Act was crafted to "restore the compelling interest test as set forth in *Sherbert*

---

modate an employee's Sabbath observance where that statute failed to take into account the burden such an accommodation would impose on the employer or other employees). Notably, in construing the Religious Land Use and Institutionalized Persons Act of 2000 (RLUIPA), 42 U.S.C. § 2000cc *et seq.*, the Court has cautioned that "adequate account" must be taken of "the burdens a requested accommodation may impose on nonbeneficiaries." *Cutter* v. *Wilkinson*, 544 U.S. 709, 720 (2005); see *id.*, at 722 ("an accommodation must be measured so that it does not override other significant interests"). A balanced approach is all the more in order when the Free Exercise Clause itself is at stake, not a statute designed to promote accommodation to religious beliefs and practices.

v. *Verner*, 374 U.S. 398 (1963), and *Wisconsin* v. *Yoder*, 406 U.S. 205 (1972), and to guarantee its application in all cases where free exercise of religion is substantially burdened." § 2000bb(b)(1).[9] See also § 2000bb(a)(5) ("[T]he compelling interest test as set forth in prior Federal court rulings is a workable test for striking sensible balances between religious liberty and competing prior governmental interests."); *ante*, 573 U.S., at 736 (agreeing that the pre-*Smith* compelling interest test is "workable" and "strike[s] sensible balances").

The legislative history is correspondingly emphatic on RFRA's aim. See, *e.g.*, S.Rep. No. 103–111, p. 12 (1993) (hereinafter Senate Report) (RFRA's purpose was "only to overturn the Supreme Court's decision in *Smith*," not to "unsettle other areas of the law."); 139 Cong. Rec. 26178 (1993) (statement of Sen. Kennedy) (RFRA was "designed to restore the compelling interest test for deciding free exercise claims."). In line with this restorative purpose, Congress expected courts considering RFRA claims to "look to free exercise cases decided prior to *Smith* for guidance." Senate Report 8. See also H.R.Rep. No. 103–88, pp. 6–7 (1993) (hereinafter House Report) (same). In short, the Act reinstates the law as it was prior to *Smith*, without "creat[ing] . . . new rights for any religious practice or for any potential litigant." 139 Cong. Rec. 26178 (statement of Sen. Kennedy). Given the Act's moderate purpose, it is hardly surprising that RFRA's enactment in 1993 provoked little controversy. See Brief for Senator Murray et al. as *Amici Curiae* 8 (hereinafter Senators Brief) (RFRA was approved by a 97-to-3 vote in the Senate and a voice vote in the House of Representatives).

B

Despite these authoritative indications, the Court sees RFRA as a bold initiative departing from, rather than restoring, pre-*Smith* jurisprudence. See *ante*, 573 U.S., at 695, n. 3, 696, 706, 714–716. To support its conception of RFRA as a measure detached from this Court's decisions, one that

---

9. Under *Sherbert* and *Yoder*, the Court "requir[ed] the government to justify any substantial burden on religiously motivated conduct by a compelling state interest and by means narrowly tailored to achieve that interest." *Employment Div., Dept. of Human Resources of Ore.* v. *Smith*, 494 U.S. 872, 894 (1990) (O'Connor, J., concurring in judgment).

sets a new course, the Court points first to the Religious Land Use and Institutionalized Persons Act of 2000 (RLUIPA), 42 U.S.C. § 2000cc *et seq.*, which altered RFRA's definition of the term "exercise of religion." RFRA, as originally enacted, defined that term to mean "the exercise of religion under the First Amendment to the Constitution." § 2000bb–2(4) (1994 ed.). See *ante*, 573 U.S., at 695–696. As amended by RLUIPA, RFRA's definition now includes "any exercise of religion, whether or not compelled by, or central to, a system of religious belief." § 2000bb–2(4) (2012 ed.) (cross-referencing § 2000cc–5). That definitional change, according to the Court, reflects "an obvious effort to effect a complete separation from First Amendment case law." *Ante*, 573 U.S., at 696.

The Court's reading is not plausible. RLUIPA's alteration clarifies that courts should not question the centrality of a particular religious exercise. But the amendment in no way suggests that Congress meant to expand the class of entities qualified to mount religious accommodation claims, nor does it relieve courts of the obligation to inquire whether a government action substantially burdens a religious exercise. See *Rasul* v. *Myers*, 563 F.3d 527, 535 (C.A.D.C. 2009) (Brown, J., concurring) ("There is no doubt that RLUIPA's drafters, in changing the definition of 'exercise of religion,' wanted to broaden the scope of the kinds of practices protected by RFRA, not increase the universe of individuals protected by RFRA."); H.R.Rep. No. 106–219, p. 30 (1999). See also *Gilardi* v. *United States Dept. of Health and Human Servs.*, 733 F.3d 1208, 1211 (C.A.D.C. 2013) (RFRA, as amended, "provides us with no helpful definition of 'exercise of religion.'"); *Henderson* v. *Kennedy*, 265 F.3d 1072, 1073 (C.A.D.C. 2001) ("The [RLUIPA] amendments did not alter RFRA's basic prohibition that the '[g]overnment shall not substantially burden a person's exercise of religion.'").[10]

Next, the Court highlights RFRA's requirement that the government, if its action substantially burdens a person's religious observance, must

10. RLUIPA, the Court notes, includes a provision directing that "[t]his chapter [*i.e.*, RLUIPA] shall be construed in favor of a broad protection of religious exercise, to the maximum extent permitted by the terms of [the Act] and the Constitution." 42 U.S.C. § 2000cc–3(g); see *ante*, 573 U.S., at 695–696, 714. RFRA incorporates RLUIPA's definition of "exercise of religion," as RLUIPA does, but contains no omnibus rule of construction governing the statute in its entirety.

demonstrate that it chose the least restrictive means for furthering a compelling interest. "[B]y imposing a least-restrictive-means test," the Court suggests, RFRA "went beyond what was required by our pre-*Smith* decisions." *Ante*, 573 U.S., at 706, n. 18 (citing *City of Boerne* v. *Flores*, 521 U.S. 507 (1997)). See also *ante*, 573 U.S., at 695, n. 3. But as RFRA's statements of purpose and legislative history make clear, Congress intended only to restore, not to scrap or alter, the balancing test as this Court had applied it pre-*Smith*. See *supra*, 573 U.S., at 746–747. See also Senate Report 9 (RFRA's "compelling interest test generally should not be construed more stringently or more leniently than it was prior to *Smith*."); House Report 7 (same).

The Congress that passed RFRA correctly read this Court's pre-*Smith* case law as including within the "compelling interest test" a "least restrictive means" requirement. See, *e.g.*, Senate Report 5 ("Where [a substantial] burden is placed upon the free exercise of religion, the Court ruled [in *Sherbert*], the Government must demonstrate that it is the least restrictive means to achieve a compelling governmental interest."). And the view that the pre-*Smith* test included a "least restrictive means" requirement had been aired in testimony before the Senate Judiciary Committee by experts on religious freedom. See, *e.g.*, Hearing on S. 2969 before the Senate Committee on the Judiciary, 102d Cong., 2d Sess., 78–79 (1993) (statement of Prof. Douglas Laycock).

Our decision in *City of Boerne*, it is true, states that the least restrictive means requirement "was not used in the pre-*Smith* jurisprudence RFRA purported to codify." See *ante*, 573 U.S., at 695, n. 3, 706, n. 18. As just indicated, however, that statement does not accurately convey the Court's pre-*Smith* jurisprudence. See *Sherbert*, 374 U.S., at 407 ("[I]t would plainly be incumbent upon the [government] to demonstrate that no alternative forms of regulation would combat [the problem] without infringing First Amendment rights."); *Thomas* v. *Review Bd. of Indiana Employment Security Div.*, 450 U.S. 707, 718 (1981) ("The state may justify an inroad on religious liberty by showing that it is the least restrictive means of achieving some compelling state interest."). See also Berg, The New Attacks on Religious Freedom Legislation and Why They Are Wrong, 21 Cardozo L.Rev. 415, 424 (1999) ("In *Boerne*, the Court erroneously said that the least restrictive means test 'was not used in the pre-*Smith* jurisprudence.'").[11]

C

With RFRA's restorative purpose in mind, I turn to the Act's application to the instant lawsuits. That task, in view of the positions taken by the Court, requires consideration of several questions, each potentially dispositive of Hobby Lobby's and Conestoga's claims: Do for-profit corporations rank among "person[s]" who "exercise . . . religion"? Assuming that they do, does the contraceptive coverage requirement "substantially burden" their religious exercise? If so, is the requirement "in furtherance of a compelling government interest"? And last, does the requirement represent the least restrictive means for furthering that interest?

Misguided by its errant premise that RFRA moved beyond the pre-*Smith* case law, the Court falters at each step of its analysis.

1

RFRA's compelling interest test, as noted, see *supra*, 573 U.S., at 746, applies to government actions that "substantially burden *a person's exercise of religion.*" 42 U.S.C. § 2000bb 1(a) (emphasis added). This reference, the Court submits, incorporates the definition of "person" found in the Dictionary Act, 1 U.S.C. § 1, which extends to "corporations, companies, associations, firms, partnerships, societies, and joint stock companies, as well as individuals." See *ante*, 573 U.S., at 707–709. The Dictionary Act's definition, however, controls only where "context" does not "indicat[e] otherwise." § 1. Here, context does so indicate. RFRA speaks of "a person's *exercise of religion.*" 42 U.S.C. § 2000bb–1(a) (emphasis added). See also §§ 2000bb–2(4), 2000cc–5(7)(A).[12] Whether a corporation qualifies as a

---

11. The Court points out that I joined the majority opinion in *City of Boerne* and did not then question the statement that "least restrictive means . . . was not used [pre-*Smith*]." *Ante*, 573 U.S., at 706, n. 18. Concerning that observation, I remind my colleagues of Justice Jackson's sage comment: "I see no reason why I should be consciously wrong today because I was unconsciously wrong yesterday." *Massachusetts* v. *United States*, 333 U.S. 611, 639–640 (1948) (dissenting opinion).

12. As earlier explained, see *supra*, 573 U.S., at 748, RLUIPA's amendment of the definition of "exercise of religion" does not bear the weight the Court places on it. Moreover, it is passing

"person" capable of exercising religion is an inquiry one cannot answer without reference to the "full body" of pre-*Smith* "free-exercise caselaw." *Gilardi*, 733 F.3d, at 1212. There is in that case law no support for the notion that free exercise rights pertain to for-profit corporations.

Until this litigation, no decision of this Court recognized a for-profit corporation's qualification for a religious exemption from a generally applicable law, whether under the Free Exercise Clause or RFRA.[13] The absence of such precedent is just what one would expect, for the exercise of religion is characteristic of natural persons, not artificial legal entities. As Chief Justice Marshall observed nearly two centuries ago, a corporation is "an artificial being, invisible, intangible, and existing only in contemplation of law." *Trustees of Dartmouth College* v. *Woodward*, 17 U.S. (4 Wheat.) 518, 636 (1819). Corporations, Justice Stevens more recently reminded, "have no consciences, no beliefs, no feelings, no thoughts, no desires." *Citizens United* v. *Federal Election Comm'n*, 558 U.S. 310, 466 (2010) (opinion concurring in part and dissenting in part).

The First Amendment's free exercise protections, the Court has indeed recognized, shelter churches and other nonprofit religion-based organizations.[14] "For many individuals, religious activity derives meaning in large measure from participation in a larger religious community," and "further-

---

strange to attribute to RLUIPA any purpose to cover entities other than "religious assembl[ies] or institution[s]." 42 U.S.C. § 2000cc(a)(1). But cf. *ante*, 573 U.S., at 714. That law applies to land-use regulation. § 2000cc(a)(1). To permit commercial enterprises to challenge zoning and other land-use regulations under RLUIPA would "dramatically expand the statute's reach" and deeply intrude on local prerogatives, contrary to Congress' intent. Brief for National League of Cities et al. as *Amici Curiae* 26.

13. The Court regards *Gallagher* v. *Crown Kosher Super Market of Mass., Inc.*, 366 U.S. 617 (1961), as "suggest[ing] . . . that for-profit corporations possess [free-exercise] rights." *Ante*, 573 U.S., at 714. See also *ante*, 573 U.S., at 709, n. 21. The suggestion is barely there. True, one of the five challengers to the Sunday closing law assailed in *Gallagher* was a corporation owned by four Orthodox Jews. The other challengers were human individuals, not artificial, law-created entities, so there was no need to determine whether the corporation could institute the litigation. Accordingly, the plurality stated it could pretermit the question "whether appellees ha[d] standing" because *Braunfeld* v. *Brown*, 366 U.S. 599 (1961), which upheld a similar closing law, was fatal to their claim on the merits. 366 U.S., at 631.

14. See, *e.g.*, *Hosanna-Tabor Evangelical Lutheran Church and School* v. *EEOC*, 565 U.S. 171 (2012); *Gonzales* v. *O Centro Espírita Beneficente União do Vegetal*, 546 U.S. 418 (2006); *Church of Lukumi Babalu Aye, Inc.* v. *Hialeah*, 508 U.S. 520 (1993); *Jimmy Swaggart Ministries* v. *Board of Equalization of Cal.*, 493 U.S. 378 (1990).

ance of the autonomy of religious organizations often furthers individual religious freedom as well." *Corporation of Presiding Bishop of Church of Jesus Christ of Latter-day Saints* v. *Amos*, 483 U.S. 327, 342 (1987) (Brennan, J., concurring in judgment). The Court's "special solicitude to the rights of religious organizations," *Hosanna-Tabor Evangelical Lutheran Church and School* v. *EEOC*, 565 U.S. 171, 189 (2012), however, is just that. No such solicitude is traditional for commercial organizations.[15] Indeed, until today, religious exemptions had never been extended

---

15. Typically, Congress has accorded to organizations religious in character religion-based exemptions from statutes of general application. *E.g.*, 42 U.S.C. § 2000e–1(a) (Title VII exemption from prohibition against employment discrimination based on religion for "a religious corporation, association, educational institution, or society with respect to the employment of individuals of a particular religion to perform work connected with the carrying on . . . of its activities"); 42 U.S.C. § 12113(d)(1) (parallel exemption in Americans With Disabilities Act of 1990). It can scarcely be maintained that RFRA enlarges these exemptions to allow Hobby Lobby and Conestoga to hire only persons who share the religious beliefs of the Greens or Hahns. Nor does the Court suggest otherwise. Cf. *ante*, 573 U.S., at 716–717.

The Court does identify two statutory exemptions it reads to cover for-profit corporations, 42 U.S.C. §§ 300a–7(b)(2) and 238n(a), and infers from them that "Congress speaks with specificity when it intends a religious accommodation not to extend to for-profit corporations," *ante*, 573 U.S., at 717. The Court's inference is unwarranted. The exemptions the Court cites cover certain medical personnel who object to performing or assisting with abortions. Cf. *ante*, 573 U.S., at 716, n. 27 ("the protection provided by § 238n(a) differs significantly from the protection provided by RFRA"). Notably, the Court does not assert that these exemptions have in fact been afforded to for-profit corporations. See § 238n(c) ("health care entity" covered by exemption is a term defined to include "an individual physician, a postgraduate physician training program, and a participant in a program of training in the health professions"); Tozzi, Whither Free Exercise: *Employment Division* v. *Smith* and the Rebirth of State Constitutional Free Exercise Clause Jurisprudence?, 48 J. Catholic Legal Studies 269, 296, n. 133 (2009) ("Catholic physicians, but not necessarily hospitals, . . . may be able to invoke [§ 238n(a)]. . . ."); cf. S. 137, 113th Cong., 1st Sess. 2–3 (2013) (as introduced) (Abortion Non-Discrimination Act of 2013, which would amend the definition of "health care entity" in § 238n to include "hospital[s]," "health insurance plan[s]," and other health care facilities). These provisions are revealing in a way that detracts from one of the Court's main arguments. They show that Congress is not content to rest on the Dictionary Act when it wishes to ensure that particular entities are among those eligible for a religious accommodation.

Moreover, the exemption codified in § 238n(a) was not enacted until three years after RFRA's passage. See Omnibus Consolidated Rescissions and Appropriations Act of 1996, § 515, 110 Stat. 1321–245. If, as the Court believes, RFRA opened all statutory schemes to religion-based challenges by for-profit corporations, there would be no need for a statute-specific, post-RFRA exemption of this sort.

to any entity operating in "the commercial, profit-making world." *Amos*, 483 U.S., at 337.[16]

The reason why is hardly obscure. Religious organizations exist to foster the interests of persons subscribing to the same religious faith. Not so of for-profit corporations. Workers who sustain the operations of those corporations commonly are not drawn from one religious community. Indeed, by law, no religion-based criterion can restrict the work force of for-profit corporations. See 42 U.S.C. §§ 2000e(b), 2000e–1(a), 2000e–2(a); cf. *Trans World Airlines, Inc.* v. *Hardison*, 432 U.S. 63, 80–81 (1977) (Title VII requires reasonable accommodation of an employee's religious exercise, but such accommodation must not come "at the expense of other[employees]"). The distinction between a community made up of believers in the same religion and one embracing persons of diverse beliefs, clear as it is, constantly escapes the Court's attention.[17] One can only wonder why the Court shuts this key difference from sight.

Reading RFRA, as the Court does, to require extension of religion-based exemptions to for-profit corporations surely is not grounded in the pre-*Smith* precedent Congress sought to preserve. Had Congress intended RFRA to initiate a change so huge, a clarion statement to that effect likely would have been made in the legislation. See *Whitman* v. *American Trucking Assns., Inc.*, 531 U.S. 457, 468 (2001) (Congress does not "hide elephants in mouseholes"). The text of RFRA makes no such statement and the legislative history does not so much as mention for-profit corporations. See *Hobby Lobby Stores, Inc.* v. *Sebelius*, 723 F.3d 1114, 1169 (C.A.10

---

16. That is not to say that a category of plaintiffs, such as resident aliens, may bring RFRA claims only if this Court expressly "addressed their [free-exercise] rights before *Smith.*" *Ante*, 573 U.S., at 716. Continuing with the Court's example, resident aliens, unlike corporations, are flesh-and-blood individuals who plainly count as persons sheltered by the First Amendment, see *United States* v. *Verdugo-Urquidez*, 494 U.S. 259, 271 (1990) (citing *Bridges* v. *Wixon*, 326 U.S. 135, 148 (1945)), and *a fortiori*, RFRA.

17. I part ways with Justice KENNEDY on the context relevant here. He sees it as the employers' "exercise [of] their religious beliefs within the context of their own closely held, for-profit corporations." *Ante*, 573 U.S., at 737 (concurring opinion). See also *ante*, 573 U.S., at 733 (opinion of the Court) (similarly concentrating on religious faith of employers without reference to the different beliefs and liberty interests of employees). I see as the relevant context the employers' asserted right to exercise religion within a nationwide program designed to protect against health hazards employees who do not subscribe to their employers' religious beliefs.

2013) (Briscoe, C.J., concurring in part and dissenting in part) (legislative record lacks "any suggestion that Congress foresaw, let alone intended that, RFRA would cover for-profit corporations"). See also Senators Brief 10–13 (none of the cases cited in House or Senate Judiciary Committee reports accompanying RFRA, or mentioned during floor speeches, recognized the free exercise rights of for-profit corporations).

The Court notes that for-profit corporations may support charitable causes and use their funds for religious ends, and therefore questions the distinction between such corporations and religious nonprofit organizations. See *ante*, 573 U.S., at 709–713. See also *ante*, 573 U.S., at 738 (Kennedy, J., concurring) (criticizing the Government for "distinguishing between different religious believers—burdening one while accommodating the other—when it may treat both equally by offering both of them the same accommodation").[18] Again, the Court forgets that religious organizations exist to serve a community of believers. For-profit corporations do not fit that bill. Moreover, history is not on the Court's side. Recognition of the discrete characters of "ecclesiastical and lay" corporations dates back to Blackstone, see 1 W. Blackstone, Commentaries on the Laws of England 458 (1765), and was reiterated by this Court centuries before the enactment of the Internal Revenue Code. See *Terrett* v. *Taylor*, 13 U.S. (9 Cranch) 43, 49 (1815) (describing religious corporations); *Trustees of Dartmouth College*, 17 U.S. (4 Wheat.), at 645 (discussing "eleemosynary" corporations, including those "created for the promotion of religion"). To reiterate, "for-profit corporations are different from religious non-profits in that they use labor to make a profit, rather than to perpetuate [the] religious value[s] [shared by a community of believers]." *Gilardi*, 733 F.3d, at 1242 (Edwards, J., concurring in part and dissenting in part) (emphasis deleted).

---

18. According to the Court, the Government "concedes" that "nonprofit corporation[s]" are protected by RFRA. *Ante*, 573 U.S., at 708. See also *ante*, 573 U.S., at 709, 712, 718. That is not an accurate description of the Government's position, which encompasses only "churches," "*religious* institutions," and "*religious* non-profits." Brief for Respondents in No. 13–356, p. 28 (emphasis added). See also Reply Brief in No. 13–354, p. 8 ("RFRA incorporates the longstanding and common-sense distinction between religious organizations, which sometimes have been accorded accommodations under generally applicable laws in recognition of their accepted religious character, and for-profit corporations organized to do business in the commercial world.").

Citing *Braunfeld* v. *Brown*, 366 U.S. 599 (1961), the Court questions why, if "a sole proprietorship that seeks to make a profit may assert a free-exercise claim, [Hobby Lobby and Conestoga] can't ... do the same?" *Ante*, 573 U.S., at 710 (footnote omitted). See also *ante*, 573 U.S., at 705–706. But even accepting, *arguendo*, the premise that unincorporated business enterprises may gain religious accommodations under the Free Exercise Clause, the Court's conclusion is unsound. In a sole proprietorship, the business and its owner are one and the same. By incorporating a business, however, an individual separates herself from the entity and escapes personal responsibility for the entity's obligations. One might ask why the separation should hold only when it serves the interest of those who control the corporation. In any event, *Braunfeld* is hardly impressive authority for the entitlement Hobby Lobby and Conestoga seek. The free exercise claim asserted there was promptly rejected on the merits.

The Court's determination that RFRA extends to for-profit corporations is bound to have untoward effects. Although the Court attempts to cabin its language to closely held corporations, its logic extends to corporations of any size, public or private.[19] Little doubt that RFRA claims will

---

19. The Court does not even begin to explain how one might go about ascertaining the religious scruples of a corporation where shares are sold to the public. No need to speculate on that, the Court says, for "it seems unlikely" that large corporations "will often assert RFRA claims." *Ante*, 573 U.S., at 717. Perhaps so, but as Hobby Lobby's case demonstrates, such claims are indeed pursued by large corporations, employing thousands of persons of different faiths, whose ownership is not diffuse. "Closely held" is not synonymous with "small." Hobby Lobby is hardly the only enterprise of sizable scale that is family owned or closely held. For example, the family-owned candy giant Mars, Inc., takes in $33 billion in revenues and has some 72,000 employees, and closely held Cargill, Inc., takes in more than $136 billion in revenues and employs some 140,000 persons. See Forbes, America's Largest Private Companies 2013, available at http://www.forbes.com/largest-private-companies/.

Nor does the Court offer any instruction on how to resolve the disputes that may crop up among corporate owners over religious values and accommodations. The Court is satisfied that "[s]tate corporate law provides a ready means for resolving any conflicts," *ante*, 573 U.S., at 718, but the authorities cited in support of that proposition are hardly helpful. See Del. Code Ann., Tit. 8, § 351 (2011) (certificates of incorporation may specify how the business is managed); 1 J. Cox & T. Hazen, Treatise on the Law of Corporations § 3:2 (3d ed. 2010) (section entitled "Selecting the state of incorporation"); 3 *id.*, § 14:11, p. 48 (observing that "[d]espite the frequency of dissension and deadlock in close corporations, in some states neither legislatures nor courts have provided satisfactory solutions"). And even if a dispute settlement mechanism is in place, how is the arbiter of a religion-based intracorporate controversy to resolve the disagreement, given this Court's instruction that "courts have no business addressing [whether an asserted religious belief] is reasonable," *ante*, 573 U.S., at 724?

proliferate, for the Court's expansive notion of corporate personhood—combined with its other errors in construing RFRA—invites for-profit entities to seek religion-based exemptions from regulations they deem offensive to their faith.

2

Even if Hobby Lobby and Conestoga were deemed RFRA "person[s]," to gain an exemption, they must demonstrate that the contraceptive coverage requirement "substantially burden[s] [their] exercise of religion." 42 U.S.C. § 2000bb–1(a). Congress no doubt meant the modifier "substantially" to carry weight. In the original draft of RFRA, the word "burden" appeared unmodified. The word "substantially" was inserted pursuant to a clarifying amendment offered by Senators Kennedy and Hatch. See 139 Cong. Rec. 26180. In proposing the amendment, Senator Kennedy stated that RFRA, in accord with the Court's pre-*Smith* case law, "does not require the Government to justify every action that has some effect on religious exercise." *Ibid.*

The Court barely pauses to inquire whether any burden imposed by the contraceptive coverage requirement is substantial. Instead, it rests on the Greens' and Hahns' "belie[f] that providing the coverage demanded by the HHS regulations is connected to the destruction of an embryo in a way that is sufficient to make it immoral for them to provide the coverage." *Ante*, 573 U.S., at 724.[20] I agree with the Court that the Green and Hahn families' religious convictions regarding contraception are sincerely held. See *Thomas*, 450 U.S., at 715 (courts are not to question where an individual "dr[aws] the line" in defining which practices run afoul of her religious beliefs). See also 42 U.S.C. §§ 2000bb–1(a), 2000bb–2(4), 2000cc–5(7)(A).[21] But those beliefs, however deeply held, do not suffice to

---

20. The Court dismisses the argument, advanced by some *amici*, that the $2,000-per-employee tax charged to certain employers that fail to provide health insurance is less than the average cost of offering health insurance, noting that the Government has not provided the statistics that could support such an argument. See *ante*, 573 U.S., at 720–722. The Court overlooks, however, that it is not the Government's obligation to prove that an asserted burden is *in*substantial. Instead, it is incumbent upon plaintiffs to demonstrate, in support of a RFRA claim, the substantiality of the alleged burden.

21. The Court levels a criticism that is as wrongheaded as can be. In no way does the dissent "tell the plaintiffs that their beliefs are flawed." *Ante*, 573 U.S., at 724. Right or wrong in this

sustain a RFRA claim. RFRA, properly understood, distinguishes between "factual allegations that [plaintiffs'] beliefs are sincere and of a religious nature," which a court must accept as true, and the "legal conclusion . . . that [plaintiffs'] religious exercise is substantially burdened," an inquiry the court must undertake. *Kaemmerling* v. *Lappin*, 553 F.3d 669, 679 (C.A.D.C. 2008).

That distinction is a facet of the pre-*Smith* jurisprudence RFRA incorporates. *Bowen* v. *Roy*, 476 U.S. 693 (1986), is instructive. There, the Court rejected a free exercise challenge to the Government's use of a Native American child's Social Security number for purposes of administering benefit programs. Without questioning the sincerity of the father's religious belief that "use of [his daughter's Social Security] number may harm [her] spirit," the Court concluded that the Government's internal uses of that number "place[d] [no] restriction on what [the father] may believe or what he may do." *Id.*, at 699. Recognizing that the father's "religious views may not accept" the position that the challenged uses concerned only the Government's internal affairs, the Court explained that "for the adjudication of a constitutional claim, the Constitution, rather than an individual's religion, must supply the frame of reference." *Id.*, at 700–701, n. 6. See also *Hernandez* v. *Commissioner*, 490 U.S. 680, 699 (1989) (distinguishing between, on the one hand, "question[s] [of] the centrality of particular beliefs or practices to a faith, or the validity of particular litigants' interpretations of those creeds," and, on the other, "whether the alleged burden imposed [by the challenged government action] is a substantial one"). Inattentive to this guidance, today's decision elides entirely the distinction between the sincerity of a challenger's religious belief and the substantiality of the burden placed on the challenger.

Undertaking the inquiry that the Court forgoes, I would conclude that the connection between the families' religious objections and the contraceptive coverage requirement is too attenuated to rank as substantial. The

---

domain is a judgment no Member of this Court, or any civil court, is authorized or equipped to make. What the Court must decide is not "the plausibility of a religious claim," *ibid.* (internal quotation marks omitted), but whether accommodating that claim risks depriving others of rights accorded them by the laws of the United States. See *supra*, 573 U.S., at 745–746; *infra*, 573 U.S., at 765–766.

requirement carries no command that Hobby Lobby or Conestoga pur-
chase or provide the contraceptives they find objectionable. Instead, it
calls on the companies covered by the requirement to direct money into
undifferentiated funds that finance a wide variety of benefits under comprehensive health plans. Those plans, in order to comply with the ACA,
see *supra*, 573 U.S., at 741–744, must offer contraceptive coverage without
cost sharing, just as they must cover an array of other preventive
services.

Importantly, the decisions whether to claim benefits under the plans
are made not by Hobby Lobby or Conestoga, but by the covered employees
and dependents, in consultation with their health care providers. Should
an employee of Hobby Lobby or Conestoga share the religious beliefs of
the Greens and Hahns, she is of course under no compulsion to use the
contraceptives in question. But "[n]o individual decision by an employee
and her physician—be it to use contraception, treat an infection, or have a
hip replaced—is in any meaningful sense [her employer's] decision or
action." *Grote* v. *Sebelius*, 708 F.3d 850, 865 (C.A.7 2013) (Rovner, J., dissenting). It is doubtful that Congress, when it specified that burdens must
be "substantia[l]," had in mind a linkage thus interrupted by independent
decisionmakers (the woman and her health counselor) standing between
the challenged government action and the religious exercise claimed to be
infringed. Any decision to use contraceptives made by a woman covered
under Hobby Lobby's or Conestoga's plan will not be propelled by the
Government, it will be the woman's autonomous choice, informed by the
physician she consults.

3

Even if one were to conclude that Hobby Lobby and Conestoga meet
the substantial burden requirement, the Government has shown that the
contraceptive coverage for which the ACA provides furthers compelling
interests in public health and women's well being. Those interests are con-
crete, specific, and demonstrated by a wealth of empirical evidence. To
recapitulate, the mandated contraception coverage enables women to
avoid the health problems unintended pregnancies may visit on them and
their children. See IOM Report 102–107. The coverage helps safeguard
the health of women for whom pregnancy may be hazardous, even life

threatening. See Brief for American College of Obstetricians and Gynecologists et al. as *Amici Curiae* 14–15. And the mandate secures benefits wholly unrelated to pregnancy, preventing certain cancers, menstrual disorders, and pelvic pain. Brief for Ovarian Cancer National Alliance et al. as *Amici Curiae* 4, 6–7, 15–16; 78 Fed.Reg. 39872 (2013); IOM Report 107.

That Hobby Lobby and Conestoga resist coverage for only 4 of the 20 FDA-approved contraceptives does not lessen these compelling interests. Notably, the corporations exclude intrauterine devices (IUDs), devices significantly more effective and significantly more expensive than other contraceptive methods. See id., at 105.[22] Moreover, the Court's reasoning appears to permit commercial enterprises like Hobby Lobby and Conestoga to exclude from their group health plans all forms of contraceptives. See Tr. of Oral Arg. 38–39 (counsel for Hobby Lobby acknowledged that his "argument . . . would apply just as well if the employer said 'no contraceptives'" (internal quotation marks added)).

Perhaps the gravity of the interests at stake has led the Court to assume, for purposes of its RFRA analysis, that the compelling interest criterion is met in these cases. See *ante*, 573 U.S., at 728.[23] It bears note in this regard that the cost of an IUD is nearly equivalent to a month's full-time pay for workers earning the minimum wage, Brief for Guttmacher Institute et al. as *Amici Curiae* 16; that almost one-third of women would change their contraceptive method if costs were not a factor, Frost & Darroch, Factors Associated With Contraceptive Choice and Inconsistent Method Use, United States, 2004, 40 Perspectives on Sexual & Reproductive Health 94, 98 (2008); and that only one-fourth of women who request an IUD actually

---

22. IUDs, which are among the most reliable forms of contraception, generally cost women more than $1,000 when the expenses of the office visit and insertion procedure are taken into account. See Eisenberg, McNicholas, & Peipert, Cost as a Barrier to Long-Acting Reversible Contraceptive (LARC) Use in Adolescents, 52 J. Adolescent Health S59, S60 (2013). See also Winner et al., Effectiveness of Long-Acting Reversible Contraception, 366 New Eng. J. Medicine 1998, 1999 (2012).

23. Although the Court's opinion makes this assumption grudgingly, see *ante*, 573 U.S., at 726–728, one Member of the majority recognizes, without reservation, that "the [contraceptive coverage] mandate serves the Government's compelling interest in providing insurance coverage that is necessary to protect the health of female employees." *Ante*, 573 U.S., at 737 (opinion of KENNEDY, J.).

have one inserted after finding out how expensive it would be, Gariepy, Simon, Patel, Creinin, & Schwarz, The Impact of Out-of-Pocket Expense on IUD Utilization Among Women With Private Insurance, 84 Contraception e39, e40 (2011). See also Eisenberg, *supra*, at S60 (recent study found that women who face out-of-pocket IUD costs in excess of $50 were "11-times less likely to obtain an IUD than women who had to pay less than $50"); Postlethwaite, Trussell, Zoolakis, Shabear, & Petitti, A Comparison of Contraceptive Procurement Pre- and Post-Benefit Change, 76 Contraception 360, 361–362 (2007) (when one health system eliminated patient cost sharing for IUDs, use of this form of contraception more than doubled).

Stepping back from its assumption that compelling interests support the contraceptive coverage requirement, the Court notes that small employers and grandfathered plans are not subject to the requirement. If there is a compelling interest in contraceptive coverage, the Court suggests, Congress would not have created these exclusions. See *ante*, 573 U.S., at 726–728.

Federal statutes often include exemptions for small employers, and such provisions have never been held to undermine the interests served by these statutes. See, *e.g.*, Family and Medical Leave Act of 1993, 29 U.S.C. § 2611(4)(A)(i) (applicable to employers with 50 or more employees); Age Discrimination in Employment Act of 1967, 29 U.S.C. § 630(b) (originally exempting employers with fewer than 50 employees, 81 Stat. 605, the statute now governs employers with 20 or more employees); Americans With Disabilities Act of 1990, 42 U.S.C. § 12111(5)(A) (applicable to employers with 15 or more employees); Title VII, 42 U.S.C. § 2000e(b) (originally exempting employers with fewer than 25 employees, see *Arbaugh* v. *Y & H Corp.*, 546 U.S. 500, 505, n. 2 (2006), the statute now governs employers with 15 or more employees).

The ACA's grandfathering provision, 42 U.S.C. § 18011, allows a phasing-in period for compliance with a number of the ACA's requirements (not just the contraceptive coverage or other preventive services provisions). Once specified changes are made, grandfathered status ceases. See 45 CFR § 147.140(g). Hobby Lobby's own situation is illustrative. By the time this litigation commenced, Hobby Lobby did not have grandfathered status. Asked why by the District Court, Hobby Lobby's counsel explained that the "grandfathering requirements mean that you can't make a whole menu of changes to your plan that involve things like the amount of co-pays, the amount of co-insurance, deductibles, that sort of thing." App. in No. 13–354, pp. 39–40. Counsel acknowledged that, "just because of economic realities, our plan has to shift over time. I mean, insurance plans, as everyone knows, shif[t] over time." *Id.*, at 40.[24] The percentage of employees in grandfathered plans is steadily declining, having dropped from 56% in 2011 to 48% in 2012 to 36% in 2013. Kaiser Family Foundation & Health Research & Educ. Trust, Employer Benefits 2013 Annual Survey 7, 196. In short, far from ranking as a categorical exemption, the grandfathering provision is "temporary, intended to be a means for gradually transitioning employers into mandatory coverage." *Gilardi*, 733 F.3d, at 1241 (Edwards, J., concurring in part and dissenting in part).

The Court ultimately acknowledges a critical point: RFRA's application "*must* take adequate account of the burdens a requested accommodation may impose on nonbeneficiaries." *Ante*, at 573 U.S., 729, n. 37 (quoting *Cutter* v. *Wilkinson*, 544 U.S. 709, 720 (2005); emphasis added). No tradition, and no prior decision under RFRA, allows a religion-based exemption when the accommodation would be harmful to others—here, the very persons the contraceptive coverage requirement was designed to protect. Cf. *supra*, 573 U.S., at 745–746; *Prince* v. *Massachusetts*, 321 U.S. 158, 177 (1944) (Jackson, J., dissenting) ("[The] limitations which of necessity bound religious freedom . . . begin to operate whenever activities begin to affect or collide with liberties of others or of the public.").

4

After assuming the existence of compelling government interests, the Court holds that the contraceptive coverage requirement fails to satisfy RFRA's least restrictive means test. But the Government has shown that there is no less restrictive, equally effective means that would both (1) satisfy the challengers' religious objections to providing insurance coverage for certain contraceptives (which they believe cause abortions); and (2)

---

24. Hobby Lobby's *amicus* National Religious Broadcasters similarly states that, "[g]iven the nature of employers' needs to meet changing economic and staffing circumstances, and to adjust insurance coverage accordingly, the actual benefit of the 'grandfather' exclusion is *de minimis* and transitory at best." Brief for National Religious Broadcasters as *Amicus Curiae* in No. 13–354, p. 28.

carry out the objective of the ACA's contraceptive coverage requirement, to ensure that women employees receive, at no cost to them, the preventive care needed to safeguard their health and well being. A "least restrictive means" cannot require employees to relinquish benefits accorded them by federal law in order to ensure that their commercial employers can adhere unreservedly to their religious tenets. See *supra*, 573 U.S., at 715–746, 764.[25]

Then let the government pay (rather than the employees who do not share their employer's faith), the Court suggests. "The most straightforward [alternative]," the Court asserts, "would be for the Government to assume the cost of providing . . . contraceptives . . . to any women who are unable to obtain them under their health-insurance policies due to their employers' religious objections." *Ante*, 573 U.S., at 728. The ACA, however, requires coverage of preventive services through the existing employer-based system of health insurance "so that [employees] face minimal logistical and administrative obstacles." 78 Fed.Reg. 39888. Impeding women's receipt of benefits "by requiring them to take steps to learn about, and to sign up for, a new [government funded and administered] health benefit" was scarcely what Congress contemplated. *Ibid.* Moreover, Title X of the Public Health Service Act, 42 U.S.C. § 300 *et seq.*, "is the nation's only dedicated source of federal funding for safety net family planning services." Brief for National Health Law Program et al. as *Amici Curiae* 23. "Safety net programs like Title X are not designed to absorb the unmet needs of . . . insured individuals." *Id.*, at 24. Note, too, that Congress declined to write into law the preferential treatment Hobby Lobby and Conestoga describe as a less restrictive alternative. See *supra*, 573 U.S., at 744.

And where is the stopping point to the "let the government pay" alternative? Suppose an employer's sincerely held religious belief is offended by health coverage of vaccines, or paying the minimum wage, see *Tony*

---

25. As the Court made clear in *Cutter*, the government's license to grant religion-based exemptions from generally applicable laws is constrained by the Establishment Clause. 544 U.S., at 720–722. "[W]e are a cosmopolitan nation made up of people of almost every conceivable religious preference," *Braunfeld*, 366 U.S., at 606, a "rich mosaic of religious faiths," *Town of Greece* v. *Galloway*, 572 U.S. 565, 628 (2014) (KAGAN, J., dissenting). Consequently, one person's right to free exercise must be kept in harmony with the rights of her fellow citizens, and "some religious practices [must] yield to the common good." *United States* v. *Lee*, 455 U.S. 252, 259 (1982).

and Susan Alamo Foundation v. *Secretary of Labor*, 471 U.S. 290, 303 (1985), or according women equal pay for substantially similar work, see *Dole* v. *Shenandoah Baptist Church*, 899 F.2d 1389, 1392 (C.A.4 1990)? Does it rank as a less restrictive alternative to require the government to provide the money or benefit to which the employer has a religion-based objection?[26] Because the Court cannot easily answer that question, it proposes something else: Extension to commercial enterprises of the accommodation already afforded to nonprofit religion-based organizations. See *ante*, 573 U.S., at 692–693, 698–699, 730–732. "At a minimum," according to the Court, such an approach would not "impinge on [Hobby Lobby's and Conestoga's] religious belief." *Ante*, 573 U.S., at 731. I have already discussed the "special solicitude" generally accorded nonprofit religion-based organizations that exist to serve a community of believers, solicitude never before accorded to commercial enterprises comprising employees of diverse faiths. See *supra*, 573 U.S., at 752–755.

Ultimately, the Court hedges on its proposal to align for-profit enterprises with nonprofit religion-based organizations. "We do not decide today whether [the] approach [the opinion advances] complies with RFRA for purposes of all religious claims." *Ante*, 573 U.S., at 731. Counsel for Hobby Lobby was similarly noncommittal. Asked at oral argument whether the Court-proposed alternative was acceptable,[27] counsel

---

26. Cf. *Ashcroft* v. *American Civil Liberties Union*, 542 U.S. 656, 666 (2004) (in context of First Amendment Speech Clause challenge to a content-based speech restriction, courts must determine "whether the challenged regulation is the least restrictive means among *available*, effective alternatives" (emphasis added)).

27. On brief, Hobby Lobby and Conestoga barely addressed the extension solution, which would bracket commercial enterprises with nonprofit religion-based organizations for religious accommodations purposes. The hesitation is understandable, for challenges to the adequacy of the accommodation accorded religious nonprofit organizations are currently *sub judice*. See, *e.g.*, *Little Sisters of the Poor Home for the Aged* v. *Sebelius*, 6 F. Supp. 3d 1225 (Colo. 2013), injunction pending appeal granted, 571 U.S. 1171 (2014). At another point in today's decision, the Court refuses to consider an argument neither "raised below [nor] advanced in this Court by any party," giving Hobby Lobby and Conestoga "[no] opportunity to respond to [that] novel claim." *Ante*, 573 U.S., at 721. Yet the Court is content to decide this case (and this case only) on the ground that HHS could make an accommodation never suggested in the parties' presentations. RFRA cannot sensibly be read to "requir[e] the government to . . . refute each and every conceivable alternative regulation," *United States* v. *Wilgus*, 638 F. 3d 1274, 1289 (CA10 2011), especially where the alternative on which the Court seizes was not pressed by any challenger.

responded: "We haven't been offered that accommodation, so we haven't had to decide what kind of objection, if any, we would make to that." Tr. of Oral Arg. 86–87.

Conestoga suggests that, if its employees had to acquire and pay for the contraceptives (to which the corporation objects) on their own, a tax credit would qualify as a less restrictive alternative. See Brief for Petitioners in No. 13 356, p. 64. A tax credit, of course, is one variety of "let the government pay." In addition to departing from the existing employer-based system of health insurance, Conestoga's alternative would require a woman to reach into her own pocket in the first instance, and it would do nothing for the woman too poor to be aided by a tax credit.

In sum, in view of what Congress sought to accomplish, *i.e.*, comprehensive preventive care for women furnished through employer-based health plans, none of the proffered alternatives would satisfactorily serve the compelling interests to which Congress responded.

IV

Among the pathmarking pre-*Smith* decisions RFRA preserved is *United States* v. *Lee*, 455 U.S. 252 (1982). Lee, a sole proprietor engaged in farming and carpentry, was a member of the Old Order Amish. He sincerely believed that withholding Social Security taxes from his employees or paying the employer's share of such taxes would violate the Amish faith. This Court held that, although the obligations imposed by the Social Security system conflicted with Lee's religious beliefs, the burden was not unconstitutional. *Id.*, at 260–261. See also *id.*, at 258 (recognizing the important governmental interest in providing a "nationwide . . . comprehensive insurance system with a variety of benefits available to all participants, with costs shared by employers and employees").[28] The Government urges that *Lee* should control the challenges brought by Hobby Lobby and Conestoga. See Brief for Respondents in No. 13–356, p. 18. In contrast,

---

28. As a sole proprietor, Lee was subject to personal liability for violating the law of general application he opposed. His claim to a religion-based exemption would have been even thinner had he conducted his business as a corporation, thus avoiding personal liability.

today's Court dismisses *Lee* as a tax case. See *ante*, 573 U.S., at 733–734. Indeed, it was a tax case and the Court in *Lee* homed in on "[t]he difficulty in attempting to accommodate religious beliefs in the area of taxation." 455 U.S., at 259.

But the *Lee* Court made two key points one cannot confine to tax cases. "When followers of a particular sect enter into commercial activity as a matter of choice," the Court observed, "the limits they accept on their own conduct as a matter of conscience and faith are not to be superimposed on statutory schemes which are binding on others in that activity." *Id.*, at 261. The statutory scheme of employer-based comprehensive health coverage involved in these cases is surely binding on others engaged in the same trade or business as the corporate challengers here, Hobby Lobby and Conestoga. Further, the Court recognized in *Lee* that allowing a religion-based exemption to a commercial employer would "operat[e] to impose the employer's religious faith on the employees." *Ibid.*[29] No doubt the Greens and Hahns and all who share their beliefs may decline to acquire for themselves the contraceptives in question. But that choice may not be imposed on employees who hold other beliefs. Working for Hobby Lobby or Conestoga, in other words, should not deprive employees of the preventive care available to workers at the shop next door,[30] at least in the absence of directions from the Legislature or Administration to do so.

Why should decisions of this order be made by Congress or the regulatory authority, and not this Court? Hobby Lobby and Conestoga surely do not stand alone as commercial enterprises seeking exemptions from generally applicable laws on the basis of their religious beliefs. See, *e.g.*, *Newman* v. *Piggie Park Enterprises, Inc.*, 256 F. Supp. 941, 945 (D.S.C.

---

29. Congress amended the Social Security Act in response to *Lee*. The amended statute permits Amish sole proprietors and partnerships (but not Amish-owned corporations) to obtain an exemption from the obligation to pay Social Security taxes only for employees who are co-religionists and who likewise seek an exemption and agree to give up their Social Security benefits. See 26 U.S.C. § 3127(a)(2), (b)(1). Thus, employers with sincere religious beliefs have no right to a religion-based exemption that would deprive employees of Social Security benefits without the employee's consent—an exemption analogous to the one Hobby Lobby and Conestoga seek here.

30. Cf. *Tony and Susan Alamo Foundation* v. *Secretary of Labor*, 471 U.S. 290, 299 (1985) (disallowing religion-based exemption that "would undoubtedly give [the commercial enterprise seeking the exemption] and similar organizations an advantage over their competitors").

1966) (owner of restaurant chain refused to serve black patrons based on his religious beliefs opposing racial integration), aff'd in relevant part and rev'd in part on other grounds, 377 F.2d 433 (C.A.4 1967), aff'd and modified on other grounds, 390 U.S. 400 (1968); *State by McClure* v. *Sports & Health Club, Inc.*, 370 N.W.2d 844, 847 (Minn. 1985) (born-again Christians who owned closely held, for-profit health clubs believed that the Bible proscribed hiring or retaining an "individua[l] living with but not married to a person of the opposite sex," "a young, single woman working without her father's consent or a married woman working without her husband's consent," and any person "antagonistic to the Bible," including "fornicators and homosexuals" (internal quotation marks omitted)), appeal dismissed, 478 U.S. 1015 (1986); *Elane Photography, LLC* v. *Willock*, 309 P.3d 53 (N.M. 2013) (for-profit photography business owned by a husband and wife refused to photograph a lesbian couple's commitment ceremony based on the religious beliefs of the company's owners), cert. denied, 572 U.S. 1046 (2014). Would RFRA require exemptions in cases of this ilk? And if not, how does the Court divine which religious beliefs are worthy of accommodation, and which are not? Isn't the Court disarmed from making such a judgment given its recognition that "courts must not presume to determine . . . the plausibility of a religious claim"? *Ante*, 573 U.S., at 724.

Would the exemption the Court holds RFRA demands for employers with religiously grounded objections to the use of certain contraceptives extend to employers with religiously grounded objections to blood transfusions (Jehovah's Witnesses); antidepressants (Scientologists); medications derived from pigs, including anesthesia, intravenous fluids, and pills coated with gelatin (certain Muslims, Jews, and Hindus); and vaccinations (Christian Scientists, among others)?[31] According to counsel for Hobby Lobby, "each one of these cases . . . would have to be evaluated on its own . . . apply[ing] the compelling interest-least restrictive alternative test." Tr. of Oral Arg. 6. Not much help there for the lower courts bound by today's decision.

---

31. Religious objections to immunization programs are not hypothetical. See *Phillips* v. *City of New York*, 27 F. Supp.3d 310, (E.D.N.Y. 2014) (dismissing free exercise challenges to New York's vaccination practices); Liberty Counsel, Compulsory Vaccinations Threaten Religious Freedom (2007), available at http://www.lc.org/media/9980/attachments/memo_vaccination.pdf.

The Court, however, sees nothing to worry about. Today's cases, the Court concludes, are "concerned solely with the contraceptive mandate. Our decision should not be understood to hold that an insurance-coverage mandate must necessarily fall if it conflicts with an employer's religious beliefs. Other coverage requirements, such as immunizations, may be supported by different interests (for example, the need to combat the spread of infectious diseases) and may involve different arguments about the least restrictive means of providing them." *Ante*, 573 U.S., at 733. But the Court has assumed, for RFRA purposes, that the interest in women's health and well being is compelling and has come up with no means adequate to serve that interest, the one motivating Congress to adopt the Women's Health Amendment.

There is an overriding interest, I believe, in keeping the courts "out of the business of evaluating the relative merits of differing religious claims," *Lee*, 455 U.S., at 263, n. 2 (Stevens, J., concurring in judgment), or the sincerity with which an asserted religious belief is held. Indeed, approving some religious claims while deeming others unworthy of accommodation could be "perceived as favoring one religion over another," the very "risk the Establishment Clause was designed to preclude." *Ibid.* The Court, I fear, has ventured into a minefield, cf. *Spencer* v. *World Vision, Inc.*, 633 F.3d 723, 730 (C.A.9 2010) (O'Scannlain, J., concurring), by its immoderate reading of RFRA. I would confine religious exemptions under that Act to organizations formed "for a religious purpose," "engage[d] primarily in carrying out that religious purpose," and not "engaged . . . substantially in the exchange of goods or services for money beyond nominal amounts." See *id.*, at 748 (Kleinfeld, J., concurring).

*   *   *

For the reasons stated, I would reverse the judgment of the Court of Appeals for the Tenth Circuit and affirm the judgment of the Court of Appeals for the Third Circuit.

JUSTICE RUTH BADER GINSBURG

RECENT SPEECHES

What follows are three speeches given by Justice Ginsburg in 2016 and 2018 in which she talks about many aspects of her life and work.

In the first, Justice Ginsburg describes her litigation strategy as an advocate in the 1970s working to dismantle institutionalized gender discrimination and shares how lessons learned from Justice Louis D. Brandeis's successful advocacy and judicial career influenced her course. As Justice Ginsburg explains, in his innovative approach to brief-writing, Brandeis sought to educate the Supreme Court Justices with facts about the lived experiences of those affected by the law. In *Muller* v. *Oregon*, Brandeis wielded this skill in support of restrictions on the rights of women in the workplace, grounding his arguments in the need to preserve traditional gender stereotypes. More influenced by his strategy than endgame, Justice Ginsburg explains how she filed her own "Brandeis briefs" in the Supreme Court—in her case, to dismantle gender stereotypes and open up opportunities for women, and men. Likewise, she explains how his jurisprudence as a Justice helped her frame her remedial arguments in these cases. Finally, Justice Ginsburg speaks here of Justice Brandeis's influence upon how she thinks of her role as a Justice.

In the second speech, Justice Ginsburg explains how her Jewish heritage and her role as a judge come together to inspire her to be "steadfast in the service" of the "demand for justice, for peace, and for enlightenment [that] runs through the entirety of Jewish history and Jewish tradition." She also reflects upon the influence of several important Jewish women on her life.

In the final speech included here, Justice Ginsburg offers remarks at a naturalization service held at the National Archives in December 2018. Justice Ginsburg speaks of the American dream that drew her own family to this country and invites the newest citizens of the United States to join her and all Americans in committing themselves to work toward achieving "a more perfect Union."

LESSONS LEARNED FROM LOUIS D. BRANDEIS

BRANDEIS UNIVERSITY, WALTHAM, MASSACHUSETTS
(JANUARY 28, 2016)

Ruth Bader Ginsburg, Associate Justice,
Supreme Court of the United States

THE BRANDEIS BRIEF

In these remarks, I will try to convey Brandeis' impact on me in my years as a lawyer, and then as a judge. I will speak first, and longest, of the Brandeis Brief famously filed in *Muller* v. *Oregon*.[1] The Supreme Court decided that case in 1908. The Court upheld, as constitutional, a 1903 Oregon law that prohibited employment of women in industrial jobs for more than ten hours per day. In briefs filed in the 1970s, I described the *Muller* decision as obstacles to Supreme Court recognition of the equal citizenship stature of men and women as constitutional principle. While the *Muller* decision was a precedent I sought to undo, the method Brandeis used to prevail in that case is one I admired and copied. Let me explain why I applauded Brandeis' method but not the decision he sought and gained.

In 1903, Oregon adopted a law setting ten hours as the maximum work day for women "employed in any mechanical establishment, factory, or laundry." Promoters of Oregon's law limiting hours for women workers included labor reformers who first proposed an eight-hour day for all workers. When that proposal failed to gain legislative support, the proponents settled on a measure limiting the hours blue-collar women could engage in paid labor. Their hope was that a law protecting women would serve as an "opening wedge," leading, in time, to protection of all workers.

Portland laundry owner Curt Muller insisted that laundress Emma Gotcher work more than ten hours on September 4, 1905. That date, it seems, was not fortuitous. It was the day the State had designated Labor Day to encourage employers to give their workers a holiday. The timing, and Emma Gotcher's membership in the Laundry Workers Union, suggest that Muller and fellow members of the Laundry-Owners' Association aimed to create a test case. As it turned out, they did. Oregon prosecuted Muller for violating the State's law. After an unsuccessful defense in Oregon's courts, Muller asked the U.S. Supreme Court to take the case and declare the State's 1903 law unconstitutional.

Muller had cause to be hopeful. In 1905, the Supreme Court had ruled, 5-4, in *Lochner* v. *New York*,[2] that New York had acted unconstitutionally when it enacted a law limiting the hours bakers could work to ten per day, 60 per week. According to the Court, the hours limitation interfered with the right of bakery owners and bakery workers to contract freely, a liberty the Court lodged in the Fourteenth Amendment's Due Process Clause, which reads: "[No] State shall deprive any person of life, liberty, or property, without due process of law."

The National Consumers League, led by social reformer Florence Kelley, wanted to ensure that Oregon would have the best possible representation. Kelley's first choice was Brandeis, but the League, while Kelley was out of town, had set up an appointment for her with a celebrated New York bar leader, Joseph H. Choate. To Kelley's relief, Choate declined to take the case. He told Kelley he saw no reason why "a big husky Irishwoman should [not] work more than ten hours a day . . . if she and her employer so desired." Kelley next went to Boston to enlist Brandeis. She was accompanied by Josephine Goldmark, who was Brandeis' sister-in-law and Kelley's associate in the Consumers League.

Brandeis, then age 51, said yes to the League, on one condition. He wanted to be Oregon's counsel, not relegated to a friend-of-the-Court role, and he wanted to argue the case orally on the State's behalf. Kelley and Goldmark made that happen. Brandeis then superintended preparation of a brief unlike any the Court had yet seen. It was to be loaded with facts and spare on formal legal argument.

Josephine Goldmark, aided by her sister Pauline and several volunteer researchers, scoured the Columbia University and New York Public Libraries in search of materials of the kind Brandeis wanted—facts and figures on dangers to women's health, safety, and morals from working excessive hours, and on the societal benefits shortened hours could yield. Data was extracted from reports of factory inspectors, physicians, trade unions, economists, and social workers. Within a month, Goldmark's team compiled information that filled 98 of the 113 pages in Brandeis' brief.

To show that Oregon was no outlier, Brandeis first set out the statutes of the 20 States that had restricted women's on-the-job hours. He also listed similar hours laws in force in Europe. His basic contention: The due process right to contract for another's labor is subject to reasonable restraints to protect health, safety, morals, and the general welfare.

To convince the Court, Brandeis had to distinguish *Lochner* v. *New York*. Bakers, the Court had commented in *Lochner*—a job category overwhelmingly male—were "in no sense wards of the state." Women, Brandeis urged, were more susceptible than men to the maladies of industrialization, and their unique vulnerabilities warranted the State's sheltering arm. The brief's pattern: After a line or two of introduction, Brandeis quoted long passages from the sources Goldmark and her associates had supplied.

Some of those sources would hardly pass go today. For example, Brandeis quoted a medical expert who reported: "[I]n the blood of women, so also in their muscles, there is more water than in those of men." Less imaginary, Brandeis emphasized the effect of overworking women on the general welfare: "Infant mortality rises," he told the Court, "while the children of married working-women, who survive, are injured by the inevitable neglect. The overwork of future mothers," he added, "directly attacks the welfare of the nation."

On the benefit side, Brandeis stressed that shorter hours allowed women to attend to their family and household responsibilities. According to a source he quoted: "[F]ree time [for a woman] is not resting time, as it is for a man. . . . For the working-girl on her return from the factory, there is a variety of work waiting. She has her room to keep clean . . . , her laundry work to do, clothes to repair and clean, and, besides this, she should be learning to keep house if her future household is not to be [a] disorderly . . . failure." To allay the concern that shorter hours were bad for business, Brandeis excerpted studies of more contemporary resonance showing that maximum hours laws improved productivity.

The brief's bottom line: Decades of well documented experience at home and abroad showed that Oregon's Legislature had good reason to believe that public health, safety, and welfare would be advanced by limiting women's paid work to ten hours per day.

Counsel for laundry owner Muller scarcely anticipated the mountain of social and economic material the State, through Brandeis, would present. But Muller's brief made a point equal rights advocates of my day embraced: Most of the disadvantages facing women in the labor market derive from society, not biology, Muller argued. "Social customs [not inferior ability]," he urged, "narrow the field of [their] endeavor." "[O]stensibly," the brief continued, Oregon's law was "framed in [women's] interest." But was it intended, Muller asked, perhaps "to limit and restrict [their] employment," in order to give a boost to "[women's] competitor[s] [for blue-collar jobs] among men?"

The Supreme Court heard argument in the *Muller* case only five days after receiving the voluminous Brandeis brief. (Such short time between briefing and argument would not occur today.) Less than six weeks post argument, the Supreme Court unanimously upheld Oregon's law. Justice Brewer, who was a member of the 5-4 majority that invalidated New York's maximum hours legislation in *Lochner*, authored the Court's relatively short opinion. Brewer took the unusual step of acknowledging the "copious collection" of statutes and reports, domestic and foreign, in Brandeis' brief.

Then, Brewer put his own spin on the materials Brandeis presented. The Justice found in those materials confirmation of eternal, decidedly unscientific, truths about men and women. According to Brewer, "history [shows] that woman has always been dependent upon man." "[I]n the struggle for subsistence," he wrote, "she is not an equal competitor with her brother." "[S]he is so constituted that she will rest upon and look to him for protection." Brewer then switched images from man as protector to man as predator. Woman's "physical structure and a proper discharge of her maternal functions," he wrote, "justify legislation to protect her from the greed as well as the passion of man."

Did the Justices rule in Oregon's favor in *Muller* because they were impressed by the extraordinary quality of the Brandeis brief? Or did they hold for Oregon because the Brandeis brief shored up their own preconceptions about the relationship between the sexes, the physical superiority of men, women's inherent vulnerability, and society's interest in "the well-being of wom[e]n" as actual or potential mothers? Would Brandeis' technique work when social and economic data was inconsistent with traditional views about "the way women are" and was used to challenge, not defend, sex-based classifications in the law?

As a law student in the late 1950s, I learned in my Constitutional Law class that *Muller* marked a first break from the Court's refusal to uphold social and economic legislation attacked as invading the liberty to contract once thought to be secured by the Fifth and Fourteenth Amendments' Due Process Clauses. *Muller* was a decision to applaud, New Deal oriented professors taught us.

Just over a decade later, briefing gender discrimination cases in or headed for the U.S. Supreme Court, I looked at *Muller* differently. The decision, I appreciated, was responsive to "turn of the 20th century conditions when women labored long into the night in sweat shop operations." But, I observed in 1970s briefs, "[a]s the work day [for industrial workers, male and female] shortened from twelve hours to eight, and the work week from six days to five," laws limiting only women's work were in many instances "'protecting' [women] from better-paying jobs and opportunities for promotion." However well intended, such laws could have a perverse effect—they could (and all too often did) operate to protect men's jobs from women's competition. (Recall that the same point was made by Curt Muller's lawyer, but it carried less credibility in 1908, when unregulated work weeks, with no overtime pay, could run 72 hours or more.)

In briefs and commentary, I included *Muller* in a trilogy of cases that "b[ore] particularly close examination for the support they appear[ed] to give [to] ... perpetuation of the treatment of women as less than full persons within the meaning of the Constitution." The other decisions in the trilogy were *Goesaert* v. *Cleary*,[3] which, in 1948, upheld a Michigan statute prohibiting women from working as bartenders, citing moral concerns;

and *Hoyt* v. *Florida*,[4] which, in 1961, upheld a state statute excluding women from the obligation to serve on juries because of their place at "the center of home and family life."

While equal rights advocates attacked the substance of the *Muller* decision, they were hugely inspired by Brandeis' method. The aim of the Brandeis brief was to educate the Judiciary about the real world in which the laws under inspection operated. That same aim motivated brief writers in the turning point gender discrimination cases, *Reed* v. *Reed*,[5] decided in 1971, and *Frontiero* v. *Richardson*,[6] decided in 1973. *Reed* was the first case ever in which the U.S. Supreme Court disapproved a classification based on gender. The Idaho statute involved in *Reed* was once typical; it provided: As between persons "equally entitled to administer [a decedent's estate], males must be preferred to females." Two federal statutes, also typical of the time, were involved in *Frontiero*. Both laws granted fringe benefits to married male military officers but withheld them from most married female officers.

The Brandeis brief presented economic and social realities in justification of protective labor legislation challenged as unconstitutional. In *Reed*, *Frontiero*, and later 1970s gender discrimination cases, Brandeis-style briefs explained that, as the economy developed and society evolved, laws premised on women's subordinate status violated the Constitution's guarantee of "the equal protection of the laws" to all persons.

The social and economic facts urged in *Reed* and *Frontiero* aimed to open jurists' eyes. Copying Brandeis' method was useful to that end. Laws once thought to operate benignly in women's favor—keeping them off juries and relegating them to "women's work" in the military, for example—in time, came to be seen as measures impeding women's opportunity to participate in and contribute to society based on their individual talents and capacities.

JUDICIAL AUTHORITY TO REPAIR UNCONSTITUTIONAL LEGISLATION

Another lesson learned from Brandeis. Much legislation into the 1970s was based on the premise that men were breadwinners, women, men's dependents. So, for example, when Stephen Wiesenfeld's wage earning wife died in childbirth, he sought the social security benefits that would enable him to care personally for his infant son. They were called "child in care" benefits, available when a wage earner dies with a spouse and young child surviving. If the deceased wage earner was a man, there were monthly benefits for widow and child. But if the wage earner was a woman, as Paula Wiesenfeld was, there were no benefits for the widower.

On behalf of Stephen Wiesenfeld, I asked the Court essentially to write into the statute the fathers Congress had left out, to convert the "mother's benefit" into a "parent's benefit." Can't be done, some of my academic colleagues told me. The Court might nullify the mother's benefit, leaving it to Congress to start over from scratch. But it would be out of bounds for the Court, lacking the power of the purse, to order payments to widowed fathers.

That is just what the Government initially argued. In the district court, the Government urged dismissal of Stephen Wiesenfeld's complaint. "It is clear," the Government maintained, that the "plaintiff does not complain about what Congress enacted [a mother's benefit], he complains about what Congress [did] not enact, [a father's benefit]. [He] has therefore chosen the wrong forum [for] the relief he seeks. He should take his complaint to Congress." That argument, had it been accepted, would have immunized from judicial review statutes that confer benefits unevenly— on women only or men only. The legislature would have power, unchecked by the judiciary, to diminish the equal protection principle.

Was my position radical? Precedent was slim, but what there was had heft. It started with Brandeis in a case decided in 1931 involving state taxation, *Iowa-Des Moines National Bank* v. *Bennett*.[7] Complainants were a national and a state bank. Their complaint, Iowa officials taxed them at a rate higher than the rate charged corporations in competition with them. Brandeis wrote for a unanimous Court that the banks were entitled to a "refund of the excess taxes exacted from them." He explained:

> The petitioners' rights were violated . . . when taxes at the lower rate were collected from their competitors. It may be assumed that all ground for a claim for refund would have fallen if the State, promptly upon discovery of the discrimination, had removed it by collecting the additional taxes from the favored competitors. By such collection the petitioners' grievances would have been redressed. . . . The right invoked is that to equal treatment; and such treatment will be attained if either their competitors' taxes are

increased or their own reduced. But it is well settled that a taxpayer who has been subjected to discriminatory taxation through the favoring of others in violation of federal law, cannot be required himself to assume the burden of seeking an increase of the taxes which the others should have paid. . . . Nor may he be remitted to the necessity of awaiting such action by the state officials upon their own initiative.

Typically clear expression from Brandeis' pen.

In a 1970 decision, *Welsh* v. *United States*,[8] Justice Harlan followed and expanded upon Justice Brandeis' lead, explaining: "Where a statute is defective because of under inclusion, there exist two remedial alternatives: a court may either declare it a nullity . . . or it may extend the coverage of the statute to include those who are aggrieved by exclusion."

Thanks in part to the Brandeis and Harlan opinions, the Court saw the light. In *Frontiero*, it did not nullify benefits enjoyed by married male officers; instead, it extended those benefits to married female officers. And in *Wiesenfeld*, instead of nullifying benefits enjoyed by widowed mothers, it extended them to widowed fathers. In several later cases, the Court followed the same path.

BRANDEIS' LEGACY

In connection with a soon to be published book titled *Louis D. Brandeis: American Prophet*,[9] author and head of the Constitution Center in Philadelphia, Jeffrey Rosen, asked me about Brandeis' influence on me. I spoke, of course, about the Brandeis brief and the brief written in the turning point 1971 *Reed* v. *Reed* case. Self-consciously Brandeisian, the *Reed* brief attempted to document, through citation to economic, social, and historical sources, the artificial barriers imposed on women by law and custom, suppressing their aspirations and opportunities to achieve.

I also spoke of Brandeis as Justice, his craftsmanship, sense of collegiality, ability to combine a dedication to judicial restraint with a readiness to defend civil rights and liberties when the values our Constitution advances required it. "Brandeis worked hard on his opinions," I responded to Jeff, "as evidenced by the number of drafts he composed. He cared not only about reaching the right bottom line judgment; he cared as much about writing opinions that would enlighten other people."

I also admired Brandeis, I told Jeff, "for his determination to dissent or concur separately only when he felt the public really needed to hear his separate views." Alexander Bickel published a book in 1957 compiling Brandeis' unpublished opinions. "Not many jurists," I observed, "would go through the hard labor of writing an opinion, then step back and ask, Is this opinion really needed." His dissents were all the more influential because of his self-imposed restraint.

A further admirable quality, Brandeis' views could change when information and experience showed his initial judgment was not right. In the 1880s he opposed extending suffrage to women. Men were doing well enough in conducting the nation's political affairs, he thought, and they had obligations women escape. Military service, for example. He might have added jury duty.

By the 1910s, however, Brandeis had become a strong supporter of votes for women. Perhaps it was the influence of his wife and a daughter who took a year off between college and law school to campaign for women's suffrage. Perhaps it was the able women he encountered among social reformers: Jane Addams, Florence Kelly, his sister-in-law, Josephine Goldmark, and a number of others. Voting was a citizen's right, he recognized, but it was also a citizen's obligation. No class or section of the community is so wise or just, he came to see, that it can safely be trusted to govern without the participation of other classes or sections.

What of interpretive approach, Jeff asked. "[Brandeis'] purposive interpretation of statutes and our fundamental instrument of government place him high among jurists who interpret legal texts sensibly," I answered. "He certainly was not an admirer of what was once called legal classicism, which seems to me similar to today's originalism." As an example, I mentioned the June 2015 health care decision. Brandeis, I have no doubt, would have agreed with the majority's decision to salvage, not destroy, the Affordable Care Act.[10] He would not say, as the dissenters did, that because the Act used the words "exchange established by the state," the text must be interpreted in a way that would undermine the entire Act. One could not attribute to a responsible member of Congress an outcome so bizarre.

I ventured, too, that Brandeis would have deplored the Court's 2010 decision in *Citizens United* v. *FEC*,[11] which struck down restrictions on corporate campaign spending. Brandeis had pointed out in 1933, in his dissent in *Louis K. Liggett Co.* v. *Lee*,[12] that legislatures throughout the nineteenth and early twentieth century had imposed a host of regulations designed to ensure that the corporate form would not threaten equality of opportunity and the autonomy of individuals.

When Brandeis retired in 1939 after 23 years of distinguished service on the Supreme Court bench, he had written 448 opinions of the Court, ten concurring opinions, and 64 dissenting opinions. It is fitting to conclude these remarks with the appraisal of his work at the Court by his colleagues, expressed in their farewell letter:

> Your long practical experience and intimate knowledge of affairs, the wide range of your researches and your grasp of the most difficult problems, together with your power of analysis and your thoroughness in exposition, have made your judicial career one of extraordinary distinction and far-reaching influence.

That influence, I can attest, continues to this day.

NOTES

1. *Muller* v. *Oregon*, 208 U.S. 412, 422 (1908).
2. *Lochner* v. *New York*, 198 U.S. 45 (1905).
3. *Goesaert* v. *Cleary*, 335 U.S. 464, 466 (1948).
4. *Hoyt* v. *Florida*, 368 U.S. 57 (1961).
5. *Reed* v. *Reed*, 404 U.S. 71 (1971).
6. *Frontiero* v. *Richardson*, 411 U.S. 677 (1973).
7. *Iowa-Des Moines National Bank* v. *Bennett*, 284 U.S. 239, 247 (1931).
8. *Welsh* v. *United States* 398 U.S. 333, 362 (1970) (Harlan, J., concurring in the result).
9. Jeffrey Rosen, *Louis D. Brandeis: American Prophet* (New Haven: Yale University Press, 2016).
10. *King* v. *Burwell*, 576 U.S. 473 (2015).
11. *Citizens United* v. *Federal Election Commission*, 558 U.S. 310 (2010).
12. *Louis K. Liggett Co.* v. *Lee*, 288 U.S. 517, 541 (1933) (Brandeis, J., dissenting in part).

REMARKS AT THE GENESIS FOUNDATION LIFETIME ACHIEVEMENT AWARD CEREMONY

TEL AVIV (JULY 4, 2018)

Ruth Bader Ginsburg, Associate Justice,
Supreme Court of the United States

I am pleased beyond the capacity of words to convey that Aharon Barak has presented this award to me. He is one of the world's most brilliant, humanitarian jurists. I am proud to count him and his wife, Elika, treasured colleagues and friends.

Huge thanks, too, to the Genesis Foundation for creating a lifetime achievement award conferred by former Genesis Prize winners, an award I am permitted to accept.

I appreciate so very much the kind words just said about me. Yet I know that, more than anything else, good fortune—"mazal"—accounts for my part in the effort to achieve equal citizenship stature for women, also for the office I now hold, including the praise it garners. An Isaac Bashevis Singer remembrance bears retelling.

Singer's grandfather was a renowned orthodox rabbi who, in a sermon, put this question to his congregation: Why is the Almighty so eager for praise? Three times a day we pray to him, we say how great He is, how wonderful. Why should the creator of all the stars, all the planets, be so eager for praise? The sage rabbi's answer: The Almighty knows from experience, from divine experience, that when people stop praising him, they begin to praise one another. This, Singer's grandfather said, is what the

Almighty does not like. But small people that we are, Singer added, we enjoy sometimes some praise, especially when it comes from the mouths of good people. Just so, I am enjoying this event and my revisit to Israel.

It is fitting, on this occasion, to speak of two Jewish women raised in the USA whose humanity and bravery inspired me in my growing up years.

First, Emma Lazarus, elder cousin to the great jurist Benjamin Nathan Cardozo. Emma Lazarus was a Zionist before that word came into vogue. Her love for humankind, and especially for her People, is evident in all her writings. She wrote constantly, from her first volume of poetry published in 1866 at age 17, until her death from cancer far too soon, at age 38. Her poem, "The New Colossus," etched on the base of the Statue of Liberty, has welcomed legions of immigrants, including my father and grandparents, people seeking in the USA shelter from fear and longed-for freedom from intolerance.

My next inspirer, Hadassah founder Henrietta Szold. Born in 1860, eleven years after Emma Lazarus, Szold lived until 1945. My mother spoke of her glowingly, also of Henry Street Settlement House founder Lillian Wald (who lived from 1867 until 1940). Szold knew how to say "No" better than any other person whose words I have read. Szold had seven sisters, but no brother. When her mother died, a man well known for his community-spirited endeavors, Haym Peretz, offered to say the Kaddish— the mourner's prayer that, ancient custom instructed, could be recited only by men. Szold responded to that caring offer in a letter dated September 16, 1916. You can read it in full in *Four Centuries of Jewish Women's Spirituality* and in the Jewish Women's Archive curriculum, *Making Our Wilderness Bloom*. The key passages:

> It is impossible for me to find words in which to tell you how deeply I was touched by your offer to act as "Kaddish" for my dear mother. . . . What you have offered to do [is beautiful beyond thanks]—I shall never forget it.
>
> You will wonder, then, that I cannot accept your offer. . . . I know well, and appreciate what you say about, the Jewish custom [that only male children recite the prayer, and if there are no male survivors, a male stranger may act as substitute]; and Jewish custom is very dear and sacred to me. [Y]et I cannot ask you to say Kaddish after my mother. The Kaddish means to me that the survivor publicly . . . manifests his . . . intention to assume the relation to the Jewish community which his parent had, [so that] the chain of tradition remains unbroken from generation to generation, each adding

its own link. You can do that for the generations of your family, I must do that for the generations of my family. . . .

My mother had eight daughters and no son; yet never did I hear a word of regret pass the lips of either my mother or my father that one of us was not a son. When my father died, my mother would not permit others to take her daughters' place in saying the Kaddish, [and so I am sure] I am acting in her spirit when I am moved to decline your offer. But beautiful your offer remains nevertheless, and, I repeat, I know full well that it is much more in [harmony] with the generally accepted Jewish tradition than is my or my family's conception. You understand me, don't you?

Szold's plea for celebration of our common heritage while tolerating— indeed, appreciating—the differences among us concerning religious practice, is captivating, don't you agree? I recall her words even to this day when a colleague's words betray a certain lack of understanding.

When I became active in the movement to open doors to women, enabling them to enter occupations once closed to them—lawyering and judging, bartending, policing, and firefighting, for example—I was heartened by the words of a girl of my generation. She wrote:

One of the many questions that have often bothered me is why women have been, and still are, thought to be so inferior to men. It's easy to say it's unfair, but that's not enough for me; I'd really like to know the reason for this great injustice!

Men presumably dominated women from the very beginning because of their greater physical strength; it's men who earn a living, beget children, [and] do as they please. . . . Until recently, women silently went along with this, which was stupid, since the longer it's kept up, the more deeply entrenched it becomes. Fortunately, education, work and progress have opened women's eyes. In many countries they've been granted equal rights; many people, mainly women, but also men, now realize how wrong it was to tolerate this state of affairs for so long. . . .

Yours,

Anne M. Frank

This insightful comment was one of the last entered in her diary. Anne Frank, Diary readers in this audience know, was born in the Netherlands in July 1929. She died in 1945, while imprisoned at Bergen-Belsen, three months short of her 16th birthday.

I was asked some years ago by the American Jewish Committee (AJC) to supply a statement on how my heritage as a Jew and my occupation as a judge fit together. I responded this way:

> I am a judge, born, raised, and proud of being a Jew. The demand for justice, for peace, and for enlightenment runs through the entirety of Jewish history and Jewish tradition. I hope, in all the years I have the good fortune to continue serving on the bench of the Supreme Court of the United States, I will have the strength and courage to remain steadfast in the service of that demand.

With thanks for your patient audience, and once again, deepest appreciation to Aharon Barak and to the Genesis Foundation, may I say to all gathered here: Shalom v'todah rabah.

REMARKS AT A NATURALIZATION CEREMONY

NATIONAL ARCHIVES, WASHINGTON, D.C.
(DECEMBER 14, 2018)

Ruth Bader Ginsburg, Associate Justice,
Supreme Court of the United States

My fellow Americans, it is my great privilege to welcome you to citizenship in the democracy that is the USA. You number 31 and came here from 26 countries, alphabetically, from China to Venezuela. Today, you join more than 20 million current citizens, born in other lands, who chose, as you have, to make the United States of America their home. We are a nation made strong by people like you who traveled long distances, overcame great obstacles, and made tremendous sacrifices—all to provide a better life for themselves and their families.

My own father arrived in this land at age 13, with no fortune and speaking no English. My mother was born four months after her parents, with several children in tow, came by ship to Ellis Island. My father and grandparents reached, as you do, for the American dream. As testament to our nation's promise, the daughter and granddaughter of immigrants sits on the highest Court in the land. In America, land of opportunity, that prospect is within the realm of the achievable. What is the difference between a bookkeeper in New York City's garment district and a Supreme Court Justice? One generation, my life bears witness, the difference between opportunities available to my mother and those afforded me.

You have studied our system of government and know of its twin pillars. First, our government has limited powers; it can exercise only the authority expressly given to it by the Constitution. And second, citizens of this country enjoy certain fundamental rights. Those rights are our nation's hallmark. They are set forth in the Bill of Rights, and other provisions of, or amendments to, the Constitution. They are inalienable, yielding to no governmental decree. Our Constitution opens with the words: "We the People of the United States." By limiting government, specifying rights, and empowering the people, the founders of the United States proclaimed that the heart of America would be its citizens, not its rulers.

After the words "We the People of the United States," the Constitution sets out the aspiration "to form a more perfect Union." At the start, it is true, the union very much needed perfection. The original Constitution permitted slavery and severely limited who counted among "We the People." When the nation was new, only white, property-owning men had the right to vote, the most basic right of citizenship. But over the course of our history, people left out at the beginning—people held in human bondage, Native Americans, and half the population, women, came to be embraced as full citizens. A French observer of early America, Alexis de Tocqueville, wrote that "[t]he greatness of America lies not in being more enlightened than . . . other nation[s], but rather in her ability to repair her faults." Through amendments to our Constitution, and court decisions applying those amendments, we abolished slavery, prohibited racial discrimination, and made men and women people of equal citizenship stature. In the vanguard of those perfections were people just like you—new Americans of every race and creed, making ever more vibrant our national motto: *e pluribus unum*—out of many, one.

Though we have made huge progress, the work of perfection is scarcely done. Many stains remain. In this rich land, nearly a quarter of our children live in poverty, nearly half of our citizens do not vote, and we still struggle to achieve greater understanding and appreciation of each other across racial, religious, and socioeconomic lines. Yet we strive to realize the ideal—to become a more perfect union. As well informed new citizens, you will play a vital part in that endeavor by, first and foremost, voting in elections, also serving on juries, and engaging in civic discourse.

We sing of America, "sweet land of liberty." Newcomers to our shores, people like you, came here, from the earliest days of our nation to today, "[seeking] liberty—freedom from oppression, freedom from want, freedom to be [you and me]." I would like to convey to you, finally, how a great American jurist—Judge Learned Hand—understood liberty. He explained in 1944 what liberty meant to him when he greeted a large assemblage of new Americans gathered in New York City's Central Park to swear allegiance to the United States. These are Judge Hand's words: Just what is this sacred liberty that "must lie in the hearts of men and women? It is not the ruthless, the unbridled will; it is not freedom to do as one likes."

> I cannot define [the spirit of liberty]; I can only tell you my own faith. The spirit of liberty is the spirit which is not too sure that it is right; the spirit of liberty is the spirit which seeks to understand the minds of other men and women; the spirit of liberty is the spirit which weighs their interest alongside its own without bias.

May the spirit of liberty, as Judge Hand explained it, be your beacon. May you have the conscience and courage to act in accord with that high ideal as you play your part in helping to achieve a more perfect Union.

AFTERWORD

OCTOBER 2020

Amanda L. Tyler

This part of the book was not supposed to exist. On September 18, 2020, shortly after Justice Ginsburg and I submitted this book for publication, she succumbed to complications from cancer and passed away at her home surrounded by her family and loved ones.

It is impossible to put into words how devastating her loss is for those of us who were lucky enough to know her. As the outpouring of grief that gripped the United States following news of her death vividly illustrated, the country she loved and spent a lifetime serving also suffered a great loss with her passing. Justice Ginsburg was a national treasure—someone who through her life and work made ours a better, more just society. Indeed, as Justice Sonia Sotomayor wrote after her passing, she was nothing short of an "American hero."

In trying to process her loss, I keep coming back to the passage from Deuteronomy that hung on a wall in her chambers:

"Justice, justice thou shalt pursue."

This calling drove Justice Ginsburg in all she did.

Indeed, Justice Ginsburg's life's work was defined by her dedication to making sure the United States Constitution leaves no one behind and truly is a document for all of us, "We the People."

This book covers only a small part of the impact Justice Ginsburg's life and work had on American law and society. And what an impact it was. From dismantling institutionalized gender discrimination as an advocate in the 1970s through forty years as a federal judge, including twenty-seven years on the Supreme Court, Justice Ginsburg worked tirelessly to advance the principle that the United States Constitution is an inclusive document that promises everyone "equal opportunity to aspire, achieve, participate in and contribute to society based on their individual talents and capacities."[1]

Justice Ginsburg was also an inspiration. As someone who had confronted adversity throughout her life and bulldozed countless roadblocks thrown in her path along the way, her strength and determination fueled her forward time and again. I keep thinking back, for example, to how she went to the Court to announce an opinion from the bench the morning after she lost her beloved life partner, Marty. Profoundly dedicated to her role as a public servant, she insisted the work always had to go on. Right up until the very end, she battled cancer with courage and grace, keeping it at bay so many times that many of us began to believe she was invincible.

On this score, I think back in particular to the events at the heart of this book. When I telephoned the Justice to invite her to deliver the first Herma Hill Kay Memorial Lecture in her friend's honor, she instantly accepted and suggested that we make it a conversation between the two of us. As originally scheduled, we would have held the event in January 2019. But in light of the Justice's December 2018 surgery to address lung cancer her doctors had discovered, we had to postpone. I recall trying to talk her into canceling the January event well before we actually did. She was so committed to honoring her friend that she resisted. When, under the advice of her doctors, she finally relented, she insisted that we immediately set a new date. When that date arrived ten months later, she made the trip despite not being back at full speed. During her visit, I witnessed first-hand the Justice's awe-inspiring resilience. Nothing—not even cancer—was going to keep her from honoring her dear friend. That is who Justice Ruth Bader Ginsburg was.

Less than a year later, the news came that we had lost her. It felt like a gut punch.

Her law clerks knew what we had to do. Despite the ongoing Covid-19 pandemic, some 120 of us who had worked for her at the Supreme Court and at the United States Court of Appeals for the D.C. Circuit traveled from all over the country to stand as honorary pallbearers as her casket returned to the Supreme Court one final time. It was our solemn duty to stand by her side as she passed under and later lay in repose below the Court's portico at its west entrance that so fittingly reads "Equal Justice Under Law."

We drew great comfort from being together during those difficult days, all of us holding her close in our hearts. She did so much for so many of us as a mentor and friend that it is simply impossible to convey her incredible generosity and kindness in this afterword. Beyond all that she taught us when we clerked for her, there were the job recommendations that followed, the encouraging notes that arrived to mark both personal and professional milestones (including "RBG grandclerk" t-shirts when new children joined our families), the support she offered as we struggled through our own periods of adversity, and the visits in which we cemented memories we will cherish forever.

After we received her at the Court, her clerks kept vigil by her side for the next forty-eight hours, two clerks at a time in twenty-minute shifts. We stood outside with her during the day, bearing witness to the droves of mourners who came, often with children in tow, to pay their respects. In their grief, we saw just how enormous Justice Ginsburg's impact on this country has been. Overnight, we came inside the Court to be alone with her, while she lay in the vast Great Hall, and there we stood by her side, just two clerks and one Honor Guard from the Supreme Court Police. It was a time to reflect and to tell her how much she changed our lives and how much we loved her. I served on the last clerk vigil before we returned her to her family, after which she departed the Supreme Court for the final time to lie in state at the Capitol. It is fitting that she was still making history, even in death, as the first woman and first Jewish person to be so honored. All the same, watching her leave the Supreme Court, knowing she would never return, was heartbreaking.

Over the spring and summer of this year, as Justice Ginsburg and I assembled this book, I had the special privilege of working closely with her one last time. She was excited about this project as well as the forthcoming publication of her dear friend Herma Hill Kay's important work chronicling the lives of the first women law professors in the United States.[2] As we exchanged drafts of various parts of this book, the Justice was every bit as rigorous an editor as she had been twenty years ago when I clerked for her. Right up until the end, she was still teaching me about the craft of writing, how important precision is, and to never use four words when three will do.

During our last conversation, we talked about this project and how she was holding up as she endured numerous medical challenges. Then, the Justice asked about my children. In light of the ongoing pandemic, she wanted to know whether they would be returning to school this fall for in-person instruction or would be attending their classes online from home. More generally, she expressed deep concern for children everywhere who were being profoundly affected by the ongoing pandemic.

That, too, was Justice Ginsburg—always thinking about others and always looking toward the future.

Writing at this moment, that future seems uncertain. But in reflecting on her legacy as told in this book, we can all draw inspiration from the wisdom she imparted in her historic dissent in *Shelby County*. If she were here with us today, I think she would tell us never to forget, as she said in announcing her opinion from the bench, what "[t]he great man who led the march from Selma to Montgomery" told us: "'The arc of the moral universe is long,' he said, but 'it bends toward justice,' if there is a steadfast commitment to see the task through to completion."

It is now the responsibility of all of us to take up this charge.

NOTES

1. The quote is from Justice Ginsburg's opinion for the Court in the *VMI* case, *United States* v. *Virginia*, 518 U.S. 515, 532 (1996), reproduced in the third section of this book.

2. Herma Hill Kay, *Paving the Way: The First American Women Law Professors*, Patricia A. Cain, ed. (forthcoming, University of California Press). Justice Ginsburg wrote the foreword to Kay's book. [The University of California Press published Kay's book in the spring of 2021.]

TIMELINE:
THE LIFE OF JUSTICE
RUTH BADER GINSBURG

1933	March 15: Born Joan Ruth Bader, Brooklyn, New York
1934	June 6: Older sister Marilyn dies of meningitis at age six
1950	June 25: Mother Celia Bader dies of cancer
	June 27: Graduates from James Madison High School, Brooklyn, New York (does not attend graduation due to mother's death)
1950	Enrolls in Cornell University and meets sophomore Martin D. ("Marty") Ginsburg on a blind date
1954	June 14: Graduates from Cornell University
	June 23: Marries Marty at his parents' home on Long Island
1954	Moves to Fort Sill, Oklahoma, for Marty's Army service as an artillery school instructor; works in several clerical positions
1955	Daughter Jane is born
1956	Enrolls at Harvard Law School, one year behind Marty, as one of nine women students in a class of over 550
1957–1958	Marty battles cancer during his final year of law school
1958	Following Marty's graduation from Harvard Law School, the family moves to New York and Justice Ginsburg transfers to Columbia Law School

269

1959	Graduates from Columbia Law School tied for first in her class
1959–1961	Serves as law clerk to the Honorable Edmund L. Palmieri, United States District Court for the Southern District of New York
1961–1963	Serves as research associate and then associate director of Columbia Law School Project on International Procedure
1963	Joins the faculty at Rutgers School of Law, State University of New Jersey (one of two women on the faculty)
1965	Son James is born
1968	June 20: Father Nathan Bader dies
1971	With Marty, represents Charles Moritz and co-authors first brief in a gender discrimination case
	Co-authors first Supreme Court brief, *Reed* v. *Reed*
1972	Joins the faculty of Columbia Law School with tenure
	Named first director of the American Civil Liberties Union's newly created Women's Rights Project
1973	First Supreme Court oral argument, *Frontiero* v. *Richardson*
1974	With Kenneth M. Davidson and Herma Hill Kay, publishes *Cases and Materials on Sex-Based Discrimination*
1975	Argues *Weinberger* v. *Wiesenfeld*
1978	Argues her last case before the Supreme Court, *Duren* v. *Missouri*
1980	Appointed by President Jimmy Carter to the United States Court of Appeals for the District of Columbia Circuit
1993	Appointed by President Bill Clinton to the Supreme Court of the United States
1996	Writes for the Supreme Court majority in *United States* v. *Virginia*
1999	First bout with cancer (colorectal)
2007	Dissents in *Ledbetter* v. *Goodyear Tire & Rubber Co.*
2009	Second bout with cancer (pancreatic)
2010	June 27: Marty dies of cancer
2013	Dissents in *Shelby County* v. *Holder*
2014	Dissents in *Burwell* v. *Hobby Lobby Stores, Inc.*

2018   Has surgery to address cancerous nodules on left lung discovered
        while being treated for fractured ribs sustained in a fall

2019   Recurrence of pancreatic cancer

2020   September 18: Passes away from complications of metastatic
        pancreatic cancer